PERCEPTUAL-MOTOR BEHAVIOUR

Developmental Assessment and Therapy

Judith I. Laszlo
University of Western Australia

Phillip J. Bairstow
University of London

HOLT, RINEHART AND WINSTON
London · New York · Sydney · Toronto

Holt, Rinehart and Winston Ltd: 1 St Anne's Road,
Eastbourne, East Sussex BN21 3UN

155.412

British Library Cataloguing in Publication Data

Laszlo, Judith I.
  Perceptual-motor behaviour: developmental
  assessment and therapy.
  1. Perceptual-motor learning   2. Perception in children
  I. Title   II. Bairstow, Phillip J.
  155.4'12   BF723.M6

ISBN 0-03-910612-8

Phototypesetting by Georgia Ltd, Liverpool.
Printed in Great Britain by Mackays of Chatham Ltd.

Last digit is print no: 9 8 7 6 5 4 3 2 1

CONTENTS

This book is dedicated to the memory of the late Dr A. J. Marshall, Reader in Psychology, one of the great pioneers of psychology in Australia, and the wisest and best teacher.

FOREWORD

Movements of many different kinds are essential components of our daily lives, yet all too often we accept them without any thought of how they are made possible. We marvel at the performance of those with exceptional skills such as the swift athlete and the dexterous pianist, without realising that even the everyday movements we perform ourselves are also manifestations of complex interactions between the brain, nervous system, and muscles of the body and limbs. Those who most appreciate the benefits of movements are the unfortunate ones who, paralysed by disease or injury, have lost them in whole or part.

Although considerable knowledge of motor skills exists, it is incomplete and imperfect. In order to advance our understanding we need both scientific studies of different aspects of motor skills together with an encompassing overview of the whole phenomenon. In this book Judith Laszlo and Phillip Bairstow have attempted such a task, and I commend it to the enquiring reader as a work of considerable scholarship.

As a paediatrician seeking to help crippled and disabled children I greatly appreciate their developmental approach, and also their desire to provide a sound basis for therapeutic techniques. The insights into the mechanisms of motor skills and disorders which I have obtained through studying their work will be of great value to me in improving the treatment of disabled children.

Within these pages there is much material which the pure scientist, the clinician and the therapist can all find of help in their work.

Judith Laszlo and Phillip Bairstow have pursued their research studies in Perth, Australia, and London. I am proud to have been able to support the London end of this fine Anglo-Australian effort.

K. S. HOLT

PREFACE

Perceptual-motor behaviour has been investigated extensively within a number of scientific disciplines. Anatomists, physiologists, biochemists, psychologists and medical scientists have contributed to our understanding of the various factors involved in the development of motor control. Teaching of motor skills and the diagnosis and management of motor dysfunction is of central concern to educationalists, medical practitioners, educational and clinical psychologists and physiotherapists and occupational therapists. In the present book an attempt is made to bridge the gap between academic and applied interests.

Outlined below is a brief review of our background, showing how academic interests can lead to applied work, and indeed how they can be combined.

While we started our university studies many years apart and in different corners of the world, there are some notable similarities in our training and interests. We both started our university studies in Medicine, and both decided that rather than practising medicine we would concentrate on research. We both chose Physiology and Psychology as our areas of study and this combination of disciplines proved valuable in our choice of research area — the control of skilled movement.

During the years we worked together the central theme of our research programme was the role of kinaesthetic information in motor control in humans, a factor in skilled behaviour not widely investigated. As the functional characteristics of kinaesthetic perception were gradually defined, the research aims were expanded to encompass other perceptual and motor factors which were hypothesised to contribute to skilled performance. Our own research findings and work reported in the literature led us to propose a closed-loop model of perceptual-motor behaviour.

All research results showed that kinaesthesis is a necessary source of information for both the acquisition and performance of skilled motor tasks. It became apparent, through reading the available literature and discussions with workers in the educational and clinical fields, that kinaesthetic development had not been investigated adequately.

The research experience gained during the years of working on kinaesthetic perception and the results collected during the research programme proved most valuable when turning to applied questions. It was decided to construct the Kinaesthetic Sensitivity Test. With the aid of the test the developmental progression in kinaesthetic perception in normal children could be measured for the first time. The test was also useful as a diagnostic tool in the evaluation of causes of motor dysfunction. The transition from theoretical to applied research was not considered as a discontinuity in the course of the experimental programme. On the contrary, it was the natural progression from collecting theoretical knowledge and refining techniques to the application of these in order to solve a practical problem.

The useful results obtained from the application of the Kinaesthetic Sensitivity Test encouraged further test construction. Instead of measuring one perceptual ability, a Perceptual-Motor Abilities Test was planned, which was to provide measures of perceptual and motor abilities.

At this point our careers diverged. Laszlo continued her work at the University of Western Australia, and Bairstow left Western Australia to join the staff of the Wolfson Centre, Institute of Child Health, University of London. It was Bairstow's experience in the applied setting and his review of the available tests of motor function which provided the final impetus for the construction of the Perceptual-Motor Abilities Test, while most of the testing and data analysis was completed in Western Australia.

This book represents the work of both of us and reflects our thoughts and opinions. We wrote Chapter 6 together, while Chapters 1, 2, 7 and 8 were written by Laszlo, and Chapters 3, 4 and 5 by Bairstow. Throughout the preparation of the book, suggestions, amicable criticisms and help from each other aided in the clarification of ideas and in bringing the book to its final form.

One additional point relating to presentation could be mentioned. We are fully aware that sex discrimination is a sensitive issue, nevertheless for the sake of clear exposition the child is designated as 'he', the therapist and psychologist are referred to as 'she', and the research worker is often described as 'he'. To some extent this sex differentiation follows the frequency of males and females in each category. We seek the indulgence of those who might find this arbitrary sex designation offensive.

JUDITH I. LASZLO
PHILLIP J. BAIRSTOW

ACKNOWLEDGEMENTS

This book is based on work conducted over a number of years. During this time we received encouragement, help and useful criticism from many people and we express our sincere thanks to all. Some of the support we received should be acknowledged individually.

The contribution of all our subjects to the project has been invaluable. The hundreds of students of the University of Western Australia and of the University of Waterloo, Canada, who participated in the experiments willingly and cheerfully, and the many who discussed the experiments, often at debriefing parties, and gave us valuable suggestions, earned our gratitude. Without the primary school children taking part in the testing and training programmes from Western Australian and London schools the construction of the Kinaesthetic Sensitivity Test and the Perceptual-Motor Abilities Test would not have been possible. More than just taking part, many of the children delighted us with their enthusiasm, cheerful acceptance of our considerable demands, persistence and delightful personalities. We wish we could thank them all individually here, but over 2000 names would take up too much space — so *Thank you* one and all. We do not underestimate the consideration we received from the teaching staff of the schools, who may have had reasons to, but who did not, complain about interruptions to their teaching schedules, or the support from parents who consented to their children's participation in the project. We appreciate all the help we received from children, their parents and the teaching and clerical staff of the following Western Australian primary schools: Claremont, Dalkeith, Hollywood, Nedlands, Rosalie, Subiaco, Bluff Point and Mount Tarcoola; and London schools: Branwood, Coldharbour, Ethel Davis, Franklin Delano Roosevelt, Holy Trinity, Richard Cloudesley, St Marks and St Marks Priory.

The construction of the Perceptual-Motor Abilities Test was made possible by the work of the two Research Officers, Ms Pia Broderick and Mr Victor J. Manyam. Not only did they share the heavy testing load, scoring and data analysis work but they contributed ideas, suggestions and insightful criticism. We were indeed fortunate to have their unfailing and devoted participation which greatly enhanced the success of the project.

To our colleagues, to whom we turned for advice, go our heartfelt thanks: Associate Professor Imre Kaldor who up to his untimely death was one of our greatest supporters — he encouraged us, argued with us and helped us over periods of discouragement — we miss him badly; Associate Professor Lumsden who advised us on the measurement and statistical problems we encountered and who critically reviewed the description of the Kinaesthetic Sensitivity Test;

and finally, the late Dr A. J. Marshall, Reader in Psychology, who taught us so much, and who showed us how to ask questions and how to evaluate the answers.

The equipment used in the studies and tests was built by members of the Psychology and Preclinical Workshops of the University of Western Australia. Our thanks go to all the technicians who translated our ideas into reliable, practical and simple instruments, and who maintained the equipment in working order throughout testing despite the heavy-handed treatment it suffered from both testers and children. We are greatly appreciative of the design and construction of the computerised systems built for the pattern perception studies and the 'Video game' by Mr Paul M. Laszlo. He worked on the 'Video game' through many nights and weekends to produce an innovative and robust yet sensitive instrument, and an enjoyable game. Thanks are due to Dr Gary R. Ward for conceiving the Ward game.

The work described in this book was carried out at the University of Western Australia, Departments of Psychology and Physiology; University of Waterloo, Canada, Department of Kinesiology; University of London, (i) Department of Developmental Paediatrics, The Wolfson Centre, Institute of Child Health and (ii) Department of Child Development and Educational Psychology, Institute of Education. The research was supported by TVW Telethon Foundation of Western Australia, National Health and Medical Research Council (Australia), Australian Research Grants Scheme, and Medical Research Council (UK).

Finally, we acknowledge the help and support we received during the writing and production of this manuscript. Our thanks go to: the staff of Holt-Saunders Ltd, and Dr Barend ter Haar, in particular, for helping us to develop the idea for a book of this nature; Professor K. S. Holt for providing space in The Wolfson Centre while writing, and for the help and encouragement given to us by him and his staff; Dr Sheila Henderson, Dr Michael Huntley, Dr J. Lumsden, Dr Neil O'Connor, and three anonymous reviewers for providing valuable criticisms and suggestions on drafts of chapters; Miss Christine Pfaff for typing the manuscript, and for never complaining about our handwriting and the changes and reorganisation of material that we asked for; Mr Victor J. Manyam for his suggestions, criticisms, assistance with revision editing and willingness to proof read; Ms Pia Broderick for her patience and uncomplaining help with proofreading; Mr Tony Hayes for drawing some of the figures; Mr Herb Jurkiewicz for the photography; and the children who submitted so cheerfully to the photographic demands placed on them: Emil Mandyczewsky, Damon Manyam and Claire Spencer, featuring in Chapter 7.

1 INTRODUCTION

THE AIM OF THE BOOK

Effective interaction between a child and the environment depends on the child's ability to explore and manipulate that environment. Any interference with the natural development of perceptual-motor abilities can restrict such interaction and can have far-reaching consequences for the child's physical and psychological well-being. It follows that the understanding of normal perceptual-motor behaviour, and the reasons for retarded or abnormal behaviour, is important for parents, teachers, psychologists and therapists. The aim of this book is to provide a framework for the analysis and understanding of perceptual-motor development, and to apply this analytical approach to the diagnosis and correction of motor dysfunctions.

Two major themes are developed in the book. The first is the interdependence of theoretical and applied work is demonstrated and an attempt is made to show the benefits of cooperation between research, educational and clinical workers. Various considerations dealt with in the book lead to the conclusion that through an interaction between workers in different professions interested in normal or abnormal perceptual-motor behaviour, significant advances may be made in the following areas: (a) a more detailed understanding of perceptual-motor behaviour; (b) the formulation of teaching programmes for normal children; and (c) the design of better diagnostic and therapeutic methods for handicapped children.

The second major theme relates to the benefits which spring from an analytical approach to the study and assessment of behaviour. Going beyond the measurement of motor behaviour, identifying underlying factors and processes, and designing tests that measure abilities in relation to these factors, will advance our understanding of the bases for motor behaviour, clarify the reasons for individual differences and generate new methods of diagnosis and therapy with specific applications.

PERCEPTUAL-MOTOR BEHAVIOUR

Skilled motor behaviour is essential in many aspects of life. Interaction with the physical and social environment is established through movement. The capability to execute purposive

1

movements is often taken for granted, and only the acquisition of specific skills is considered an achievement. For instance, adults speak, handle cutlery, dress themselves and turn knobs on their radios without much thought for the processes underlying the performance of these habitual tasks. They do however become aware of difficulties when perceptual and motor factors have to be integrated to form a new combination when learning a new activity, like driving a car, or perfecting a tennis stroke. All motor skills, whether well practised or in the process of being mastered, demand a balanced interaction between many physiological and psychological processes.

Skilled motor behaviour can be assessed at two levels, either in terms of the different tasks or activities that constitute the motor repertoire (task-orientated approach), or in terms of the processes which underlie motor behaviour (process-orientated approach). As an illustration: if one wants to assess 'fine hand control' in a child, one could measure his capability to trace over a variety of different line drawings, cut out a drawing with a pair of scissors, place pegs in a pegboard, join up dots on paper with a pencil, make a drawing, place forms in a form-board and arrange the parts of a jigsaw puzzle. Many readers will recognise these activities as items which are commonly used in the clinical assessment of hand function. All the tasks involve the fine manipulation of materials, including the accurate control of hand and finger movement, and the accurate placement of the hand in relation to a visual 'target'. Leaving aside the problem of how to measure performance objectively and of how to gain a composite view of hand function from such different items, consider an alternative approach to this task-orientated assessment. This focuses on fundamental processes which underline the performance of these and other tasks. These processes cannot be measured directly. Their function can be inferred from performance on specifically designed test items. For instance, ballet, playing a video game or football all depend to a degree on the ability to generate movements within spatial and temporal constraints, i.e. a spatio-temporal programming process. The identification of processes, and the measurement of associated abilities, enables a fundamental understanding of a child's behaviour that surpasses the results of a task-orientated assessment — an understanding which is achieved without the need for assessing him on a great number of individual tasks.

Fig. 1.1 may further assist in explaining the nature of a process-orientated approach to assessment, as distinct from a task-orientated approach. The line of boxes in the bottom row represents a series of individual everyday tasks, some of which may be superficially similar (e.g. tasks that involve fine hand control) and others that form an apparently different class of tasks (e.g. gross body skills like running to kick a ball). A task-orientated assessment seeks to measure the child's behaviour in these individual tasks and, perhaps, seeks to summarise the results of the assessment in terms of a fine and gross motor index. The line of boxes on the top row represents a series of fundamental perceptual-motor processes or factors that underlie or determine behaviour on the individual tasks. The lines joining the bottom row to the top row are intended to convey three notions: that performance on any one task may be dependent on a number of underlying processes; that different tasks may share some common underlying processes; and the converse, that any one process may have a role in many tasks which, superficially, may appear to have little in common. These notions will be taken up at various points throughout the book, and the major point to be made here is that the goal of a process-orientated approach to assessment is two-fold: (a) the definition of fundamentally important processes which determine behaviour and (b) the design of test items which will accurately measure abilities in relation to these processes. Accordingly, the behaviour of a child on a wide variety of daily tasks can be explained in terms of abilities related to the fundamental processes which underlie these tasks.

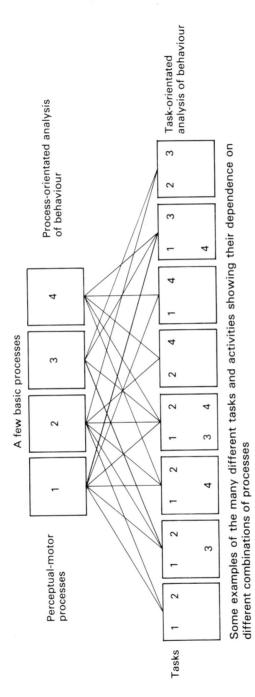

Figure 1.1 *Two levels of behavioural analysis.*

When children are compared with each other on tasks and activities, and individual differences are observed, these differences may be for two distinct reasons. They may be due to differences in the development of underlying abilities, or the children may in fact have similar abilities but differ in the levels of task proficiency. An advantage of the process-orientated analysis of behaviour is that an understanding of the reasons for individual differences can be gained. This understanding springs from the fact that the child is assessed on fundamental abilities and the results of the assessment give an indication of the child's *potential* for performing different tasks. Comparisons between children at the level of tasks and activities can be misleading. Differences in task proficiency could reflect different opportunities in practising the skill, and different interests and motivation. Yet the norms and expectancies that are quoted when considering motor development are often at this level. In the present day climate, when child-rearing practices are based on the 'normative' appraisal of a child's progress, these expectancies assume great importance. As long as the child reaches each listed milestone at the expected age (or earlier), the parents are satisfied. 'Average' ages at which certain skills should be performed are published in books of child care and in popular magazines. The quoted ages vary from publication to publication and the parents rely on the information they happen to have access to.

The 'normative' appraisal of progress can lead to some misconceptions. One major problem which can arise is the lack of understanding of the concept of average. Parents are tempted to believe that the set age for the emergence of a skill is an inflexible expectation; i.e. if the book says that a specific skill should be performed at year 3.5, their child is retarded if he acquires the skill three months later, or he is considered a promising athletic talent if he performs it three months earlier. The concept of individual differences, the normal distribution about the mean or standard deviation is either not explained or not understood (Miller, 1975). Nor is the fact emphasised that within the limitations imposed by basic processes children develop differently, depending on their interests and opportunities. One child might spend more time on manipulative activity than gross motor activity and hence be ahead in such skills as bead threading and building, but behind in ball catching, while his brother might prefer ball games to building and be ahead in the former and behind in the latter. Both children would be 'normal', yet the difference in their development might cause some concern to parents if they do not conform to the normative expectations.

Another effect of the 'normative' approach is that it might lead to unfair comparison and competition between children, and to possibly unwise early 'streaming' in their education. For example, the child who learns to swim early might be considered to be a more promising swimmer than a second child who learns to swim later. The parents of the first child might hope for a career in swimming for him and demand extensive training. This is especially likely if a parent expects sporting excellence from his children, either because he himself was a great sportsman in his youth, or because he always wanted to become a great sportsman but could never fulfil this ambition. The second child on the other hand might be subjected to long training sessions in order to 'catch up'. The result could be similar for both children — a dislike of swimming, tension, anxiety, and more importantly, a loss of time in which to play and develop skills of their own choosing.

Acceptance of the different rates at which abilities develop from child to child, and approval and encouragement in whatever skill the child is interested in, can accelerate progress in particular areas and eliminate anxiety about areas of weakness. There is a need for acknowledgement of normal individual differences in terms of underlying abilities and an appreciation of the importance of these differences.

The importance of perceptual-motor behaviour

Motor development influences intellectual, social and emotional development (Gelman, 1978; Holt, 1975; Rosenbloom, 1975). Exploration leads to knowledge about the environment, and this, in turn, to formulation of concepts. Later, ideas and concepts can be expressed through the skills of drawing, writing and playing music.

Social and emotional development is facilitated by an interaction with others through the complex skills of gesturing, playing and speech. The development and nature of self-concept and self-confidence play an important role in these areas. Gallahue (1982) discusses the relationship between motor development and the development of self-concept and self-confidence. A child who moves with ease and performs motor tasks skilfully tends to have confidence in himself and builds a positive self-image. If given freedom of choice he will select activities which he judges he can perform successfully and this further strengthens his self-concept. Cratty (1967) argues that a child who cannot control his movements adequately develops a poor self-concept and encounters difficulties in social and emotional adjustments.

While a relationship between motor proficiency and self-concept undoubtedly exists, the relationship is far from simple. The child can judge his motor performance by comparing his own skill at various tasks with those of his playmates, and through the approval or disapproval that he receives from his parents and teachers. It might not be the actual performance level which is important but the way the child evaluates his own performance. The encouragement of activities which the child is good at leads to the development of self-confidence. Once self-confidence is firmly established, the child is ready to experiment with and practise the skills which he finds difficult without much threat to his self-concept. It follows that parents and teachers can help a child most effectively if they allow and encourage him to find his own strengths and talents, and assist him to develop at his own pace; that is, to recognise and encourage him as an individual. One might even suggest that children would benefit if the mythical 'normal child' was forgotten, together with the 'average performance levels' to which all children are expected, according to the normative viewpoint, to conform to.

The effects of motor difficulties and their evaluation

Holt (1975) points to the fact that the importance of motor control is most often perceived when the development of motor capabilities are retarded, or halted. The child who suffers from motor disability cannot acquire the skills which would be ordinarily expected of him. He may judge himself inferior to others and may be perceived by others as inferior, thus he cannot develop confidence in himself. Consequently, his social and emotional development may be retarded, or permanently disrupted.

Gubbay (1975) describes the difficulties a clumsy child encounters in many everyday situations, such as the evening meal, and the effect this clumsy behaviour might have on his family. Frequent accidents, like drinks being upset or forks dropped can irritate the father and embarrass the older sister. If the child finds the handling of eating utensils difficult and is worried about the criticism he receives, he is likely to become tense and anxious at every meal and consequently accidents occur with even greater frequency than before. To avoid accidents the child might decide to eat before the family meal and withdraw from the potentially threatening social situation, or pretend indifference and give up trying to improve the skill altogether. The danger to the child's development lies in the fact that he might generalise to include other skills as well as the specific task for which he was criticised, and perceive himself as generally clumsy and inadequate. This generalisation might not be warranted, however.

The case of seven-year-old David is described here to give an example of problems that children can encounter when motor proficiency is considered without appreciation of the underlying abilities and individual differences that are to be expected in these abilities. David was thought of by his family as a 'one man disaster area' at meal times. Drinks were upset, chicken pieces came alive and 'jumped' off his plate and peas and crumbs were spread all around him. He was an untidy dresser, indifferent at ball games and frequently sustained minor injuries during play. Academically he was well advanced, being top of his class. He was a quiet, withdrawn and lonely boy. On examination he was diagnosed as a clumsy child, suffering from minimal brain dysfunction. Soon after his parents were told of the diagnosis, David, observing his sister at her ballet lesson, developed a sudden and unexpected interest in ballet and asked to be allowed to join the ballet school. His parents felt apprehensive that in view of his medical condition, ballet would be beyond his motor capacity. Not wanting to discourage him, however, they enrolled him for ballet lessons. Within six months he proved himself an outstandingly talented pupil and continued to develop at a fast rate to achieve artistic and technical excellence. He also found a number of friends and became socially skilled. Thus the diagnosis of clumsiness and minimal brain dysfunction, which was based on difficulties David experienced in some isolated skills, was unwarranted. More than that, the diagnosis could have been counterproductive but for the lucky accident of David's discovery of ballet and his parents' decision that despite the diagnosis, he should be allowed to follow his interest. While David proved that he was highly skilled in some activities, he never improved his eating and dressing skills, which initially drew most criticism and disapproval from his parents.

David's story illustrates two important points. Firstly, it shows that the concept of a general motor disability can be misleading and is best avoided in the clinical setting. Skilled motor behaviour depends on a number of underlying perceptual and motor abilities. Even in a seemingly clumsy child, a cluster of abilities might be sufficiently developed to allow the acquisition of some specific skills. Labelling a child as clumsy, in general, is counterproductive to optimal development. If censure cannot be avoided, it is best related to a specific response, not to the child; i.e. this act was clumsy, not, you are clumsy, since any derogatory label given by parent, teacher or peers must undermine the child's confidence. Not only must he overcome the primary difficulty of controlling his movements, and hence his physical environment, but he must learn to cope with the secondary social and emotional problems resulting from a lack of self-confidence.

Secondly, it supports the notion that perceptual-motor behaviour should be analysed in terms of abilities which underlie motor performance, rather than relying on the evaluation of motor behaviour or proficiency at different tasks. The analysis of behaviour in relation to underlying processes can lead to a deeper understanding of individual differences and will help to encourage the full development of each child according to his abilities, as well as his interests and opportunities. It does not lead to a demand for conformity with expectations which might not meet the needs or capabilities of the individual child.

DEVELOPMENTAL ASSESSMENT, DIAGNOSIS AND THERAPY

Perceptual-motor development is of crucial importance for the general development of children. Books dealing with the development of motor behaviour have been mostly descriptive in nature, listing developmental milestones and concentrating on normative data, or have been written from the educational viewpoint, giving some guidelines on methods of training.

There is a need to depart from the descriptive approach, and rather than restrict the enquiry to observations of motor behaviour, to adopt an analytical approach. Perceptual-motor development can be examined in terms of processes which are responsible, or contribute to the overt responses. This process-orientated approach would lead directly to new causal diagnostic methods.

There are a number of tests available today which claim to differentiate the mildly or severely motor-handicapped child from normal children. These tests, in the main, are task-orientated rather than paying attention to the reasons for the malfunction. This is not surprising since the tests are based on descriptions of motor development and the ages at which motor milestones are expected. They offer more or less complex test procedures to establish whether the child is, or is not, performing each task according to expectations with his age.

This type of diagnosis provides limited guidance for the therapist. Knowing that the child is behind his age in some tasks is taken as an indication that these tasks should be practised. It does not, however, define the underlying cause for the difficulties, nor does it reveal the reason why the specific group of tasks should be affected, yet there may be one single underlying cause for failure at all the motor tasks. If one can discover the cause of the problem, training programmes can be devised which focus on the relevant process or processes with the aim to correct the diagnosed deficiency. Tasks depending on the ability will improve as a consequence of the treatment. Thus, rather than attempting to treat each symptom, i.e. each task, individually, the underlying problem causing the symptoms can be attacked.

In the assessment and treatment of motor problems, the aim should be to approach the standards of the 'medical model' which is illustrated in the following example: a doctor is confronted with a feverish, coughing child, and he diagnoses pneumonia. Rather than prescribing aspirin and cough mixture — achieving, at best, temporary relief from the symptoms — he would prescribe the appropriate antibiotic, cure the disease and the symptoms would disappear. It can be argued that, by applying recent findings relevant to perceptual-motor development, the causes of motor problems can be diagnosed and treated with specific therapy programmes. Certainly, if the medical model could be approximated, significant improvements in the management of perceptual-motor disorders would be anticipated in terms of increased efficiency and effectiveness.

THE NEED FOR COOPERATION BETWEEN THEORETICAL AND APPLIED WORKERS

In the present book, recent research findings in physiology, the neurosciences and psychology are amalgamated to provide a theoretical framework for perceptual-motor function. This framework incorporates the different types of processes which are necessary for the acquisition and performance of motor activities. The framework is of service in a number of ways. It is useful for identifying the basis of perceptual-motor development and describing its progress. It indicates processes which develop and underlie the observed improvement in motor proficiency with age.

For the successful execution of a process-orientated assessment and therapy programme, constant communication and close cooperation between theoretical and applied workers is of particular benefit. The research worker is trained to design and carry out experiments, and to analyse the results and evaluate them for the generation of theories of behaviour. The methods employed by the applied worker can depend on the results of basic research and the applied worker is in the position of applying theoretical knowledge to serve the practical needs of the children she is dealing with, either in the educational or clinical setting. Working with children on a day to day basis, she is in the best position to recognise recurrent problems and locate areas where theory does not aid the clarification of everyday problems. Consequently, she can point to issues which the research worker can investigate. This, in turn, can lead to changes in or refinement of the theory. A two-way reciprocal interaction would be of mutual benefit.

The theoretical research worker, by training and inclination, and due to the nature of the research process is confined to investigations of specific, strictly delineated questions. The experiments are reported in learned journals or books, and are written to be intelligible, in the main, for a reader whose background and interests are similar to those of the researcher. The applied worker has restricted access to and scant opportunity to evaluate the findings and conclusions reported in the scientific journals of the various disciplines. Yet, it is often said that regardless of all the theorising and deliberations, the 'buck stops with the therapist' who is responsible for improving the child's condition, whatever the cause for the difficulty.

What is needed is direct communication between theoretical and applied workers. Inter-communication would enable the applied worker to assess new theoretical advances in terms of their practical value. On the basis of her findings she would be in the position to recommend areas in which further research would be useful.

The barriers could be eliminated if the mutual dependence and complementary nature of theoretical and applied areas were recognised, and if efforts were made to discuss theoretical issues, experimental findings, and diagnostic and therapeutic problems in single publications. The present book is such an attempt.

THE PLAN OF THE BOOK

The book deals with the processes and functions which contribute to perceptual-motor behaviour, the development of perceptual-motor abilities from five years of age to adult, and the diagnosis and treatment of perceptual-motor dysfunction. The topics of the book are organised to progress from theoretical research-based descriptions of behaviour and development to the consideration of applied problems of diagnosis and therapy.

In Chapter 2 a closed-loop theory of perceptual-motor behaviour is presented and some of the supporting research findings are discussed briefly.

Perceptual-motor development is described in Chapter 3. Development is not considered in terms of normative steps, rather an attempt is made to discuss parallel development of perceptual and motor abilities. One representative skill, that of catching a moving object, is selected for analysis. This is the only part of the book where development is examined from the neonate, rather than from age five onwards. The aim is to trace the emergence of abilities and their gradual development.

The decision to restrict the scope of the book to children from age five was governed by practical considerations. Under five years of age, finely graded perceptual-motor skills are only poorly developed, testing for perceptual and motor abilities is extremely difficult, and predictions of future development based on the test results are unreliable.

Once the theoretical structure underlying perceptual-motor behaviour is described, and the development of the perceptual and motor abilities is outlined, it becomes possible to specify the causes for individual differences. Individual differences might be due to the differential rate of development or the different level attained in any one of the perceptual or motor abilities. A diagnostic test should aim at measuring abilities in relation to well-defined processes, and to specify those functions which are deviant.

In Chapter 4 the general problems of test construction and test usage are described, and the criteria used in designing a perceptual-motor test are discussed.

In Chapter 5 specific tests are evaluated with reference to the criteria established in the previous chapter. In addition, the theoretical background on which the tests are based, and their ease of administration, method of presentation of the results and usefulness as diagnostic tools are appraised.

Chapter 6 describes the construction of the Kinaesthetic Sensitivity Test. The rationale on which the test is based is discussed, the method used to achieve a measure of perceptual ability, uncontaminated by motor involvement, is reported, and the administration, scoring and usefulness of the test as a diagnostic tool is outlined.

The test construction theme is further developed in Chapter 7. The development of the Perceptual-Motor Abilities Test, the test programme and the results obtained are described. The test is evaluated, considering both theoretical and practical issues. New evidence on ability development which could lead to significant changes in many aspects of the evaluation of motor development is discussed. The test results could have a bearing on school curricula at the lower primary level, and the test is shown to be a viable and useful diagnostic tool in revealing specific foci of perceptual or motor difficulties which can be responsible for motor dysfunction.

Finally, in Chapter 8 the direct link between process-orientated assessment and the design of effective therapy programmes are demonstrated. The relationship between kinaesthetic dysfunction, writing difficulties and clumsiness are discussed. The therapeutic method devised to improve kinaesthetic sensitivity, where kinaesthetic difficulty is diagnosed, is detailed. The chapter ends on an optimistic note, showing the marked improvement in motor performance following successful kinaesthetic training.

WHO THE BOOK IS WRITTEN FOR

The book is directed at readers interested in motor behaviour in children, from the theoretical and/or the applied aspect. It is hoped that developmental and clinical psychologists, medical practitioners, kinesiologists, therapists, teachers of physical education and of primary school children, and teachers with responsibility for children with special needs, along with students of these varied disciplines will find the book useful.

The varied background of the potential readers makes it necessary to introduce each topic fully, without presupposing familiarity or detailed knowledge of the area under discussion. 'Scientific jargon' is avoided as far as possible, and where scientific terms are introduced, their meaning is explained.

2 CONTROL OF SKILLED MOVEMENT; PROCESSES UNDERLYING ACQUISITION AND PERFORMANCE

All overt behaviour is expressed through movement; this is true whether the individual is interacting with the environment or involved in social communication. The complex processes responsible for efficient performance of the large variety of motor acts which constitute everyday behaviour are often taken for granted. The importance of motor control becomes apparent when normal perceptual-motor development is disrupted, or when illness or accident interferes with the system. The extreme case of the patient whose entire voluntary motor system is paralysed illustrates the paramount importance of motor control. The patient might perceive and understand the environmental input he receives but be unable to respond to it. He cannot satisfy his needs, nor can he communicate his needs to others. Sometimes such a patient is misnamed as a 'poor vegetable', yet he retains his mental faculties, thoughts and feelings, only the overt manifestations are lost.

All movements, whether simple or complex, depend, for their efficient and smooth performance, on a number of perceptual and motor processes. In this chapter a model is presented, providing the theoretical framework within which perceptual-motor behaviour is discussed. Some of the perceptual and motor processes are described in detail to establish their roles in the system.

Before presenting experimental evidence in support of the model it might be helpful to analyse an everyday motor task in order to highlight the perceptual and motor processes which underlie such tasks, and which form the components of the model. The task chosen is pouring tea from a teapot into a cup. Where appropriate, terms that will be discussed in later sections are given in brackets (see Fig. 2.1).

The task analysis begins with a factor that provides the focus for many processes involved in the generation of a motor action, namely the goal. In the present case, the goal may be operationally defined as: pouring a full cup of tea without spillage. Next the relative position of cup and pot are observed (visual input) and the position of body and limbs perceived (kinaesthetic input). The teapot is a well-used favourite, hence its weight when full of tea, the speed at which tea pours out of the spout and the fact that the lid falls off easily, can be predicted. From previous experience it is known how best to hold the handle, how much effort or muscle tension is necessary to lift and tilt it, what the best tilt angle is and that the lid must be held with the free hand (memory traces stored in the Standard). These memories of previous experiences, together with the goal and current sensory input, are used in the generations of a plan of action (by the Standard). The plan of action is translated into movement by activating the necessary muscles (motor programming).

The movement (output) of reaching for the pot, curling the fingers round its handle, lifting it up and carrying it to the cup, tilting it to pour the tea, straightening it when the cup is full and replacing it on the table is a chain of movements which can only be performed successfully if information about its progress is monitored (sensory feedback). The tension in the muscles, the direction and extent of the movements and the velocity with which they are executed is provided by position and movement sense (kinaesthetic feedback) while the eyes are focused on the position of the spout over the cup and the amount of tea in the cup (visual feedback). The entire movement sequence is perceived as being voluntary or intentional (corollary discharge).

The described chain of events appears smooth and error-free to the observer. Yet when the movements are recorded in fine detail, by taking video recordings for instance, ongoing corrections or modifications to the path and speed of the movement become apparent. Such corrections might occur, for example, when approaching the handle, to make a fine adjustment prior to grasping the handle. The need for adjustment is detected through constant monitoring of sensory information (error detection) and the necessary corrections are implemented (error corrective programming).

The specific task of pouring tea cannot be regarded as an isolated event, but rather as part of ongoing activity demanding continuous postural adjustment. The continuous monitoring of postural information anchors each movement to past and future activity (closed-loop system).

Pouring tea from a new teapot, for the first time, differs from using the old teapot in a number of ways: (a) the weight of the full pot cannot be estimated with accuracy — hence the effort necessary to lift the pot cannot be predicted accurately; (b) the best grip on the handle, to achieve a well-balanced hold, has not been established; and (c) the speed at which the tea pours from the spout is not known. Due to the lack of past experience with the new pot, there is a dearth of stored memory traces relevant to the specific task demands. However, from past experience with many types of teapots the most likely plan of action is formulated and the task is performed accordingly (transfer of training). Depending on how closely previous experience relates to the task at hand and how well the characteristics of the pot have been predicted the tea is poured with more or less requirement for ongoing correction.

Lastly, the young child's first attempt at pouring tea could be considered. The child has no previous experience with teapots, but has some knowledge about pouring water from buckets, bottles and bath toys. The memory traces relevant to these situations can be retrieved and an inexact, generalised plan of action is formulated. The ensuing movements are far from perfect: tea is likely to be poured not only into the cup, but also into the saucer and over the table. The most frequently occurring errors are due to the overinclusiveness of the plan; excessive muscle involvement, i.e. too much force is generated; the movements might include the whole trunk, along with shoulder, arm and wrist movements; and spatial and temporal characteristics of the movement are not kept within acceptable limits.

THE CLOSED-LOOP MODEL; FUNCTIONAL PROPERTIES OF THE PERCEPTUAL-MOTOR PROCESSES

A number of closed-loop models have been proposed in the literature in an attempt to provide the theoretical framework within which acquisition and performance of motor skills can be described and investigated (Anokhin, 1969; Bernstein, 1967; Laszlo and Bairstow, 1971a; Pew, 1974a). All closed-loop models have one essential component in common, the sensory feedback loop. This loop forms the connection between output and input, thus providing the means for error detection and error correction within the system.

In the following discussion the authors present a closed-loop model of movement control which is shown in Fig. 2.1.

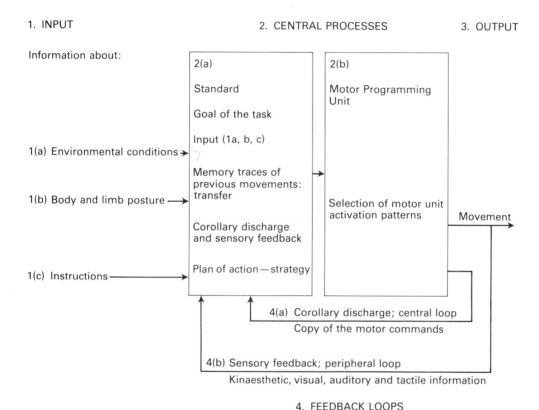

Figure 2.1   *The closed-loop model of motor control.*

In discussing the component processes of the closed-loop system the input variables are considered first. The numbers in brackets refer to the numbers shown in Fig. 2.1.

Input (1)

Environmental conditions (1a)

All motor acts are performed within the constraints imposed by the environment on the performer. While some aspects of the environment remain constant and are predictable, environmental conditions can also vary in many ways, some of which are unexpected. Before planning and execution of the motor act can begin, the environmental conditions need to be perceived. The relationship of objects to each other and the intrinsic properties of the target object must be evaluated. For example, in aiming tasks the position and size of the target must be observed, and its distance from the performer judged. The type and amount of visual information available about the target has a systematic influence on both the acquisition and performance level of the aiming task (Carlton, 1981; Henderson, 1977; Whiting and Cockerill, 1974). The texture of an object to be manipulated can be judged by touch. Sound emitted by a moving target might give information about target characteristics, e.g. the different sounds ping-pong balls and tennis balls give when hitting a hard surface. All this information is encoded, stored and used by the Standard when planning the motor action.

Body and limb posture (1b)

Information about the posture of body and limbs prior to commencement of an action is no less important than processing of environmental cues. The motor programme must generate postural adjustments, enabling the operator to perform a particular task. The necessity for postural adjustment can be illustrated by considering an example. The task is that of making a telephone call. The caller might be sitting near the telephone, with the phone book held in both hands, or he might be standing in the far corner of the room looking at the telephone. In the former case gross body posture might not need changing but the hand used in dialling must be freed and brought to the dial. In the latter instance, the caller must walk to the telephone and raise his hand to the dial.

Not only is the position of body and limbs perceived, but also the tension maintained in the various muscles. Some of the postural information can be obtained from vision, but a sensitive and detailed picture of body posture and muscle tension can only be provided by the kinaesthetic modality (Cordo and Nashner, 1982; Marsden, Merton and Morton, 1981; Nashner and Cordo, 1981).

Kinaesthesis provides information about body and limb position, the direction, extent and velocity of movements, and the level of tension in the muscles. There are three main classes of kinaesthetic receptors: the muscle spindle, tendon organ and joint receptor. Each receptor type is specialised to generate well-defined aspects of muscle function, and limb position and movement (for detailed discussion see Crago, Houk and Rymer, 1982; Matthews, 1972; Schaible and Schmidt, 1983). The sensory information from all these receptors is integrated to provide global kinaesthetic information. This information is continuously monitored and processed by the Standard. Thus, when the plan of action is formulated it incorporates the necessary postural adjustments which will place the operator into the appropriate position to perform the skill.

Instructions (1c)

The last input channel to be discussed relates to the instructions given to the individual. In some tasks the importance of instructions cannot be stressed too strongly. Through instructions the goal of the task is defined, the instruments and tools to be used in the task are described and explained, and the task strategy is indicated. Incomplete or unsatisfactory instructions can retard the acquisition of the skill and might prevent satisfactory performance. How appropriate the instructions are, and whether they are given in quantitative or qualitative terms, can influence the performance of a task at many levels, i.e. at the physiological and attentional levels and with regard to the strategy adopted.

Instructions can be given verbally, by demonstrating the task or by combining these two methods. Whether verbal instruction or demonstration is more efficient depends on the task to be acquired and performed. A task with high cognitive loading such as car driving, must be explained verbally, while a task which is predominantly motor in nature, such as swimming or ballet, is often best understood when demonstrated.

In the Standard the instructions are stored and the goal defined as clearly as the instructions permit. In some skills, description of the goal is best achieved by an explanation of the scoring method used, e.g. in a darts game. On the other hand, some skills cannot be scored quantitatively and demand complex goal descriptions. In car driving, for instance, the goal is seemingly easy to understand, yet it is a multifaceted goal, depending on a large number of task conditions and demands. In the case of accuracy of handwriting, the goal can only be described in qualitative terms, and hence the learner has to adopt a trial and error approach during acquisition of the task.

For the reader interested in neurophysiology some relevant studies could be mentioned briefly. Instructions have been shown to have a direct influence on motor cortex neurons in monkeys in a 'push–pull' lever moving task (Tanji and Evarts, 1976), on rapid, reflexively controlled movements, on the transcortical long-loop reflex (Evarts and Granit, 1976; Evarts and Tanji, 1976), and on the electromyogram (EMG) pattern generated during the movement. In a visually guided tracking task Brown and Cooke (1981) demonstrated that the EMG pattern is systematically varied according to the instructions given to the subject, even though the task remains the same.

The attention of the subject can be focused on various aspects of the task through instructions (Keele, 1973). Often, in experiments where attentional demands are investigated, the subject is instructed to perform two tasks concurrently. The instructions direct the subject's attention to one or other of the tasks. The overall conclusions drawn from these studies (Klein, 1976; Wickens and Gopher, 1977) point to the fact that attention can be allocated according to instructions for the two tasks.

A strong, and often observed, effect of instructions relates to the emphasis placed on the accuracy or speed of the performance. The well-known speed–accuracy trade-off phenomenon can be influenced, to some extent, by instructions. There is a negative correlation between speed and accuracy: the greater the accuracy demand imposed by the task, the slower is the performance (Livesey and Laszlo, 1979); the faster a task is performed, the less accurately it is done.

The trade-off effect is not task-specific, it is a general trend across most tasks. Individuals show characteristic preference for fast or accurate performance (Pew, 1969). The limiting factor in speed of performance is the subject's individual rate of information processing (Kay, 1970) and this cannot be affected by instructions. However, below this limitation, performance can conform to instructional demands, i.e. instructions can induce a speed or accuracy bias as is shown in Goodman's (1979) experiment in which he introduced speed–accuracy conflict through instructions in a mirror-drawing task.

The most effective method for influencing the speed–accuracy bias is to include, in the instructions, the scoring method to be used when evaluating performance on the task. For instance, in a dress-making factory manufacturing cheap garments, the machinist might be told that the number of garments completed each day is counted, while in a workshop producing high quality dresses, the machinist might be informed that each garment is inspected for precision machine work at the end of the day. In the first factory a speed bias is introduced and in the second an accuracy bias. The Standard, on receiving this information, will incorporate the instructional bias in the plan of action.

Central processes (2)

Two conceptually distinct central processes contribute to the control of motor behaviour; cognitive-perceptual and motor programming. While in psychological terms these two facets of the control system can be clearly distinguished, there are no corresponding brain centres which can be shown to serve either of these functions exclusively. Indeed, the central nervous system acts as a functionally integrated neural network. There is overwhelming evidence in support of the dual sensory-motor role of the classically labelled motor and sensory areas (Fetz and Cheney, 1980; Fromm and Evarts, 1982; Godschalk *et al*, 1981), the supplementary motor area (Macpherson *et al*, 1982; Tanji, Taniguchi and Saga, 1980) and the cerebellum (Brooks, 1979). Thus, the two central processing units of the closed-loop model, the Standard and the Motor Programming Unit, do not refer to anatomical entities, but are used for convenience to describe functionally, though not anatomically, distinct systems.

Standard (2a)

Processing and storage of all information relevant to motor activity takes place in the Standard (see Fig. 2.1).

Besides the input information (described above) the Standard incorporates memory traces of previous attempts at the task, and of similar tasks. In addition the Standard receives corollary discharge and sensory feedback. How these multiple factors are integrated, how they contribute to the plan of the action and how they lead to the generation of a motor programme is now to be considered.

Motor memory. Firstly, the memory component of the Standard is examined. Short-term motor memory has been investigated extensively by many workers interested in motor skill research (Poulton, 1981; Welford, 1976). Most studies employed a lever positioning task where the subject was required to move a slide, or lever which was positioned between parallel rails, to a set location and/or distance (Laabs, 1974; Schmidt, 1982). The lever was constrained to allow only unidimensional excursions. In some studies the force required to manipulate the lever was varied (Pepper and Herman, 1970). Kinaesthetic and/or visual information was transmitted to the Standard during the criterion movement. Based on this stored information, the subject was asked either to recognise or reproduce the criterion movement. Recognition or reproduction might be performed under the same information conditions as the criterion movement, i.e. intramodally, or by changing the information conditions, i.e. cross-modal recall (Diewert and Stelmach, 1977). The results obtained from the lever studies are often contradictory and provide only limited definition of motor memory characteristics. While the task is easy to administer and score, it bears little resemblance to everyday skills. Few, if any, skilled movements are as restrictive as lever positioning, allowing the subject only a single choice, either the choice of the endpoint or the extent of the movement.

An everyday example of such a restricted movement is shifting the carriage on a manual typewriter by pushing the carriage-shift lever. Although the laboratory task of lever positioning has limited ecological validity, the lever studies have provided an experimental vehicle for investigating the way in which simple movements are remembered over retention intervals, and whether practice of different tasks during the retention interval would interfere with the memory trace of the lever positioning movement.

The investigation of complex movement patterns might lead to a better understanding of motor memory processes than could be achieved from studies using unidimensional movements. In studies of the perception and memory of complex, two-dimensional movements, arbitrary curved patterns were presented to the subject either kinaesthetically or visually (Bairstow and Laszlo, 1978a,b, 1979a,b, 1980). The experimental situation is shown in Fig. 2.2.

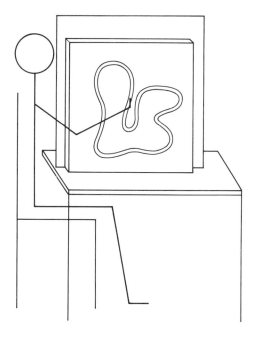

Figure 2.2 *Schematic illustration of the experimental set-up for the kinaesthetic condition.*

In the kinaesthetic condition the blindfolded subject was required to trace a grooved stencil using a hand-held stylus to guide his hand round the pattern. In the visual condition, the subject observed a pinpoint light moving round the pattern; the light was moved by the experimenter. The Standard received kinaesthetic or visual information about the size and the shape of the pattern. The sequentially received information was integrated into a global image which was stored in memory. This memory trace could be retrieved when necessary for recognition or reproduction of the pattern. The task was related to many everyday skills, such as drawing and writing.

It was demonstrated that the moment to moment perception of the sensory input was accurate (Bairstow and Laszlo, 1979a), and that the major source of error in recognition and recall performance lay in the process of integrating the sequentially received sensory information into a global image of the movement pattern (Bairstow and Laszlo, 1978a,b, 1979b). The resultant memory trace, once stored, seemed to be relatively stable. With increasing retention intervals, only minor deterioration in performance was observed.

Transfer of training. How and when are memory traces of previous movements used in the performance of a skilled task? The answer is two-fold: they are necessary in the between task transfer situation, and in the trial by trial improvement within any one task.

There are anatomical limitations to the number of movements possible around any one joint. Early in a child's life all possible elements of movements are produced, albeit in uncoordinated sequences. Skilled performance differs from these uncoordinated movements, not by the range of the movements used, but by the orderly sequence and well-defined character of the movements which contribute to the task. However, even uncoordinated actions generate sensory information and this can be stored in motor memory. It follows that, whenever a new skill is attempted, memory traces of all necessary movement components may have already been stored and may be recalled. Certainly no skill is completely novel, the degree of novelty depends on the degree to which movements previously performed are recombined. Often, a skill which is similar to the task to be learned has already been practised and can be recalled. The memory traces stored during the previously practised skill are helpful in planning the movements necessary in the new task. This reliance on a learned task in the performance of a novel skill is called transfer, or transfer of training (Holding, 1976). If transfer of training in motor skills occurs, it is most often positive, i.e. practice in one task usually enhances performance on the second related task. However, the presence and degree of transfer between two tasks cannot be predicted. The theoretical principles governing transfer effects are not fully understood as yet, though a number of studies have addressed the question of the nature of transfer principles (Laszlo and Baguley, 1971; Laszlo, Baguley and Bairstow, 1970; Laszlo and Pritchard, 1969, 1970; Laszlo, Shamoon and Sanson-Fisher, 1969; Livesey and Laszlo, 1979). When one considers that educational procedures rely heavily on transfer of training, this lack of theoretical knowledge is not reassuring. For instance, it would be helpful if the beneficial effects of prewriting exercises were known, rather than accepted at face value. Are the hours of labour spent by primary school children in drawing loops and 'Jack and Jill' patterns well spent? Do these tasks transfer positively to printing and writing skills? Would it not be more efficient to start the children on the target task of printing? Some of these questions could be answered by conducting the relevant transfer experiments. These experiments would answer the question of whether these particular drawing exercises are beneficial or not in terms of printing skill, but could not be generalised to any other tasks in the absence of theoretical principles governing transfer. Until the theoretical principles of transfer can be clarified, *ad hoc* expectations of transfer effects should not form the basis of the teaching methods employed, not without experimental verification of the expectations.

Retrieval of memory traces might be important in the between tasks transfer situation. However, memory traces of previous experiences must be used in the situation when a task is repeated in order to bring about an improvement in performance. Information about the success of the movement, or about errors which might have occurred during the movement, is stored in memory. When next attempting the task, the information is retrieved and used in the formulation of the subsequent trial.

Plan of action. The Standard is responsible for the formulation of the plan of action of the task. All information received, processed and stored in the Standard, which is relevant to the task, might be included in the formulation of the plan of action (Marteniuk, 1976). Supporting the psychological findings relevant to movement planning, neurophysiological evidence shows that overt performance of a task is preceded by neural activity in task-related cell assemblies (Brooks, 1981).

The complexity of the plan depends on the task characteristics. In skills performed within severe environmental constraints, e.g. lever positioning tasks, the plan is simple since there are only limited numbers of responses to choose from. At the other end of the scale, where spatial and temporal constraints are few (Bruner, 1970), and the possible choice of responses are numerous, the plan of action must be complex and would need to take into account many cognitive, perceptual and motor factors. Any team ball game could be considered as an example of such a skill. To pass the ball efficiently in football, the player (in terms of the present discussion of the Standard) should remember the rules of the game, previous games played, and the performance style of his team mates and his opponents. He should perceive prevailing field conditions, the position of other players on the field, the approach velocity of the ball, and his own body and limb position. He needs to recall his previous responses made in similar conditions and their success or failure. Based on all this information he must decide on the optimal plan of action or response strategy, taking into account his level of motivation, e.g. weighing the importance of his next move against possible injury. With experience, the potentially useful information becomes more extensive, while at the same time selection of relevant information becomes easier and faster.

Once the plan of action is completed the Standard activates or 'instructs' the Motor Programming Unit to initiate the required movement.

Motor Programming Unit (2b)

The same skill can be performed in many different ways. Individual movement styles are accepted, indeed expected in everyday life, e.g. a person's gait can be recognised, and a hairbrush is held and moved in characteristic ways. Even within the style adopted by an individual, variations in performance of a task occur from occasion to occasion. The motor system allows for the flexibility in the performance of skilled movements and for varied approaches to identical goals.

The Motor Programming Unit is the executor of the system. It is responsible for the selection and activation of the relevant muscles required for the performance of a specific movement if, for instance, the forearm is to be bent, the flexor muscles of the upper arm are called into action, the muscle fibres contract and the forearm is bent upwards. At the same time the opposing extensor muscles are in a relatively relaxed state to allow unopposed flexion.

Motor units. Motor units are the smallest building blocks of the motor system. It is through the activation of motor units (Basmajian, 1962) that the initiation and execution of a movement is achieved. A motor unit consists of one motor nerve fibre and all the muscle fibres supplied by it. The label 'unit' indicates that each motor unit can be activated independently from other neighbouring units. The impulses sent down along the nerve fibre from the central nervous system activate all the muscle fibres supplied by that nerve.

Different muscles differ in the number and size of motor units they contain. Muscles which participate in finely graded movements (e.g. muscles moving the thumbs and fingers) comprise relatively numerous, small motor units, i.e. each nerve fibre is connected to a few muscle fibres only. Muscles involved in supportive action, such as postural muscles of the back and thigh, are built of large motor units; large numbers of muscle fibres are supplied by a nerve fibre.

Pattern of activation. Fine motor control is achieved by graded motor unit activation patterns. Motor activities differ from each other in direction, extent, velocity and force. The Motor Programming Unit selects the appropriate motor units to be activated, the number of units and the temporal sequence of their activation, and the frequency of nerve impulses sent to each motor unit. The combination of these activation parameters defines the characteristics of the intended movement. Spatial parameters (direction and extent of movement), temporal characteristics (speed and rhythm of movement) and force production (the amount of effort needed) rely, to some extent, on independent central control mechanisms (Brooks, 1981; Desmedt and Godaux, 1978, 1979; Evarts *et al*, 1983; Fetz and Cheney, 1980; Freund, 1983; Georgopoulos, Kalaska and Massey, 1981).

The selection of motor unit activation patterns is a complex and flexible process. The flexibility of this process can best be illustrated when considering that the same goal can be reached in many different ways. While the plan of action, formulated by the Standard, defines the overall approach which should be used to arrive at the goal, it is the Motor Programming Unit which determines how the goal will be achieved. In all movements only a certain proportion of all available motor units are activated at any one time. Overtly identical, repeated movements are executed by different motor units. Analysis of each individual movement reveals that different motor unit combinations are activated for the performance of each movement (Paillard, 1960).

Motor unit activation patterns are generated not only for the specific target muscles, but for the synergist and antagonist muscles as well, in order to achieve finely graded, well-balanced movements. In addition, postural adjustments need to be initiated and continuously upgraded during the entire course of the movement.

Thus, the Motor Programming Unit, does not trigger set programmes for set movements but can use the wide freedom of choice which is at its command (Pew, 1974a).

Output (3)

The output from the system is the muscle response. Two types of responses can occur as the result of motor unit activation, isometric and isotonic. In isometric contraction the length of the muscles do not change, but the tension is increased. In an isotonic response, the tension is maintained at a constant level, but muscle length varies: shortening in the agonist and lengthening in the antagonist. Holding an object in a constant position exemplifies isometric activity, while bending an elbow is an isotonic activity. Only seldom can the two response types be observed in isolation. In most everyday movements isometric response is followed by isotonic contraction as in the case of picking up a baby from her pram. In the first stage of the response, isometric tension is generated in the arm and postural muscles until the tension is in balance with the weight of the upper limbs and of the baby. When the required tension is reached, the isotonic phase is entered, resulting in elbow flexion and lifting of the baby.

Feedback loops (4)

Two feedback loops can be distinguished in the closed-loop model under consideration, the corollary discharge (central loop) and the sensory feedback (peripheral loop). The corollary discharge loop is important in providing a record or template of the ongoing motor programme to be stored in memory. The sensory feedback loop carries information about the progress of the movement and its outcome.

The central loop, corollary discharge (4a)

Whenever a neural impulse is sent to the muscle, a copy of this motor command is also relayed back to higher central nervous system centres, i.e. to the Standard. In a number of studies the anatomical (Wiesendanger, 1969) and functional properties of corollary discharge have been investigated (Bairstow and Laszlo, 1980; Gandevia and McCloskey, 1976; Hulliger and Vallbo, 1979; Hulliger, Nordh and Vallbo, 1982; Vallbo *et al*, 1979).

The corollary discharge is thus a copy of the intention or is the programme which activates the motor units. It conveys to the Standard a record of the number of units activated, the temporal sequence and the frequency at which the units are activated. Whenever a movement is actively performed, the subject, through receiving corollary discharge, is aware of the intentional nature of the movement. Conversely, when the movement is imposed on the subject (e.g. the arm of a car driver is jogged by a pothole which induces a turn of the steering wheel), the absence of corollary discharge denotes the lack of intention. Subjectively, active movement is reported as 'I moved my arm' and passive movement as 'my arm was moved'. This difference is due to the presence or absence of corollary discharge respectively.

The information about the motor programme conveyed by the corollary discharge is stored in memory (Laszlo and Ward, 1978). Without this record of the motor commands, repetition or selective alteration of the motor programme would not be possible, and hence constancy in motor performance or improvement in motor performance could not occur.

Sensory, or peripheral, feedback loop (4b)

Corollary discharge conveys detailed information about the motor programme, but does not carry information about the progress and outcome of the movement. It is the sensory feedback loop which conveys to the Standard, information about the success or the errors in performance throughout the entire duration of the movement.

There are two possible sources of error in movement. Firstly, the Motor Programming Unit might generate an inadequate programme. Inappropriate programming occurs most frequently during the acquisition of a skill. At the beginning of training, the motor programme is often overinclusive, activating muscle groups which need not participate in the performance of the task, generating excessive muscle tension and poorly controlling the temporal aspects of the movement. Secondly, the environmental conditions might not conform to expected conditions, or might change during the course of the movement.

It is the sensory feedback information which cues the Standard about the progress of the movement. The returning sensory feedback can be compared with the corollary discharge and any discrepancy between intended and actual movement detected. When errors are detected, the Standard 'instructs' the Motor Programming Unit to generate the necessary corrective programme. The outcome of the corrective programme is, in turn, conveyed to the Standard and the efficacy of error correction is monitored.

Improvement in performance during acquisition, and maintenance of high performance level in skilled performance, depends on the functional integrity of the sensory feedback loop. Feedback information can be generated through kinaesthetic, visual, auditory and tactile sensory modalities. Kinaesthesis is always present and is possibly the most important source of feedback information. There is an intimate and unique relationship between movement and kinaesthesis. While one can move in silence, in the dark, without touching any objects, i.e. in the absence of auditory, visual and tactile feedback, kinaesthesis is always present, conveying information about posture and movement to the Standard.

Clinical evidence (Sanes and Evarts, 1984) gained from patients suffering from kinaesthetic loss has shown that these patients were grossly inaccurate in the performance of small movements and would not maintain stable posture. Kinaesthesis can also be eliminated experimentally, in human subjects, by the technique known as ischaemic block (Laszlo and Bairstow, 1971b). In the ischaemic block a blood pressure cuff is applied to the subject's upper arm, and the cuff is inflated to exert a pressure of 180 mmHg. This pressure prevents the blood from entering the arm below the cuff, and hence depriving the tissues of oxygen. Due to this anoxia developing in the tissues of forearm, hand and fingers, tactile and kinaesthetic sensations are reduced after 20–25 minutes of continuous block. The suitability of this technique for studying movement control in the absence of kinaesthesis lies in the fact that at the time of sensory loss the motor apparatus is functional. Studies using this technique show that kinaesthesis is essential for the control of movements demanding accuracy in performance especially after a task has been practised (Laszlo and Bairstow, 1971a), and that kinaesthetic feedback is stored in long-term memory, while visual feedback is only held in short-term store (Laszlo and Baker, 1972).

The importance of visual, auditory and tactile feedback varies from task to task. For instance, in handwriting, vision but not audition, and in violin playing, audition but not vision, provide feedback information in addition to kinaesthesis.

Some workers (Fitts and Posner, 1967) claim that the importance of feedback diminishes as the task becomes well learned. Performance is said to become automatic and independent of feedback; the closed-loop system becomes open loop. However, both experimental evidence and everyday observation of skilled performance contradicts this theoretical standpoint. Studies can be cited (Laszlo, Bairstow and Baker, 1979; MacKay, 1982; Pew, 1974b) which present data in support of the increased rather than decreased reliance on sensory feedback as performance of a task becomes progressively more skilful. The notion of automation may have originated from the observation that skilled performance appears smooth and free of obvious ongoing corrections.

detection and correction resulting in performance improvement.

Is there a difference between the adult learning a new skill and the development of motor behaviour with age? The young child has a less extensive store of well-learned skills to draw on when attempting a new task. Accordingly in the earlier years the child's first attempts at a skill are often based on trial and error and less dependent on transfer.

Thus acquisition of a task is shown to depend on similar processes as performance of the task. Only the degree of dependence on the various processes, rather than the presence or absence of these processes, distinguishes acquisition from performance.

3 PERCEPTUAL-MOTOR DEVELOPMENT

As children grow older, they gradually show qualitative and quantitative changes in motor behaviour, and they steadily acquire a broad repertoire of motor skills. It is common for authors writing on motor development to embark on a detailed description of this progressive change in motor behaviour. Development is predictable enough to permit what amounts to a sketch of a collective child, including estimates of the chronological age at which particular motor characteristics should appear.

There is no shortage of this *what-happens-when* account of motor development, with Gesell being one of the earliest and most prominent authors. Chapters by Halverson and Thompson in Gesell (1954) detail the development of categories of behaviour such as walking, prehension, manipulation, drawing and block building over the first five years of life, while Gesell and Ilg (1946) discuss the development of motor behaviour over the second five years of life (see Chapter 5). More recently, Gallahue (1982) describes the development of 'rudimentary movements' associated with stability, locomotion and manipulation over the first two years, and 'fundamental movements' such as walking, jumping, skipping, throwing, catching, striking, rolling and balancing over the ages of two to six years. There are other reports of the description and measurement of motor development over the years two to six (Hottinger, 1973), four to 12 (Cratty and Martin, 1969), five to 10 (Keogh, 1973) and six to nine (Rarick and Dobbins, 1975) which collectively aid the characterisation of the developmental sequence normally expected from a child.

While there are many publications on when a child acquires particular motor behaviours and when he can achieve a certain level of motor performance, there is a dearth of publications on *how* such behaviours are attained (see Kay, 1957, 1970, for early, thoughtful analyses). This lack in the literature on child development is recognised as a shortcoming (e.g. Connolly, 1981; Wade, 1982) and as a challenge to research. Gallahue (1982) commented on the scarcity of developmental models and said, 'it is appropriate that a comprehensive model leading to a theory of motor development be put forth in an effort to explain motor development' (p 39). In other areas of psychology — those of perceptual and social judgement and decision making, for example — Anderson (1980) said, 'virtually all thought and behaviour has multiple causes' (p 1), and he made the observation that multiple causation is difficult to study. This difficulty is nowhere more apparent than in the domain of the development of motor behaviour, since development is not only the end product or effect of a complex set of developing physical, physiological and psychological factors and processes, but also causes physical, physiological and psychological changes in the developing child.

It is the purpose of this chapter to attempt a *what-happens-how* account of motor development, i.e. to present an account of the psychological processes underlying the development of motor behaviour, albeit not a comprehensive model. It is acknowledged that a child's behaviour is expressed through the 'machinery' of his body which is both physically complex and changing. A clear review of the mechanics of human motion can be found in O'Connell and Gardner (1972); and Gallahue (1982), Tanner (1978) and Teeple (1978) describe various aspects of physical growth.

The description of the bases for motor development will be illustrated with the skill of catching a ball. Catching has been chosen from the many activities making up a normal motor repertoire for four reasons:

1. It is a skill that can provide the focus of discussion of a number of related activities. Motor activities can be classified depending on whether the body as a whole is stationary or moving, and whether the activity involves interacting with a stationary or moving object in the environment. Four types of activities can be listed in these terms, and examples can be given as follows: Type A — the subject is seated and reaches towards a stationary object (e.g. picking up a pen from the desk); Type B — the subject is seated and reaches towards, or aims at, a moving object (e.g. picking up an object from a moving conveyor belt); Type C — the subject moves to pick up a stationary object (e.g. walking across the room to pick up a bag); Type D — the subject moves to intercept a moving object (e.g. running to catch a tossed ball). Type D activity involves movement of the body and the object. It is the most complicated of the four types, and one example is the catching activity described in Fig. 3.1. Consideration of this most complicated type of activity will allow for a discussion of the other types at various points in the chapter.
2. Catching is a skill with a long developmental progression beginning in the first year of life with the grasping of stationary and moving objects, and with the potential to progress to the expression of the highest levels of skill seen in adult ball-game players.
3. As will be described, catching is the end product of many factors and therefore provides an ideal vehicle for describing the cause and effect relationships underlying motor development.
4. There is reasonably comprehensive literature relating to catching.

The plan of the chapter is as follows. A brief task analysis is made of the skill of catching as seen in adults (see also Alderson, Sully and Sully, 1974). Development is then traced from the neonatal period and is discussed in terms of the emergence of behaviour and the changes in capabilities that predispose to the normal acquisition of the fully developed skill. While the description of neonatal and early infant behaviour is, strictly speaking, outside the scope of this book (as described in Chapter 1), an overview of the relevant literature is useful for understanding the factors underlying motor behaviour and its development. There is a discussion of individual differences and the old 'nature or nurture' controversy, leading to the conclusion that the inherent physical and physiological nature of a child determines how he behaves in his environment, and conversely, the child's interactions with his environment leads to changes in his physical and physiological nature. A conceptual framework interrelating the development of motor, perceptual and cognitive factors is presented, which shows how the basis for behaviour becomes progressively broader as development goes on.

TASK ANALYSIS OF CATCHING IN ADULTS

The parabolic flight path of a tossed ball depends on a number of parameters, two of which are the projection angle and the projection velocity. The ball undergoes continuous changes in velocity as it moves along a curved trajectory from its point of projection. Its motion can be described by a fairly complicated series of mathematic relationships (O'Connell and Gardner, 1972), but its basic characteristics — its path and changing speed — become familiar to everyone after years of experience of observing tossed balls.

A skilled adult can catch a ball on a wide variety of trajectories, including direct frontal and lateral approaches, as well as trajectories not aimed directly at the subject. Fig. 3.1 represents a subject running to catch a ball tossed directly at him.

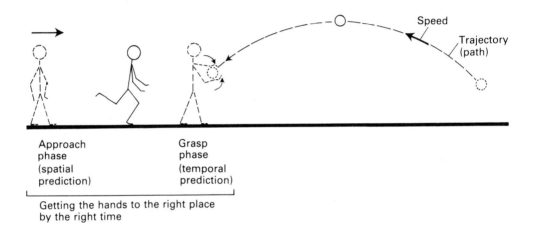

Figure 3.1 illustration labels:

Speed

Trajectory (path)

Approach phase (spatial prediction)

Grasp phase (temporal prediction)

Getting the hands to the right place by the right time

Figure 3.1 *Diagrammatic representation of a subject running to catch a tossed ball.*

Catching is typical of a wide variety of tasks in which movement is performed in an environment where the conditions are constantly changing (Type D activity, p 27). The ball is moving and the subject must move to position his body and arms to intercept the path of the ball, and the hands must be shaped to accommodate the size of the ball: the *approach phase*. The hands must then grasp at the appropriate time to halt the flight of the ball, and the arms may have to 'give' on contact to absorb the force of the ball: the *grasp phase*.

Movements of the eyes, head, arms and hands are correlated and synchronised with movement of the ball — and therein lie a number of important relationships.

1. The eyes are typically on the ball (Alderson, 1972) and head and eye movements are synchronised with the movement of the ball. This enables a visual analysis of the ball's movement and the perception of its path and speed, along with the relative position of the subject and the ball.
2. Knowledge about body and hand movements is derived from the sense of kinaesthesis. This

sense enables the subject to analyse his own movements and hov̶
what he intended.

3. The synchronous picking up of visual and kinaesthetic input rele̶
    catching the ball, leads to the correlation of input from the two so̶
    experienced at catching, the visual appearance of the approachin̶
    feeling of the body's motion form a perceptual unity — the task ̶
    like a unified action, even though there are clearly identifiable c̶

(After much practice, the external events and the motor actions become 'tied together' through the synchronous use of sensory input from various sources) thus justifying the labelling of the act of catching as a *perceptual-motor* task (Kay, 1970).

It is obvious simply by virtue of the fact that the subject begins a complex series of preparatory movements long before the arrival of the ball to the vicinity of his body, that catching involves a great deal of prediction on the part of the subject. The anticipatory movements are performed because the subject knows from past experience that he will not have time to execute the appropriate grasping movements if he does not prepare himself in advance, and his preparations are possible because of the above described perceptual analysis of ball and body movement. Both head and eye tracking of ball movement, and the placement of the body and shaping of the hands to intercept the path of the ball (the approach phase), depends on the prediction of the path of the ball, i.e. a *spatial* predictive judgement is implied. In addition, the approach phase and, more importantly, the grasp phase are timed in advance, and this depends on the prediction of the time of arrival of the ball in the hands, i.e. a *temporal* predictive judgement is implied. The grasping action begins before ball contact and there is very little latitude for error; an action that is either too early or too late will result in the ball being dropped. The later the important placement and timing decisions are made, the more difficult is the task. The fact that a skilled performer can make early decisions gives rise to the subjective impression that he moves smoothly, seems unhurried and has 'all the time in the world' (Kay, 1957). The capacity to predict enables the synchronisation of ball movement and motor actions.

Two modes of control or methods of bringing the hands to intercept the ball can be identified. One involves a rather bold prediction of the future location of the ball on the basis of a visual analysis of its motion, and a bold prediction of the future location of the body on the basis of a kinaesthetic analysis of body movement. The future course of action is planned well in advance and the catch is executed without the need for modifications 'en route'. This could be called a 'planning strategy' or a 'prediction strategy'. The other method involves making short-term predictions. The hands are brought to the ball in short successive steps by noting where the hands are in relation to the ball and by constantly updating the action. This could be called an 'error correction strategy'. Each strategy has its advantages. Being able to predict the motion of the ball, and being able to predict the movement of the body, releases the subject from the need to *constantly* have his 'eyes on the ball' or his 'mind's eye on his own movements'. He has time to attend to factors that identify the highly skilled performer; for example, he can generate the taxing movements associated with a difficult catch, or he can give thought to the broader strategies that can bring success in the competitive playing of a ball game. On the other hand, being able to update the action (error correction strategy) allows the subject to take into account an unforeseen event (e.g. another player getting in the way), or a misjudgement (e.g. the motion of the ball was not accurately predicted in the first place). In practice, a combination of these two modes of control, or ways of doing the task, will give greatest flexibility to performance. For

...le, a large part of the distance to be travelled by the body and hands may be covered on the ...s of a bold prediction (with associated advantages of the type listed above), while a correction ...t the last moment is allowed for. There is of course a 'point of no return', i.e. a point on the ball's trajectory beyond which no modification to the current catching action can be made. If something unforeseen should happen during these last milliseconds, like a deflection of the ball, no corrective action can be taken that will permit a catch. A corollary to this is that losing sight of the ball at the last moment may not affect the outcome as long as he has had sufficient time to observe the ball and the ball continues moving along the same path (Sharp and Whiting, 1974).

NEONATAL AND EARLY INFANT REACHING AND GRASPING BEHAVIOUR

In this discussion of neonatal and early infant behaviour the emergence of behaviours and the change in capabilities that lead to the normal acquisition of the fully developed ball catching skill will be reviewed. There will be a description of the way babies visually regard stationary and moving objects, and of how their visual skills in fixating and following indicate an early sensitivity to the location and path of motion of objects. One 'object' they spend much time visually regarding is their own hand, and it is suggested that this is the origin of a 'perceptual unity' between vision and kinaesthesis. There follows a description of the way babies respond to stationary and moving objects with their hands, including evidence of an early development of predictive behaviour in reaching to and grasping objects. The purpose of this discussion is to lead into a section dealing with how perceptual factors underly the transition from uncontrolled to controlled behaviour.

Before proceeding, it is necessary to introduce two terms which relate to different types of knowledge. In doing so, some material in this chapter will be pre-empted. When an infant preferentially reaches towards graspable objects that are placed within reach, it can be said that he demonstrates a sensitivity to, or an *implicit knowledge* of, location, distance and solid three-dimensionality. Likewise, when a child reaches ahead of a moving object, he demonstrates an implicit knowledge of motion — that a moving object tends to continue moving along its current path. This 'sensitivity', implicit knowledge or tacit understanding shows in behaviour, although behaviour is not the result of judgement or reasoning: the child performs as if he has made a judgement, or as if he has an understanding of, for example, distance and motion. This understanding is quite different from the *explicit knowledge* that an older child demonstrates when he makes an estimate (a verbal judgement, for example) of the distance, speed or future location of an object. Explicit knowledge (being able to make an evaluative judgement) can also show in behaviour, and the behaviour in this situation is the result of reasoning and judgement. Performing 'as if' one has knowledge (implicit knowledge) and performing 'because' one has knowledge (explicit knowledge) is an important distinction that will be taken up at various points in the following sections. In passing, it should be said that an individual may perform because he has knowledge *and* as if he has knowledge, at various points in the one action. For example, a modification is made to an ongoing reaching action on the basis of an explicit predictive judgement, followed by the continuation of that (now) modified action.

In what way do babies visually regard stationary and moving objects?

In the first months following birth babies develop a number of visual skills. They fixate on stationary objects in the first weeks and show an early preference for looking at particular features (Bruner, 1970; Dodwell, Muir and Di Franco, 1976; Fantz, 1961a). They have the potential for perceiving visual input and by one month their preferential looking suggests a sensitivity to some of the cues which specify depth (Pick and Pick, 1970) and solidity (Fantz, 1961b). By one-and-a-half months there is some visual accommodation of objects at different distances and by the fourth month accommodation is comparable to that of adults: the infant is capable of focusing automatically the image of an object placed at various distances from him (White and Held, 1966).

At two months of age, a looming object triggers a defensive blinking reaction (White and Held, 1966). This reaction becomes progressively more selective and by four to six months blinking is triggered only by objects moving towards them on a collision course (Yonas *et al*, 1977), suggesting an early sensitivity in infants to objects moving along different paths.

At birth the eyes of babies move laterally to follow a large laterally moving pattern of lines as well as a large single object (Gorman, Cogan and Gellis, 1957; Kremenitzer *et al*, 1979; McGinnis, 1930). There is a gradual change in the nature and accuracy of eye responses to moving objects, from an inaccurate tracking of large slow moving objects to the accurate following of faster smaller objects (Rancoux, Culee and Rancoux, 1983). By two months the eyes seem to anticipate the motion of the target and the infant seems to engage in active visual searching, rather than automatically following a moving stimulus (Bronson, 1974; Volkman and Dobson, 1976; White, Castle and Held, 1964).

The visual fixation of stationary objects, the automatic accommodative response and the visual tracking of moving objects facilitate the focusing of an image of stationary and moving objects onto the retina. The gain in visual acuity facilitates the perception of patterns and events in the array of light entering the eye from objects that are being visually regarded (Gorman *et al*, 1957; Ludvigh, 1955; Ludvigh and Miller, 1953; Mackworth and Kaplan, 1968). While at one month infants seem to respond differentially to the *content* of the array of light, and they rapidly develop a definite preference for looking at certain 'meaningful' stationary and moving visual patterns (Fantz, 1961a; Fox and McDaniel, 1982), exactly what is being seen is not known. However, they may first develop a sensitivity to depth and the location of an object; i.e. an implicit knowledge of *where* in relation to the child is the object, and is it graspable. Certainly by seven months they show a strong tendency to look at stationary objects that are within reach in preference to ones placed beyond reach (Field, 1977). These early visual skills facilitate the perception of events in the environment and it will be argued that this perceptual development enables the development of control over reaching behaviour (in terms of Chapter 2, through the development of a Standard).

In what way do babies regard their own hands?

One 'object' that babies spend much time visually regarding is their own hands, although active visual interest in the hand may develop somewhat later than visual interest in other objects. When babies are placed on their backs in the first months, they sometimes adopt a particular posture: the head is turned towards one side, and the arm is outstretched on that side. This posture is said to be due to an asymmetric tonic neck reflex (ATNR) and has been discussed as one of the antecedents of handedness (Michel, 1983). It has also been discussed as a precursor to reaching towards seen objects.

White, Castle and Held (1964) observed the spontaneous behaviour of infants lying in a crib. They gave a detailed account of how there is a gradual change from an automatic adoption of this ATNR posture with its unilateral regard of one hand, to the active and sustained regard of one hand, to the sustained active regard of two hands clasping and moving over the midline of the body. At $1-1\frac{1}{2}$ months: the infant was frequently in the ATNR posture. The hand to which the eyes were orientated was often in the centre of the visual field, but the eyes neither converged on it nor did they adjust to variations in its position. At $1\frac{1}{2}-2$ months: the eyes occasionally converged on and fixated the hand. At $2-2\frac{1}{2}$ months: the posture was not fixed. However, the infant still spent much time looking at his hand, and now the behaviour was much more varied and active as the infant shifted his hand, shifted his gaze and moved his head with comparative ease. At $2\frac{1}{2}-3$ months: the ATNR posture was seen infrequently, but active and sustained hand regard was common. At $3-3\frac{1}{2}$ months: active and sustained unilateral hand regard was common, but so also was bilateral arm activity. The hands were often clasped in the midline and the infant looked at them as they approached and engaged in mutual tactual exploration. At $3\frac{1}{2}-4$ months: sustained unilateral hand regard was seen less frequently but active visual monitoring of hand clasping over the midline was common (see also Williams, 1973). At $4-4\frac{1}{2}$ months: fascination with the hands and their movement began to wane.

There is evidence that this early visual fascination with hand movements is a precursor to the development of controlled reaching, in which the eyes are on the target while the hand approaches the object under kinaesthetic guidance. A study with infant monkeys (Held and Bauer, 1968) is a particularly useful demonstration of the importance of early hand regard. Monkeys reared under normal conditions accurately reach for and manipulate visible objects before the age of one month. Those reared from birth in an apparatus which precluded sight of their body below their neck developed very differently. They showed a normal interest in objects and orientated their head and eyes to look at them. They also demonstrated a capacity to control movements of the limbs which were out of sight and under kinaesthetic control. However, at a little over one month when one hand was exposed to view the initial reach for the feeding bottle was terminated as soon as the hand entered the visual field. The monkey immediately looked at his hand and watched it intently while moving it about — a fascination that resembled a stage in early human infant development discussed above. Visual pursuit of the hand was prolonged in comparison with visual following of other targets. During 20 days of testing, hand watching gradually decreased, and there was a later and gradual development of normal accurate reaching and grasping. In short, normal visually guided prehension had to be acquired by the infant monkey who had been deprived of early visual exposure to his own hands.

In summary, the ATNR in the neonate automatically places the hand within the infant's visual field and the potential exists for him to 'accidentally' see his hand. Subsequent developments in hand regard have the affect that babies are exposed, for the first time, to congruent visual and kinaesthetic input. It will be argued that the processing of this dual input, as an infant visually regards his hands while controlling their motion, leads to the development of a tacit understanding of the relationship between what is seen, what is felt and what is commanded. This implicit knowledge of the relationship between input from different sensory modalities (cross-modal relationships) and between input and output (sensory–motor relationships) is a prerequisite to the development of control over reaching and grasping behaviour.

In what way do babies respond with their hands to stationary and moving objects?

Most reports on the reaching behaviour of infants have suggested that controlled and accurate reaching and grasping of stationary objects (Type A activity, p 27) starts to occur at around five months of age; i.e. following the development of visual skills and visual regard of the hand discussed in the previous two sections. While an infant engages in visual and manual activity at one month, the two activities are unrelated — he does not reach towards objects that are visually regarded (e.g. White, Castle and Held, 1964). Reports that neonates intentionally reach for seen objects (e.g. Bower, 1972; Bower, Broughton and Moore, 1970a,b) have been criticised on logical and methodological grounds (e.g. Bushnell, 1981), and other workers have failed to replicate the experimental results (Di Franco, Muir and Dodwell, 1978; Dodwell, Muir and Di Franco, 1976).

It is generally agreed that an infant can approach an object with his hands before he has the capability to terminate the reach with a grasp. The first object-orientated arm movements appear to be visually triggered, fisted swipes (2–$2\frac{1}{2}$ months). Reaching that seems to be under ongoing control begins to develop later (4–$4\frac{1}{2}$ months; White, Castle and Held, 1964). A fully developed tactile grasp reflex in response to an object placed in the hand is present at 3–4 months (Twitchell, 1965), but an anticipatory opening of the hand as it approaches an object does not occur until $4\frac{1}{4}$–5 months (White, Castle and Held, 1964. See also Bruner and Koslowski, 1972; Field, 1977; Paine, Pasquali and Spegiorin, 1983). Not until the hand is controlled and opened in anticipation of contact with an object can a reaching action be smoothly terminated with a grasp. At $4\frac{1}{2}$–5 months controlled reaching movements, while still poorly coordinated, can be terminated with variable success (Halverson, 1932) by a grasping action that is probably triggered by contact with an object. By seven months all the components of the reaching and grasping action appear to be under the control of the infant. At 10–12 months the total action seems to be planned to a certain extent. At this age infants need only intermittently regard an object in order to obtain it. Two modes of control seem to be in operation; both an 'error correction' mode when the infant has his eyes on the object, and a 'planning mode' when his eyes are elsewhere and the action continues successfully. Furthermore, under these modes of control the reach is smooth and direct, the hand is opened in anticipation of contact with the object and the grasp, instead of being triggered by contact, may commence just prior to contact with the object (Castner, 1932; Field, 1977; Halverson, 1932; McDonnell, 1975).

One might intuitively predict that the act of reaching for and grasping a moving object (Type B activity, p 27), involving as it does the apparent complication of accurately aiming and timing a motor response in relation to a moving object, would be manifested somewhat later than the act of reaching and grasping a stationary object. However, a number of important prerequisites for coping with a moving object are established quite early in development: these include the capability to visually track the object, a sensitivity to its path of movement and an implicit understanding of the characteristics of motion, i.e. a moving object tends to continue moving along its current path. The first two prerequisites were discussed earlier. As far as the third prerequisite is concerned, babies anticipate the continuation of a motion at three months (Bruner, 1970) and anticipate the end location of an object as it moves towards them at six months (Halverson, 1932).

Once an infant can pursue and anticipate the motion of an object, and can reach for and grasp a stationary object, the step of putting the 'components' together in pursuing and grasping a moving object may also be manifested. The developmental progression over ages three to nine months in reaching for a moving object was documented in studies that included a condition in which infants also reached for stationary objects (Von Hofsten, 1979, 1980; Von Hofsten and Lindhagen, 1979). While the data were collected and presented in such a way that a direct comparison between development in the two situations was difficult to make, there were a number of indications that medium to fast moving objects posed difficulties for infants compared to slow moving objects and, by extrapolation, stationary objects.

The following is a summary of development over the ages three to nine months of reaching to moving objects as reported by Von Hofsten. Reaching for a moving object developed prior to the capability to terminate the reach with a grasp (Von Hofsten and Lindhagen, 1979). At $4\frac{1}{2}$ months infants aimed their reaches ahead of a moving object, especially when the object moved quickly. The authors observed that both the head and the eyes tracked the object during the reach, while the hand was directed ahead to an advanced meeting point. The 'prediction capability' (an implicit ability to predict the future of a moving object) of infants at this age seemed good. They did not catch at a fixed point and did not put their hands out and wait for the target. Rather, the initial segment of their reaching movement was aimed at the eventual meeting point with the object, and the object and the hand arrived at that point at approximately the same time (in the majority of cases within the same 40 msec as the arrival of the object, and in all but four cases within 120 msec). In a sense, reaching for a stationary object was a special case of reaching for a moving object: reaches were made in reference to a 'coordinate system' centred on the target, regardless of whether the target was moving or stationary. In the case of a moving object, the arm moved towards and with the object.

A detailed analysis of the development of reaching to moving objects (Von Hofsten, 1979) resembled in many ways the developmental progression for stationary objects reported by Halverson (1932). The incidence of reaching increased over the ages $3\frac{3}{4}$–9 months, and there were changes in the quality and success of reaching, including a gradual decrease in variability of the initial element of a multistep reach, a decrease in the number of steps per reach, an increase in the relative length of the first movement element and an overall straightening of the path of the approach. These observations together with others reported by Von Hofsten (1980, 1983) indicated that there were developmental changes in the control of the reaching action, including the development of a 'planning mode' of control.

While it has yet to be established whether there is a delay in the development of reaching for moving objects compared to reaching for stationary objects, it is likely that the capability to catch targets moving at 'moderate speed' is acquired sometime before 12 months of age.

The development of controlled, adaptive and economical movements in the first year

The very earliest motor activities seen in the neonate are of two types: (a) reflexive or automatic reactions to stimuli (e.g. ATNR, the withdrawal from a noxious stimulus) and (b) spontaneous/rhythmic movements (e.g. thrashing with the hands, kicking with the legs). It is likely that the earliest reflexes are not under the control of the neonate, and spontaneous/rhythmic movements appear to be poorly controlled. The question is, how does behaviour that is controlled, adapted to particular circumstances and economical, develop from these early activities. While there is general agreement on the old view that reflexes are at the root of motor development (Halverson, 1932), how directly they lead to the development of voluntary behaviour is a matter of debate (e.g. Donnelly and Connolly, 1983). On the one hand it has been observed that several of the reflexes existing during infancy resemble later voluntary movement and that reflexes may be a direct basis for voluntary movement (Lipsitt, 1979; Masters, 1981; Twitchell, 1965). On the other hand it has been argued that there is an appreciable gap between the disappearance of reflexes and the onset of voluntary movement, and the components of early skilled behaviours do not come directly from the repertory of neonatal reflexes (Bruner, 1970; Gallahue, 1982). The position adopted here is akin to the latter: while reflexes are at the root of development, they may not all directly evolve into voluntary movement. Rather, intentional movements that are controlled, more generally evolve from the spontaneous/rhythmic movements as a result of underlying psychological factors which are going to be discussed. These factors begin to be established by virtue of the neonatal reflexes. The existence of a physiological substratum of 'wired-in' reactions to stimuli *ensures* the responsiveness of the organism to its environment from the earliest times following conception, and the repeated stimulation of these relatively stereo-typed reactions *starts off* the developments of controlled behaviour from spontaneous activities within the first year of postnatal life.

The very first prerequisite for such development is the arousal of an intention — something that probably does not occur in the case of reflexes. The child must move on his own volition as distinct from reflexively reacting to a stimulus or being the unassenting generator of movements. *Intention* is a difficult concept to contemplate and ask questions about. Why does an infant *want* to reach for and seize an object? Halverson (1932) said, 'The answer seems to be that he wants it, not only for the sole purpose of possession, but perhaps that he may better appreciate it' (p 257). But this is not an explanation, and while the origin of intention has been the subject of discussion (e.g. Anokhin, 1969) it must be said that we are not close to understanding why it is aroused in the first place. Once it is aroused, intention has a number of features or characteristics which relate to, and affect, the movement to be generated (Bruner, 1973). The child wants to obtain something and there is an *anticipation* of the outcome of the act; there is a *selection* from several possible ways of getting to the object; there is a *sustained direction* of effort or attention during the reaching movement; there is a *stop order* that is defined by the anticipated outcome of grasping the desired object; and there is a *substitution rule* whereby the infant will try alternative ways of getting to the object if he was initially unsuccessful. It was argued by Bruner that the *capacity* for intentional behaviour exists at birth and that the earliest activities are converted into controlled actions by virtue of the above features, but only after the infant has had an opportunity to observe the results of his own acts.

The arousal of an intention (wanting to do something) is one matter, being able to satisfy one's desires (actually doing it) is quite another matter. Infants apparently have a desire or need to achieve certain ends some time before they can succeed in achieving them, and the reaching behaviour of infants illustrates this observation. The activity of reaching and grasping objects changes in two basic ways during the first year. The earliest responses to objects seem not to be planned at all, while later reaching movements show all the hallmarks of being planned and adapted to particular circumstances. The other change relates to the quality of movement; the earliest directed movements being a rather stereotyped swipe, followed by the development of slow, poorly coordinated though controlled reaching, and then a gradual development of economy in reaching, evidenced by a reduction in the number of corrections to the path of the movement and a faster, more direct approach to the object. While these refinements in 'what to do' and 'how to do it' bear on each other, they are sufficiently distinct to warrant separate discussion.

The development of motor behaviour that is planned and adapted to particular circumstances will be illustrated by the example of reaching for stationary objects. The capability to reach for and grasp a seen object, and subsequently to reach *selectively* for objects that appear to be within arm's length, depends on the development of a number of underlying psychological factors. One of the more important of these is the development of an implicit knowledge of how the visual appearance of something relates to the tactile or the kinaesthetic feeling of the same thing. In more technical terms, this means the development of a sensitivity to relationships in the sensory input from different modalities — development of a tacit understanding of cross-modal relationships. To illustrate this: a successful reach and grasp of an object is accomplished by a visual fixation of the object and a visual/kinaesthetic guidance of the reaching movement. The act depends on utilising input from the two separate sensory modalities. The infant can only relate input from different origins if he has previously experienced the separate input during a single activity and so established the intermodal relationships, e.g. by watching and manually exploring an object simultaneously.

As a neonate lies in his cot and spontaneously moves his eyes, arms and legs, there are unique relationships between the patterns of input from the kinaesthetic, visual and tactile receptors, but these relationships or cross-modal correspondences are not known to the child. They become established and become known only through experience. It was Howard's (1971) view that animals seek out invariants or correlations within modalities, and between different modalities, as well as between motor output and its associated patterns of sensory stimuli: 'the perceptual-motor system will surely correlate what it can' (p 252). Indeed, as Butterworth (1981) pointed out, 'the spatial organisation of the senses at birth should ensure that where cross-modally equivalent information is available in the infant's world, it will be rapidly detected' (p 54).

Having some record or knowledge of the relationships between the visual appearance of the location, size and shape of an object, and the kinaesthetic feel of the arm and hand in the situation of reaching to and grasping hold of that object, is important if the hand is to be aimed at the visually sensed location and if it is to be opened and shaped in accord with the visually perceived size and shape of the object. An implicit knowledge of such intermodal relationships first begins to be acquired by virtue of the earliest reflexive behaviours of the type discussed in a previous section (e.g. ATNR), and knowledge is developed as the infant visually regards his own hands and routinely reaches and touches objects that are within reach.

The development of an implicit understanding of intermodal relationship between visually and kinaesthetically sensed locations amounts to a perceptual-motor rule that can be expressed as: 'What I can see in a place I can also touch in that same place' (Bushnell, 1981, p 13). This rule is clearly useful for obtaining most objects; the infant can look at an object and bring his hand to it under kinaesthetic guidance. But the rule is not useful for all situations, and there follows a stage when it is overapplied and inappropriate reaching behaviour is seen. The infant seems to 'believe' that: (a) the path to a seen object should always be a direct one; (b) the visual and kinaesthetic location of an object should always be the same; and (c) everything that is seen should also be touchable. Up to eight months infants apparently do not understand the nature of glass which they can see through but cannot reach through; they do not understand mirrors and attempt to touch the image they see in the mirror; and they *persist* in reaching towards an intangible three-dimensional image of an object. They behave as if they expect to be able to touch everything they see within arm's reach (Field, 1977). The gradual discovery of exceptions to his overinclusive perceptual-motor rules fosters the development of a more subtle understanding of perceptual-motor relationships and is the means by which the infant learns more about the nature of his environment. His failure, for example, to always be able to reach directly to what he sees, enables him to learn about the nature of glass and mirrors and to plan his reaching behaviour to suit a particular circumstance.

From nine months, after the act of reaching has been overapplied for some time, and when reaching is reliable and performed with comparative ease, the infant can devote his attention to *why* he is doing something rather than how he can do it. He begins to recognise violations to his overinclusive perceptual-motor rule that everything that is seen can be directly touched. He learns about the nature of glass, and after the first contact with a glass barrier will not persist in pushing against it to follow the line of sight, but will reach around it (Bruner, 1970). By 18 months he understands mirrors well enough to know and remember that objects are not always where they look as though they ought to be, but may be kinaesthetically found in a different location to the visual location.

The above discussion highlights how the development of perceptual capabilities and the development of knowledge of the relationships between the senses (made possible through the establishment of memory for past experiences) underlies the development of motor behaviours that are planned and adapted to particular circumstances. Actions enable perceptual development and the development of knowledge about the environment, and these developments in turn lead to modified behaviour.

From this discussion of the development of reaching behaviour that is adapted to particular circumstances, we turn now to a consideration of economy and accuracy in movement. The development of economy and accuracy — the question of 'how to do it' — will be illustrated with the examples of: (a) the development of a direct path of movement to a stationary object and (b) the predictive reaching ahead to intercept a moving object. In general, infants behave as if they know what they want to do before they can control the necessary movement very efficiently or accurately. In infants younger than four months, the initial arousal of an intention to reach for an object is often followed by a loosely ordered sequence of actions, with occasional swiping contacts with the object. This is not to say that the infant's behaviour is random, but often the aim of the hand can scarcely be determined as the infant makes zig-zag attempts to make contact. The infant seems to want the object and he sustains his efforts in reaching for it (two of the features of intentionality listed earlier) but the object is unattainable. Occasionally his considerable efforts are rewarded. He makes contact, almost by accident, since the loosely organised sequence is hardly adequate for the purpose.

Two features of this early reaching behaviour can be identified: a reach is not accurately aimed at the object and is not smoothly terminated with a grasp; and attempts at reaching seem very demanding with the infant apparently needing to devote all his attention to controlling the action. The ideal action would be a direct and quick reach and grasp of the object that involves the minimum of 'mental effort' and allows the child to give his attention to other thoughts and activities. The 'smoothing of action' will be discussed first.

Reaching involves the serial ordering of constituent actions (Lashley, 1951), and the development of accuracy and economy of movement entails the ordering and regulation of initially poorly organised and fragmented movements into an economical and unified whole (mastery over degrees of freedom; Bernstein, 1967). How do the zig-zag movements come to be 'ironed out' into a straight reach terminated with a grasp? The single most important factor is likely to be the capability to anticipate not only the end result of the act, but also to anticipate the sequence of events during the reaching movement (Kay, 1970). This involves the establishment of an implicit understanding of a different set of relationships to that described earlier — in this case, knowledge of how one event in a sequence follows and is the forerunner of other events. These 'events' can be motor or sensory. The implicit understanding of the relationship between neighbouring events amounts to remembering the temporal pattern of the stream of motor output to the muscles and the stream of sensory input from the activity.

Many workers have suggested that serially organised movements are developed hierarchically (Bruner, 1970, 1973; Siegal, Bisanz and Bisanz, 1983; Thelen and Fisher, 1983). The essential idea is that all activities are made up of a sequence of movement fragments, many of which are individually manifested in the first month. The initial accidental ordering of fragments, that is rewarded with a successful reach and grasp, is remembered in terms of the sensory and motor order of events. There follows a period in which the act is repeated with increasing frequency of success. Modularisation takes place when the temporal pattern in the sensory–motor stream is remembered (in terms of Chapter 2, one component of the Standard). At this point, a sequence of movement can be controlled as a unit. A structural representation or central analogue of the movement develops (Mandler, 1962; Schmidt, 1975), and this representation of what has become a smooth sequence of activity can be used to plan future attempts to reach for a stationary object. It is not suggested here that every possible action is specifically and separately represented in memory. Rather, the attributes of smooth and direct movements are remembered in a way that is not specific to any particular action.

Memory of the attributes of smooth movement not only serves as a basis for exercising control

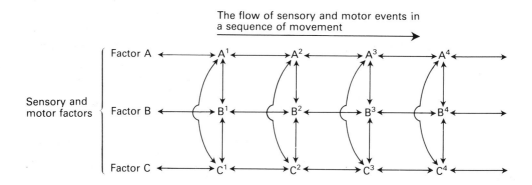

KEY
The numbered letters (e.g. A^1, A^2, A^3) represent sensory factors such as kinaesthetic input relevant to elbow joint angle as the angle changes during movement, or motor factors such as the commands to the flexor muscles of the forearm which cause changes in the angle of the elbow joint.
    Vertical arrows represent relationships at particular points in time between neural inputs arising from different sensory receptors, between neural outputs to different muscle groups, and between input and output.
    Horizontal arrows represent relationships across time between the sensory events and motor events at different points along a sequence of movement.

Figure 3.2 *Diagram illustrating that there are relationships between discrete sensory and motor events in a motor activity. Children gradually acquire an understanding of these relationships. This understanding is a basis for the development of control.*

over movement of the limb to a stationary object, but also underlies the capability to reach ahead of a moving object in order to intercept it. Implicit knowledge of the visual flow associated with a moving object enables the child to predict its future path and plan a limb movement that is aimed ahead to an eventual meeting point.

The second development in 'how to do it' relates to a reduction in the amount of 'mental effort' the child must devote to exercising control over the reaching action. This reduction in effort stems from three related developments that are going on during the first year. One development concerns the establishment of an implicit understanding of the relationship between input from different sensory modalities. This was discussed earlier in this section in terms of the development of cross-modal relationships. In Fig. 3.2, these relationships are shown as vertical arrows; one column of arrows is meant to suggest that the child has an understanding of, for example, how the visual appearance of an object at a certain location corresponds to the kinaesthetic and the tactile feeling of the arm and hand at the point of grasping hold of that object. The second development relates to the establishment of an implicit understanding of order in the sensory–motor flow of an action. This was discussed above in connection with the smoothing of an action. In Fig. 3.2, the implicit understanding of the relationship between neighbouring events is shown as horizontal arrows; one row of arrows is meant to suggest that the child has an understanding of, for example, how a discrete visually perceived location of an object on its path of movement relates to other locations along that path, or how the motor commands that have placed a limb in a certain location relate to past and future commands along the same path of limb movement. In other words, the horizontal arrows represent memory for the temporal pattern of movement, both sensed and commanded. The third development has not been explicitly discussed; it concerns the development of an understanding of the relationship between current sensory and motor events. At any point in time during a motor activity the child is generating motor commands which are responsible for the posture and movement of the body, and is also receiving sensory input. Some of this input is related to the immediately preceding motor commands and some of the input is unrelated to the activity. There is a relationship between how a posture or movement of the body is commanded and what the body looks like and what it feels like (Bairstow and Laszlo, 1980). In Fig. 3.2, these relationships are also shown as vertical arrows; a column of arrows connecting sensory and motor events is meant to suggest an implicit understanding of these sensory–motor relationships at set points in time. In summary, the grid of arrows in Fig. 3.2 conveys the notion that a child develops a global understanding of how a movement sequence looks, feels and is commanded (in terms of Chapter 2, information received by the Standard).

The question to be addressed is how this understanding leads to a reduction in the 'mental effort' a child must devote to exercising control over his actions. Each point in Fig. 3.2 represents a single sensory or motor event; for example, the visual input from an object at one point on its path or the motor output associated with the present state of the body and limbs. Before a child has an understanding of how one event relates to another, i.e. before the relationships (indicated by the arrows) are established, each event during an activity is unconnected to any other. Put another way, any given event is unexpected in terms of what else is going on at the moment, what happened before and what is likely to happen in the immediate future. This amounts to a situation in which the infant is 'bombarded' with unrelated events, any one of which could be significant; thus he is overwhelmed by information. He has no way of knowing what is significant and what can be ignored. His attempt to control his behaviour under these conditions leads to poor control because events that are unrelated to the action may be incorrectly taken into account. Control also seems laboured because he is trying to take too many events into account, any and all of which may be significant.

Relationships of the type depicted in Fig. 3.2 allow for three 'effort saving' changes to the control of behaviour. Firstly, knowing how one sensory event relates to another has the effect that when the infant attends to one aspect of sensory input, he indirectly has knowledge of other aspects of input from the same activity. For example, in the activity of reaching towards a visually fixated object, knowing the relationship between visually and kinaesthetically sensed movement enables the infant to keep his eyes on the object and bring the hand to the object essentially under kinaesthetic guidance — he does not need to have visual knowledge of hand and object movement by looking back and forth between object and hand in order to bring the two together. In other words, he does not need to attend to as many sensory events during an activity as he did before the relationships were established. Secondly, knowing how events along a sequence of action are related means that patterns of sensory input and motor output at given points are not entirely new or unexpected. This reduces the need to frequently attend to the flow of input, or the production of motor output — knowledge of the temporal pattern of events effectively 'fills the gap' caused by a lapse of attention. Thirdly, knowing how sensory and motor events are related, i.e. knowing what an action that is commanded in a certain way looks like, or what it feels like, gives the infant a 'global view' of his behaviour without the need to frequently turn his attention between the motor output that is being generated and the sensory input which is being received.

Returning now to the discussion of 'modes of control' introduced on pp 29–30, it can be noted that knowledge of sensory–motor relationships of the type depicted in Fig. 3.2 facilitates the development of a 'planning strategy' or a 'prediction strategy' in the control of behaviour. For example, the infant does not need to constantly have his 'eyes on the object', or his 'mind's eye on his own movements', nor does he need to constantly update the movement being generated. He has time to attend to other factors while a reaching action is in progress.

Another consequence of the development of knowledge of sensory–motor relationships, and the development of efficiency in the control of movement, is that the infant can use his eyes and hands more effectively to sample sensory input. Interactions with the environment are *used* by the infant to perceptually scan his environment. Perception is a process in which the infant is actively engaged (Gibson, 1983; Neisser, 1976) and the nature of the exploratory activity affects the sampling of sensory events relating to the environment (Abravanel, 1981; Heller and Myers, 1983; Wolff, 1972; Zaporozhets, 1965). The child now selectively explores his own environment and input is sampled and used to modify the exploratory process.

DEVELOPMENT BEYOND THE FIRST YEAR OF LIFE

It is useful at this stage to return to the skill of catching and review the identified capabilities that have been acquired during the first year.

Infants at one year can:

1. Visually fixate on stationary objects and visually accommodate objects at different distances.
2. Visually track moving objects, including their own hands.

3. Reach for and grasp a stationary and moving object with a direct and economical reach.
4. Demonstrate by their actions that they have an implicit knowledge of the distance, path and speed of objects that are visually regarded.
5. Reach out to a stationary object with only an intermittent visual regard of the object. This implies that they have knowledge of the relationships between sensory modalities and the relationships between motor output and sensory input.
6. (a) Anticipate an impending contact between the hand and an object, as the hand moves towards the object. (b) Anticipate the future path of a moving object. This implies that they have knowledge of the temporal pattern of motor output and sensory input associated with a sequence of activity.
7. Control a reaching movement to a stationary or a moving object that is planned and adapted to the particular circumstance. This implies the development of 'sophisticated knowledge' of their environment. For example, they are beginning to understand the nature of mirrors and glass; they also modify their behaviour depending on the speed of an object they want to grasp.

The point of immediate interest is that infants at one year *can* intercept and grasp a moving object, and they do so because they have acquired the capabilities described in the previous section. It hardly needs to be said, however, that infants at one year cannot catch a tossed ball. This capability is not typically acquired until around four years of age, and even then catching is unreliable; only large slow moving balls that are on a direct line of approach can be crudely gathered into outstretched arms and trapped against the body. Catching can undergo an extended course of development, although some adults have never acquired a high-level capability. The description of a well-developed catching skill resembles in many ways the behaviour seen many years earlier in the one year old child and already described: the subject's eyes are on the ball and the ball's movement is visually tracked. The trajectory of the ball is anticipated and the hands are aimed at an eventual meeting point. The hands and the ball arrive at this point at approximately the same time. Impending contact is predicted, the hands are opened and shaped in anticipation of receiving the ball, and closure around the ball commences shortly before contact (Alderson, Sully and Sully, 1974).

How then do the capabilities of a one year old, in relation to this illustrative skill, differ from that of adults? The singular most obvious difference is the failure of one year olds to intercept and catch *fast* moving objects. There is a sharp fall-off in catching success with only a modest increase in the speed of a target (from 3.4 cm/s to 30 cm/s; Von Hofsten and Lindhagen, 1979), and one year olds certainly cannot catch objects that move as fast as the slowest moving tossed ball (a realistic range of indoor ball speeds is 150–760 cm/s). Children aged two and three years wait until too late, often until the ball actually arrives, before initiating the necessary reaching and grasping actions (Alderson, 1972), and it has been shown that children aged four to six years do not anticipate and aim their reaching movements as far ahead of targets moving at 50–100 cm/s as do children aged nine to 11 years (Forsstrom and Von Hofsten, 1982). The other developmental change is in the capability to catch balls moving over a range of trajectories. In the studies of infant catching behaviour reported by Von Hofsten, the targets moved laterally along exactly the same trajectories trial after trial, while in the typical ball catching situation the trajectory varies. When children first show a capability to catch a ball, they can do so only when the ball is aimed directly at a convenient point immediately in front and at arm's reach. Not until much later can they catch a ball that is tossed too short, too high or to one side, demanding an extended movement or an asymmetrical reaching and grasping action of the hands.

Two superficial 'explanations' for the fall-off in catching success with increasing target speed should first be discussed. In the typical catching situation when the ball is tossed at the child, an avoidance reaction is often seen in young children consisting of turning the face away or protecting the face with the arms (McClenaghan and Gallahue, 1978). These reactions definitely interfere with the catching activity and certainly contribute to failure, but it is suggested here that they are *secondary* causes for failure, arising as they do out of a fear of being struck by the ball. The child knows from past experiences that he cannot reliably catch and therefore anticipates that the ball is likely to hit him (Fig. 3.3). The child 'knows best' and his fear and avoidance is no more unreasonable than that seen in adults who know they cannot cope with a situation. Even children who do not show an avoidance reaction fail to catch a tossed ball; hence other reasons than 'fear of being hit' must be sought.

Figure 3.3   *Example of avoidance or defensive response in ball catching by Damon, aged six years. The photograph was taken while preparing the illustrations for Chapter 7.*

The other superficial 'explanation' is that the child cannot move fast enough to catch a ball. In tasks where *maximum* speed of movement is crucial, young children are slower than adults (Sugden, 1980). However, the speed of movement that is seen when children fail to catch a ball is less than their maximum; they move more quickly in many other situations and they can certainly move quickly enough to *avoid* a moving object, but seemingly not when trying to catch a tossed ball. In any case, a skilled person does not have to move quickly when catching a ball provided he begins to interpret the movement of the ball far enough in advance, predicts when and where it is going to land, and plans the necessary movements. A child has at least two seconds to execute the movements to catch a slow moving ball tossed from a 4 m distance, and has even more time if he can interpret the throwing actions of the person tossing the ball. Thus, it is suggested that inability to catch the ball is not due to a general inability to move quickly, rather a specific inability to move quickly in this context. The explanation for failure must be found in factors other than slowness of the movements *per se*. These factors include the further development of perceptual and cognitive capabilities which will be considered in the remainder of this chapter.

The following discussion of development will occasionally divert from a strict consideration of catching a moving object. This will be necessary because of the lack of fundamental research on child development that directly relates to this skill and a corresponding lack of an explicit understanding of all the factors and events that contribute to development of the one type of behaviour.

A general feature of the literature on child development is worthwhile recounting here. While babies are the most difficult subjects for the measurement of behaviour because they cannot be verbally instructed and they cannot give a verbal report that would enable the measurement of an underlying psychological process, this difficulty is offset by the fact that their behaviours are scanty and fundamental. It is easier to design experiments for older children. However, behaviour patterns of older children are more numerous and the underlying psychological processes are more differentiated, more difficult to define and more complexly interrelated. As Keogh (1973) observed:

> it becomes increasingly difficult with each succeeding year of a child's life to describe changes and differences in motor skills. Children refine and modify their motor skills, thus producing more diverse and complex movements. Changes and differences in movements become more subtle and not as observable . . . (p 57).

It is evident that the increasing ease of experimentation does not offset the increasing diversity and complexity of behaviour, and while descriptions and theories of child development are often explicit and inclusive at the youngest ages, they tend to become specious and less rigorous at later ages. The best that can be done here is to sketch under broad headings the kinds of developments that are taking place from the first year onwards that are likely to have a bearing on catching behaviour. The picture that should emerge is that development up to one year (discussed in some detail in previous sections) is a microcosm of what continues to occur throughout life, and the developmental process is fundamentally the same beyond the first year. There is a process of progressively building on what has already been established, a development of knowledge of relationships between sensory and motor events within and across time, and a progressive differentiation and accretion of knowledge that is achieved through action, and this knowledge in turn modifies behaviour.

Perception

There are two related categories of change taking place during perceptual development: (a) the differentiation of separable perceptual dimensions within modalities — progressive discrimination where there were previously only vague impressions (Gibson, 1953; 1983; Gibson and Gibson, 1955; Masters, 1981; Pick and Pick, 1970); and (b) the development of liaisons with the establishment of relationships within and between modalities at given points in time, as well as across time during a sequence of activity — development of knowledge of the order and pattern in a sequence of events (Gelman, 1978; Gibson, 1983; Pick, 1983). In terms of Fig. 3.2, development could be likened to more rows (more separate perceptual factors) and the development of the necessary links to relate these rows (the 'columns of relationships'). The two sensory modalities most involved in catching are vision and kinaesthesis; vision will be considered first.

Vision

Catching an object depends on having knowledge of the object's distance, path of approach and its speed. The subject's knowledge may be of an implicit kind, with the activity being performed without an explicit judgement having been made. The subject may also have made an explicit judgement prior to the act of catching; and there are developmental changes in the judgement of the location and movement of objects (Pick and Pick, 1970; Wohwill, 1960). Whatever the kind of knowledge, perception of the parabolic flight path of a ball, which varies slightly every time it is tossed, poses significant problems for the developing child — problems that are not faced by a one year old infant who is presented with an object moving along a fixed trajectory, as described by Von Hofsten (1979). A brief discussion of the visual perception of velocity and acceleration of a moving object will help to highlight the fact that perceptual development continues beyond the first year as a story of the development of an understanding of the relationships that exist in the pattern of light entering the eye.

One might intuitively understand that motion of an object is perceived simply when there is movement in the image of the world projected onto the retina. However, movement of an object, of the eye and of the observer himself all produce movement in the retinal image, albeit in different ways (Gibson, 1954). Yet we readily detect movement of an object in the environment and we readily sort out whether we are stationary or moving in relation to it. Different combinations and types of eye movement, body movement and object movement produce unique sets of changes in the pattern of light entering the eye (Gibson, 1958, 1968; Lee, 1976; Nakayama and Loomis, 1974; Todd, 1981). It is not movement of an image over the retina that gives rise to the perception of movement, but specific sequences of change within the flowing pattern of light as a whole that enable us to perceive the movement of an object visually as our eyes and body move in relation to it.

One view of perception is as follows: that knowledge of the movement of an object is gained *without* interpreting the visual input because relationships that define movement are present in the input (Gibson, 1966). Neural activity in the brain corresponds in a specific way to the total pattern of input, and the pattern of this neural response is the basis for perception. This view of perception has validity at one particular age of a subject, but does not take into account perceptual development. The eyes of a one year old are essentially the same as those of a 20 year old. While both sets of eyes are presented with similar input when an object moves towards them, a one year old child sees the world in his own particular way. There is a difference in seeing which depends on age (Gibson, 1966), regardless of whether one is talking about implicit or explicit knowledge; the precise pattern of neural activity in the brain of a one year old, that results from visually following a moving object, is different from that of an adult. We can make sense of a sequence of change in the pattern of light only after our nervous system has matured, and after we learn and remember through past experience how the changing pattern relates to different types of object and body movement. Johansson (1975) observed that there is overwhelming evidence that the visual system abstracts relations from the light entering the eye and this enables the perception of rigid objects moving in three dimensions, given the two-dimensional images formed on the retina (Borjesson and Von Hofsten, 1973).

While there is evidence that adult observers are highly sensitive to many properties of the pattern of light entering the eye, they probably never become sensitive to all the relationships, and they have less knowledge than is potentially available to them (Todd, 1981), presumably because of the complexity of the relations. Indeed, as adults we do not have the benefit of a 1:1 relationship between physical events and our perception of them, and in the field of the visual perception of speed there are numerous examples of disparity between physical velocity and acceleration of an object, changes in the flowing pattern of light entering the eye, and the phenomenal (perceived) velocity and acceleration. Judgements regarding velocity are rarely accurate and are biased by many factors (Brown, 1931a; Cohen, 1962; Johansson, 1950; Richardson, 1916; Runeson, 1974, 1975) such as the size and orientation of the object, the direction of its movement relative to the observer and whether there are other stationary or moving objects nearby. It is clear that our perception of velocity depends on the overall structure and general properties of the perceptual field in which the movement takes place. What one sees may be quite different from what actually happened, and one cannot talk of a single correct phenomenal velocity associated with a physical velocity.

For there to be any degree of constancy in the perception of the velocity of an object, the general properties of the perceptual field must remain constant (Brown, 1931a) and the eyes have to remain stationary or in pursuit of the object (Gibson *et al*, 1957). But constancy is not a feature of our everyday environment. We do not follow a moving object all of the time, and many biasing contextual factors, of the type listed above, are operating. Since objects move at varying distances in a complex non-uniform environment, the observer needs some understanding of the factors that bias his perception of velocity if he is not to be grossly misled by what he sees. Such understanding, whether implicit or explicit, can develop only through the experience of actively interacting with moving objects, but judgements, even in adults, always remain labile.

The detection of acceleration or deceleration involves a perception of change in velocity. If our perception of a *constant* velocity can change depending on a multitude of factors, how tenuous then is the perception of genuine change or difference in velocity from point to point (Brown, 1931b), especially in the everyday situation? Even in the controlled and uniform laboratory situation, a large change in velocity is needed before a steady acceleration is detected (Gottsdanker, 1952a, 1952b, 1955, 1956; Gottsdanker, Frick and Lockard, 1961; Rosenbaum, 1975). In the everyday situation, factors that bias the perception of velocity do not remain constant as a ball moves through a complex environment, so the perception of true change as a ball moves along its parabolic flight path is particularly difficult.

If as adults we have difficulty in judging the velocity and acceleration of moving objects, with perception depending on relationally complex events within the flowing pattern of light entering the eye, is it any wonder that children have difficulty catching balls tossed over a variety of trajectories and at different speeds? As said earlier in this section, the eyes of a one year old receive the same visual input as the eyes of adults, and the visual relationships that define movement are present in the input to the eye. However, it is suggested that the relationships have to be learned in order to have knowledge of movement. There is a dearth of studies on the development of visual judgements of velocity and acceleration in children, and it is therefore difficult to talk in concrete terms about how the perceptual capability of adults, imperfect as it is, develops as well as it does. We do not know how a child perceives the parabolic flight path of a ball. It can be hypothesised, however, that while young children may *need* to be sensitive to many relationships in the sensory input in order to make a judgement (Wohwill, 1960), they may in fact focus their attention on isolated events which are unreliable even for adults. Only through experience do they learn *not* to rely on specific changes. They begin to take a broader view, to gain knowledge of relationships that are conducive to more reliable judgements. Later still, they may learn to attend to specific stimulus patterns which are reliable in a specific circumstance.

Kinaesthesis

While studies of kinaesthetic perception and its development are relatively rare compared to vision, it is likely that the two modalities share a common type of mechanism: the establishment of relationships between input generated by the family of receptors.

There are four anatomically and physiologically distinct classes of receptors that contribute to the sense of kinaesthesis: muscle spindles, tendon organs, joint receptors, and stretch receptors in the skin overlying the joints (McCloskey, 1978). When we move, there are relationships in the activity arising from these receptors, and the relationships vary depending on the resistance to movement or the weight of the object being lifted. What we perceive as kinaesthesis is the product of these relationships. We certainly do not perceive activity arising from the separate sources (from the muscle spindles, for example) and we do not perceive the input in discrete units during the progression of a movement (when the elbow joint is at 45°, for example). Rather, we are sensitive to the total pattern of input from the separate sources at given points in time and across time that varies depending on the amplitude, direction, velocity and acceleration of body and limb movements, as well as the resistance to movement that is encountered.

It is not known exactly in what way adults or children perceive the flow of input from the kinaesthetic receptors. While some perceptual issues have been touched on in the past, the results obtained were at best sketchy. For example, the development of body image, which includes the perception of parts of the body in relation to one another, depends partially on kinaesthesis, but methods of investigation have had the effect that the contribution of kinaesthesis was not defined, nor were normal developmental changes established since the early literature was based on clinical observations (Pick and Pick, 1970) (see Chapter 7 for developmental data on the judgement of limb positions).

It has been shown experimentally that children aged five and six years have problems with kinaesthetically discriminating the direction of a line (Over and Over, 1967), and that fine directional discrimination is only gradually acquired (see Chapter 6 for developmental data). In addition, developmental data has been gathered on kinaesthetic velocity discrimination (see Chapter 7). It is, however, fair to say that while there are many indications of marked developmental changes in the accuracy of explicit kinaesthetic judgements, we are far from an understanding of the details of the way in which this multifaceted sense develops.

Cross-modal development

While vision has a major role in the perception of the approach path, distance and speed of a moving object, reference to the two modalities of vision and kinaesthesis is normally necessary for judgements to be made, especially when the observer himself is moving. Perception of the *direction* of an environmental object relative to the body as a whole depends on both visual and extravisual factors, including the location of the object's image on the retina, the position of the eyes, the position of the head and trunk and the orientation of the entire body (Cohen, 1981). Only when all this visual and kinaesthetic activity is taken into account can the direction of an object be specified. In addition, an observer senses his own movements partly through kinaesthesis and partly through vision. The perception of *distance* in the environment is facilitated by the observer moving and noting the visual and kinaesthetic changes. An observer can judge the *speed* of an object only when he has judged its distance (see Gogel and McNulty (1983) for a consideration of this issue), and has noted whether he is moving in relation to it. In short, a sharp functional separation between the senses is not a factor in the everyday judgement of the approach path and speed of a moving object (Gibson, 1958), and there is a perceptual unity between the senses in many activities — the visual appearance of an action is often not perceived separately from the kinaesthetic feeling of the action, rather the action is perceived globally (Lackner, 1981; Ryan, 1940).

Since everyday perception of the motion of an object depends on a close cooperation between the visual and kinaesthetic modalities, it is to be expected that young children will make inaccurate judgements when they attempt to take both modalities into account, because the modalities themselves are undeveloped, and the complex cross-modal relationships have not yet been learned. There is widespread agreement that while some relationships have already been established during the first year (Bryant, 1974), development of intersensory liaisons continues throughout childhood (e.g. Alderson, 1972; Williams, 1973) and indeed into adulthood (e.g. Riesen, 1982; Welch and Warren, 1980), and developmental studies have been reported (e.g. Birch and Lefford, 1963, 1964; Connolly and Jones, 1970; Millar, 1972). The sampling and encoding mechanisms in such modalities as vision, touch and kinaesthesis have much in common, but they are far from identical. It has been hypothesised that if input is to be related from one modality to another, supramodal mechanisms have to be developed for sampling and relating events from the separate systems (Abravanel, 1981).

Some workers have said that perceptual development progresses towards a closer correspondence between our perception of the environment and its physical nature (perception becomes more veridical; e.g. Abravanel, 1981; Gibson and Gibson, 1955), while others say that such a progression is not a feature of development. Rather, a change towards the development of knowledge of the relationships between events is the crucial product of development, and the resulting total perceptual experience can be more or less veridical (Wohwill, 1960). The tendency to relate sensory events is a basic property of perceptual mechanisms, and there is unmistakable evidence that adult perceptual mechanisms retain some of the plasticity that is a feature of children, and the *maintenance* of perceptual capabilities depends on the continuous active exposure to correlated sensory events (London, 1954; Riesen, 1982; Welch and Warren, 1980).

Cognition

The term cognition means: to have knowledge, understanding, grasp or mastery of a situation. The field of cognitive development embraces such topics as the development of perception, attention, memory, language and problem solving capabilities. The sampling of sensory information relating to events which surround our activities in the world is the first step in a chain that enables us to have knowledge of our environment and our interactions with it. The study of cognition is the study of processes by which sensory inputs are transformed, reduced, elaborated, stored, retrieved and used (Neisser, 1967). As a child develops, his knowledge of the world becomes progressively less dependent on his immediate sensory–motor experiences (Keil, 1981).

As outlined in a previous discussion of implicit and explicit knowledge, we can have knowledge of a situation at many levels, and we can demonstrate our knowledge in a number of ways. As an illustration, take the example of the speed of a moving object. When an infant tracks a moving object with a controlled movement of his eyes, and adjusts the speed of his eye movements to the speed of the object, he demonstrates an implicit knowledge of speed and its variations. This knowledge does not involve much 'thought', but the fact that he adjusts his own behaviour in accord with an external event demonstrates that the infant knows something about that event. It will be some years before the child's knowledge of speed is sufficiently well established for him to know which objects in his environment move faster than others. At this level he knows that one object moves faster than another when it is seen to pass it, and this knowledge is now independent of his own immediate activities. Cars generally move faster than trucks and he may demonstrate an explicit knowledge of speed with a model car that has all the attributes of a racing car. He may also grasp the difference in meaning between the words 'fast' and 'slow' and be able to vary the speed of his own movements depending on a verbal command. Some further years of accumulated experience with moving objects (viewed, judged and interacted with in various circumstances) will be needed however before he has an abstract understanding of speed in terms of its physical nature; i.e. speed of an object relates to the distance it covers in a given period of time, or perhaps the elapsed time for it to cover a certain distance (Dembitz, cited by Gerhard, 1959; Johansson, 1950). At this level, knowledge can be far removed from an observer's immediate sensory–motor activities and past experiences, and may even be contrary to what *seems* to be the case in a situation. Only when he has grasped the relationships between distance, time and speed, and the effect of the viewing location on the appearance of distance and speed, will he cease to make what seem to be obvious errors in the explicit judgement of speed of an object (Siegler and Richards, 1979; Williams, 1973), and only then will he begin to understand that an object viewed from a distance (e.g. a satellite) may be moving very fast even though it *appears* to move slowly. Basic levels of knowledge are normally acquired without any specific tutelage. More advanced levels can also be acquired without tuition; e.g. the thoughtful observer may derive for himself the relationship defining physical velocity. However, the more advanced the knowledge the greater the effect of specific tuition.

The issue of central concern to psychologists studying cognitive development is how this progressively more abstract knowledge is built up from our actions and experiences in the world. Internal representations of external phenomena and events consist of relationships between the relevant sensory input, and relationships between these relationships, etc., forming a hierarchical structure (Fischer, 1980). The structure of the world makes certain relationships more obvious than others and cognitive development consists partly of becoming sensitive to, or aware of, regularities at higher and higher levels. The hierarchical structuring of knowledge has features that are worth recounting here.

1. In the establishment of knowledge during cognitive development, there is no separation between thought and action because thought is literally built from sensory–motor skills. On the other hand, each level of organisation has unique properties which are dependent on the properties of elements at lower levels, but appear only when these have become interrelated (Siegal, Bisanz and Bisanz, 1983).

2. Development occurs against a background of some restructuring of knowledge, but just as importantly, against a core of unchanging relationships. The highly conspicuous differences between the behaviour of children and adults tends to obscure the even more remarkable similarities (Keil, 1981). The existing knowledge structure is an invariant core which constrains the direction of future development, and individuality is maintained while developmental change goes on.

Knowledge of the world acquired during cognitive development is the result of many perceptual-motor experiences. On the other hand, this acquired knowledge affects the way we perceive the world. At no stage in our development can we be characterised as the passive recipients of sensory input. Rather, we are actively and intentionally engaged in directing our eye movements and limb movements in a visual, tactile and kinaesthetic exploration of our environment, and we thereby exercise cognitive control over the perceptual process (Heller and Myers, 1983; Neisser, 1976; Pick, 1983).

There are developmental changes in the way children direct and use their eyes and hands to explore their environment (Wolff, 1972), changes which are directed by cognitive processes and which accompany important developments in the effectiveness of perception and judgement. Perception in a young child (for instance, three years of age), confronted with a novel situation, is often limited by his exploratory activities which are too global and incomplete. Children gradually change their scanning behaviour and direct their eyes and hands in a more complete scanning activity, leading to a better capacity to integrate and unify parts of a perceptual field (Abravanel, 1981).

The steady improvement with age in the capability to direct movements of the eyes when tracking a moving object, i.e. to relate eye movement to object movement, results in an improved capability to perceive the details of the size, shape and texture of that object (Muijen, 1969). These factors are important to know about if the hands are to be shaped and closed in anticipation of contact with a tossed ball, for example.

Cognitive processes facilitate the development of intersensory liaisons. For example, the eyes and the hands of adults behave in similar ways when an object is scanned, and the separate senses of vision, touch and kinaesthesis seem to register the same phenomenal experience (Gibson, 1962) — a familiar cup with a characteristic handle can be recognised when its features are visually scanned or manually scanned. The analogous behaviour of the eyes and the hands which facilitates such commonalities in perceptual experience is gradually developed and is directed by a supramodal or cognitive process (Abravanel, 1981).

In the next sections, two aspects of cognitive development will be discussed; namely, the development of memory and the development of a capability to anticipate and predict.

Memory

A central factor in the previous discussion of perceptual development and cognitive development is the capability to remember relationships. This amounts to remembering past experiences, and it is said that the capability of young children to solve problems and to perform a variety of tasks is often affected by their limited capability to remember the past (Gelman, 1978). Remembering a sequence of events relating to a movement pattern, for example, is difficult even for adults (Bairstow and Laszlo, 1982; Franks and Wilberg, 1982), and even more so for children (see Chapter 6 for developmental data on the ability to remember a movement pattern).

Literature concerning the development of three stages of memory for mainly visual events was reviewed by Clark (1978). A short-term sensory store was said to maintain all environmental stimuli for approximately 0.5 seconds after the offset of a physical stimulus, and subjects over the age range of five to 21 years do not differ in this initial intake and storage of visual input. Certain events or relationships are abstracted from this sensory store and stored in short-term memory for approximately 30 seconds. The older the child, the better able he is to recall events after a brief delay, including visually and kinaesthetically sensed locations (Ashby, 1983; Smothergill, 1973) and kinaesthetically sensed movement patterns (see Chapter 6). This improvement in memory may relate to an improved capability to retrieve factors from the short-term sensory store, as well as an improved capability to keep what is remembered 'in mind' by mental rehearsal. There has been little systematic research on short-term memory for motor events in children. Long-term memory allows us to retain a record of sensory and motor events over a period of minutes, days or even years. Again, there has been little systematic research on the development of this capability.

We do not know exactly what underlies the obvious (but under-researched) capability to store and retrieve a record of past events, but the importance of such a capability hardly needs to be debated. If sensory and motor activities had no long-lasting effects on the central nervous system, i.e. if there was no memory, our behaviour would never progress beyond the most primitive reflexive and spontaneous behaviours of the type seen in neonates. Furthermore, there could be no chance of change or improvement in motor functioning no matter how much practice was engaged in. For example, memory for a movement pattern enables that pattern to be repeated in the future (Bairstow and Laszlo, 1982; Franks and Wilberg, 1982), while memory for predictable components within a movement pattern enables a subject to devote his attention to the control of other parts of the pattern not yet mastered (Frith and Lang, 1979). On the other hand, memory for movement can change the mode of control, leading, for example, to a heightened dependence on specific sensory input (Laszlo and Bairstow, 1971a; Laszlo, Bairstow and Baker, 1979).

Anticipation and prediction

One effect of having knowledge of the relationship between events along a sequence of action is the development of a sensitivity to, and appreciation of the flow of activity, i.e. knowledge of how one event is inevitably the outcome and forerunner of others. This underlies the capability to predict the future course of a moving object both in terms of where it is likely to go and when it is likely to arrive at a given point (spatial and temporal anticipation; Schmidt, 1968). A large number of studies with adults have reported on: (a) the accuracy of prediction of the future of an object (or oneself) moving with a constant velocity or an acceleration (e.g. Bonnet and Kolehmainen, 1969; Ebbenson, Parker and Konecni, 1977; Ellingstad, 1967; Ellingstad and Heimstra, 1969; Foot, 1969; Gerhard, 1959; Gottsdanker and Edwards, 1957; Lee, 1976; Rosenbaum, 1975; Schiff and Detwiler, 1979; Slater-Hammel, 1955, 1960; Todd, 1981); (b) the accuracy of extrapolation or continuation of motion (e.g. Franks and Wilberg, 1982; Gottsdanker, 1952a,b, 1955; Hammerton and Tickner, 1970); and (c) the effect of partial visual occlusion of a tossed ball on catching success (e.g. Nessler, 1973; Sharp and Whiting, 1974;

Whiting, Gill and Stephenson, 1970). Themes emerging from these studies include: difficulty of predicting and extrapolating the future of an accelerating target; an increase in error in spatial and temporal predictive judgements when the span of time or distance over which the future has to be predicted is increased; a decrease in catching success that comes about when the observer sees only a small part of the ball's trajectory, or when his vision of the ball is occluded too far in advance before its arrival at the hands; and restricting vision of the ball has a greater effect on the grasp phase than the approach phase (subjects can intercept the ball but not catch it), suggesting that temporal anticipation may be more difficult than spatial anticipation.

Studies on the development of the capability to predict and extrapolate motion are relatively rare, and those that have been reported relate primarily to the visual modality. Certainly an implicit knowledge of the visual order in a sequence of events is developed early (see earlier discussions on the reaction to looming objects, and avoidance reactions), and it has been suggested that there is development both in the accuracy of explicit predictive judgements and the speed with which such judgements are made by children (Wade, 1976). Children from the age of six years can, to a certain extent, predict the path of a moving object, and in a laboratory task they can 'intercept' an object after a period of visual occlusion of its motion (Dorfman, 1977; Haywood, 1977), but there is an improvement in the accurate timing of the interception up to the age of 14 years. In a study of the prediction of motion of a tossed ball, children of varying ages watched part of the ball's flight and ran to a spot where they thought it would land (Williams, 1973). The speed and accuracy of judgements changed with age. Up to eight years of age, children were quite poor at predicting the landing place, i.e. they responded quickly but inaccurately. At nine years there was a complete reversal of behaviour: children responded slowly but precisely, taking time to make a proper judgement. At 10 years children were a little less accurate but quicker, and at 11 years of age they were quick and accurate. Such findings suggest a gradual improvement in capability to predict the path of a moving object and a change in capability to use this newly developing predictive skill. In the ball catching situation, the eyes of young children seem 'glued' to the approaching ball (they cannot catch it if they look away briefly), while adults can achieve success with only intermittent 'sampling', effectively filling in the gaps by accurately anticipating the continuation of motion and predicting the future path. The development of the capability to predict and extrapolate motion almost certainly depends on active experience of pursuing moving objects with the eyes, hands and body, and is most likely not to be restricted to the visual modality, although the capability to predict from kinaesthetic input has yet to be studied in detail.

Metacognition

A higher level of cognition is metacognition, which refers to the knowledge people can have of their own cognition and to the control they are able to exercise on these cognitive activities (Lefebvre-Pinard, 1983; Masters, 1981). Metacognitive behaviour includes: checking the outcome of any attempt to solve a problem, planning the next move, monitoring the effectiveness of any attempted action, and testing, revising and evaluating one's strategy for learning (Brown, 1978; see also Chapter 2 for a description of the function of the 'Standard'). Helson (1949) identified a metacognitive attribute in adults in his hypothesis of *par* or *tolerance*. It was said that operators seem to have a standard of par or excellence representing the maximum error they will tolerate under a given set of conditions. Tolerance shows itself in a variety of ways: the amount of error which an operator will not strive to reduce; the amount of effort that will be made to overcome difficulties and defects; the degree to which the operator concentrates on the task, overcomes distractions, boredom and the like; and the amount of external encouragement or reward needed to motivate best performance.

Infants from the first year demonstrate behaviours which imply some degree of metacognition. For example, the control over reaching behaviour is a cognitive activity as defined by Fischer (1980). Infants from around four months indicate that they have knowledge of their own reaching behaviour when they do not even attempt to reach for an object that moves too quickly (Von Hofsten and Lindhagen, 1979); they seemed to attend to the fast object and there was ample time to initiate an action, but they behaved as if they knew they could not grasp it and preferred to sit and watch it pass by. There is a gradual emergence and then subsequent change in 'wanting to do it oneself' (Geppert and Kuster, 1983, p 355). For example, young children can become very impatient when offered help or guidance, while it has been observed that children aged five to six years, when presented with a diamond shape to copy with pencil and paper will exclaim, 'I can't do that!' (see Chapter 7). They know that they cannot exercise control, even before trying.

Children gradually reach an awareness and mastery over their own thoughts and actions; they gradually acquire a sharper realisation of what they know and what they can do, and develop a greater intolerance for error. As Alderson (1972) suggested, part of the reason why young children fail to catch a ball is that they have not yet realised that the problem lies within themselves and that they need to examine their own approach to the ball catching situation.

The effect of cognitive and perceptual development on motor behaviour

'Developmental psychologists tend to be only marginally interested in motor development and then only as a visual indicator of cognitive functioning' (Gallahue, 1982, p 4). One scarcely needs to do more than quote this observation which refers to the common use of motor test items for the measurement of cognitive capabilities, to illustrate the strongly held view that cognition affects behaviour. There is a relationship between the way an individual thinks about his environment and the way he acts on it (Lefebvre-Pinard, 1983), and it has been said that representational and abstract skills are instrumental in the production and control of sensory–motor actions (Fischer, 1980). However, we do not yet understand the ways, the means and the conditions under which thoughts are turned into actions. At a metacognitive level, the setting of one's own tolerance for maximum error will define the limits to one's performance in a given situation (Helson, 1949). Indeed, without metacognitive and cognitive control the high level of skill shown by, for instance, an outstanding ball player could not be attained.

An effect of cognitive processes on the current perceptual-motor behaviour of an individual can be inferred from studies which show a change or even a deterioration in behaviour at a time when a new mode of control is being acquired and employed; for example, when confronted by an object with ambiguous or unexpected features, or a gadget that they do not understand, adults and children direct their eyes and hands to an intensive exploration of its properties, movements which bring about multisensory interactions and eventual understanding (Bushnell, 1981); directing one's attention to an action that is normally performed almost without thought can produce a debilitating effect on performance but may also enable a reappraisal of the effectiveness of one's control (Lefebvre-Pinard, 1983); at one stage in the development of the capacity to predict the future of a moving object, children know their judgements are inaccurate and will direct slower responses to enable more accurate judgements (Williams, 1973); in the development of accurate pointing to visual targets, children become very inaccurate as they try to exercise control over the action based on sensory input picked up from the movement (Hay, 1978, 1979). In general, the deterioration in performance that is sometimes seen when new perceptual or cognitive skills are being acquired may be due to a diversion of attention away from motor control toward trying to understand a new set of events or a lack of capability to apply a new understanding to the control of behaviour, or both.

Returning now to the illustrative motor skill of catching, young children respond by moving their body and limbs when a ball is tossed in their direction, but their response fails in two major respects: they are slow in beginning their movements, often not commencing until after the ball has struck them; and even after they can manage to hold onto a ball that is tossed directly into their arms, they fail to catch balls that are tossed too high, too short or to one side. The remainder of this section will be devoted to discussing what this failure implies in terms of cognitive and perceptual development.

Two types of development will help to bring this motor behaviour under control so that it is appropriately aimed and timed: namely (a) the capability to have *accurate* knowledge of the conditions in which the task is being performed (this includes knowledge of the trajectory and speed of the ball, of the position and movement of the body, and of how the body relates to the ball); and (b) the capability to have this knowledge *quickly*.

The first point was discussed in detail in a previous section on perceptual development. The capability to have a global 'perceptual grasp' of the current situation undergoes a long developmental progression which continues on through adulthood. Our perception of the world is not always veridical, neither is it always complete, but as adults it is likely that the implicit and explicit judgements we make are 'closer to the mark' than are the judgements of children; our knowledge of relationships results in many factors being taken into account when a judgement is made, without being overwhelmed with a mass of significant events. We are also less prone to making use of isolated events than are children so that our judgements are more broadly based and more balanced.

When we attempt to control our behaviour in relation to an external or environmental set of events, our perception of these events must affect the adequacy of control of our movements. Some experimental studies can be quoted in support of this contention. For example, characteristics of the total perceptual field affect the way motor tasks involving the aiming for and tracking of moving objects are performed by children and adults (Laszlo *et al*, 1980), and the capability to detect differences in the speed of movement, and dynamic visual acuity, have been related to tracking (Brown, 1961) and catching (Sanderson and Whiting, 1978). The way we perceive our world determines how we respond to it.

The second point, the capability to have knowledge of a situation *quickly*, was considered in the section on neonatal development when the 'mental effort' an infant devotes to exercising control over his actions was discussed. No matter what the age of a subject, he cannot simultaneously attend to every sensory and motor event that is going on at the one time, and cannot utilise all the separate inputs. The wealth of events far exceeds a central processing limitation, and there are mechanisms that bring about a selective attention to particular factors. Prior to the establishment of relationships of the type discussed in connection with Fig. 3.2, a child is faced with the need to attend to a larger and perhaps different array of factors, than are adults; when trying to control their behaviour, they are overwhelmed with sensory events because of the uncertain relationship between them (Kay, 1970; Wade and Davis, 1983). What appears simple for an adult is complex for a child. A subject who needs to take into account many unrelated factors in order to control his behaviour will either have to devote more time to attending to each of these separately, resulting in a slow though accurate judgement being made, or else may attend to fewer factors and make a quick, ill-considered and possibly inaccurate judgement.

A major developmental change that facilitates quick judgements relates to the perceptual and cognitive organisation of events, through the establishment of relationships between events. This not only leads to more accurate judgements, but also a reduction in the number of factors that must be attended to in order to have knowledge of a situation. After the establishment of relationships, knowledge of one event enables, as an automatic concomitant, knowledge of other events that most likely happened before, are happening now and will probably happen in the immediate future — knowledge that is accrued without the need to actually attend to a multitude of factors.

The discovery of relationships and the reduction in the information load can only be effected by an active interaction with the environment and is facilitated by a number of developmental changes: (a) an improvement in capability to maintain a state of attentive readiness (Elliot, 1970; Mulder, 1983; Pick and Pick, 1970); (b) an improvement in the maintenance of attention across time (Pick and Pick, 1970); and (c) an improvement in selectivity, or degree to which a child may choose to process specific events and ignore others (Mulder, 1983). The reduction in the information load resulting from these developmental changes leads to an increase in the speed with which judgements can be made (Pew and Rupp, 1971; Wickens, 1974).

In a situation in which a child is free to choose the speed with which he moves, he may not be hampered by a need to take many unrelated factors into account because he can slow his behaviour to accommodate the information load. However, lack of knowledge of relationships and lack of redundancy among the many events is a particular handicap in a situation like ball catching; the child deals with the many sensory and motor events sequentially and therefore slowly, but he cannot slow his behaviour sufficiently because his movements have to be paced to the speed of the ball. Hence, he has to (a) make an ill-considered judgement (he moves quickly enough, but misses the ball), or (b) devote more time to dealing with the events (he begins to move too late), or (c) attend to earlier parts of a ball's flight and make a prediction over a longer span of time [increasing the span over which predictive judgements are made leads to inaccurate judgements even for adults (Schiff and Detwiler, 1979), and probably more so for children]. The child is in a 'no-win' situation and his handling of sensory and motor events inevitably leads to failure in ball catching. The development of economy and speed in the use of events to control behaviour is all important for quick and accurate control, particularly when the movement required has to be paced to an external event.

INDIVIDUAL DIFFERENCES AND THEIR BASES

There is no doubt that the genetic makeup of an individual is a primary determinant of his physical structure and is also one determinant of his behavioural characteristics. We are broadly constrained in the types of motor behaviours we can acquire, but even subtle variations in genetic makeup or genetic abnormalities can have physical and behavioural effects, and cause deviations in individuals (Carter and Fairbank, 1974). At an even finer level, variations between individuals who have no genetic abormalities account for physical differences such as height, proportion of body parts, muscle mass, etc., which predispose to excellence in certain areas of physical endeavour. Genetic factors have also been implicated in variations in intelligence and personality, and the field of 'behavioural genetics' seeks to specify and explain genetic sources of variance in such domains (Masters, 1981).

As far as the *development* of motor behaviour is concerned, the genetic makeup of a neonate must partly affect the nature of behavioural change. The sequence and rate of his physical growth and maturation (including that of the central nervous system) is guided by genetically controlled biochemical and physiological processes, and the types of behaviour that a child is capable of acquiring at any given age must be broadly constrained by his stage of physical development. Indeed, there is a broad pattern to the early emergence of motor capabilities, with an underlying tendency for cephalo-caudal, proximo-distal sequence of mastery over body parts (Gallahue, 1982) — a sequence partly determined by maturational changes within the central nervous system. For example, control over the proximal musculature for the approach phase of reaching manifests before control over the distal musculature for grasping (Halverson, 1932).

It must however be emphasised that the genetically controlled sequence of growth and maturation only defines the *potential* for development (Malina, 1973). While basic changes in the architecture of the central nervous system are genetically determined, there is no doubt that subtle changes and remodelling are induced by the experiences we have in interacting with our environment (Cotman and Nieto-Lampedro, 1982; Riesen, 1982; Spinelli and Jensen, 1979) and the realisation of potential is strongly influenced by such experiences.

Almost immediately following birth, the baby's encounters with the environment, sensed through the various modalities, induce modifications to the fine structure and function of the central nervous system. These encounters thereby affect the subsequent behaviour the baby will manifest and control. Within weeks, the behaviour of the infant is a product of genetic and environmental factors. Hence, while there is some early delay in the manifestation of visually directed grasping in premature and small-for-age babies, they seem to rapidly catch up as a result of experience, and most acquire the capability to grasp an object between the fourth and fifth month (Paine *et al*, 1983). Also, the onset of hand regard, the onset of visually directed catching and the growth of visual attentiveness are significantly affected by environmental modifications. Many authors subscribe to the view that perceptual-motor development and learning result from a complex interaction between environmental and inherited factors (e.g. Fentress, 1981; Malina, 1973; Pick and Pick, 1970; Schiller, 1952). Furthermore, since there is essentially no separation between thought and action (Fischer, 1980), cognitive development must reflect experience-induced changes in the central nervous system.

The two determiners of development, genetic and environmental, in combination, lead to large individual differences at all ages. Individual children begin to develop different capabilities at different ages, and they develop at different rates and reach different final levels. The order, rate and final level of development is so variable that the concept of the 'average' child has little meaning when trying to account for behaviour. The study and understanding of behaviour would progress a long way if it was possible to account fully for individual differences, i.e. to be able to say exactly what cognitive, perceptual or motor capabilities determine how an individual behaves the way he does (Campbell and Richie, 1983; Carroll, 1983; Fleishman, 1972; Meyers and Dingman, 1960). While individual differences at all levels of functioning begin to emerge within the first year, the relationship between capabilities that forms the structure of behaviour at different ages of development has yet to be determined.

THE BROAD PICTURE OF DEVELOPMENT

In Fig. 3.4 an overview of the nature of motor development is given. In the left hand column the progression from the neonatal uncontrolled and non-adaptive reflexive and spontaneous behaviours, to controlled, accurate and adaptive behaviours is shown. These later behaviours must include not only skills of the type seen in ball games, gymnastics and the shaping of our physical surroundings, but also the subtle movements used in the advanced communication of thoughts and emotions. The progressive refinement in capability to mobilise and control the motor system almost certainly continues over the first 20 years, and there are changes throughout life in the way we employ this system which we are mastering, to both adapt to and control our environment. In the top row of the figure another progression is shown, namely, the development of progressively more abstract knowledge of our environment and our relationship to it. The full arrows in the body of the figure are intended to indicate the building of knowledge or skills on the basis of active interactions with our environment, while the broken arrows indicate the skilled control we exert over perception, and over our actions, depending on the knowledge we have acquired. It will be seen that the term 'behaviour' is linked to motor, while the term 'skill' is reserved for perception, cognition and metacognition. This use of terms is meant to highlight the important fact that a 'motor skill' cannot exist in isolation from perceptual and cognitive processes. Rather, *skilled motor behaviour* is a reflection of underlying perceptual and cognitive skills. No time scale is given because the scale depends on the particular behaviour. For example, some communication behaviours and some metacognitive skills are acquired in the first year but these are built on over years of experiences.

Three generalisations spring from this view of development. The first is that the basis for behaviour becomes broader and broader as development progresses, and the older the individual the greater the number of perceptual and cognitive factors that can potentially affect 'what he does, how he does something and when he does it'. Reference to the overall triangular configuration of arrows in Fig. 3.4 will help to illustrate this point. A neonate has little or no control over primitive reflexes, and spontaneous movements appear to be non-purposive, non-adaptive and not well controlled. In the case of reflexes, the infant's movements are automatic reactions to stimuli, and in the case of spontaneous movements he seems to be the unassenting generator of the particular pattern of movement involved in kicking with his legs and thrashing with his arms. By the time a child or an adult can plan and control behaviour that is adapted to specific sets of circumstances, the movement he generates is controlled from a broad base of perceptual and cognitive skills — which is not to say that the capability to generate a basic reaction is ever lost. With development, everyday behaviour becomes more and more qualified by the child's perception of the world, his understanding of its physical nature and his understanding of his own capabilities to affect and control his environment. Since the progressively broader perceptual and cognitive capabilities a child acquires are in large measure a function of his specific experiences, points of possible comparison (and difference) between individuals become more numerous and difficult to define with increasing age.

The second generalisation is that a physical disability upsets the normal interaction between the child and his environment. A disability, especially one 'incurred' early in development, even motor inactivity, has wide-ranging effects on subsequent perceptual and cognitive development because such development depends on an active interaction with the environment (this is indicated by the full arrows in the body of Fig. 3.4). This compromised perceptual and cognitive

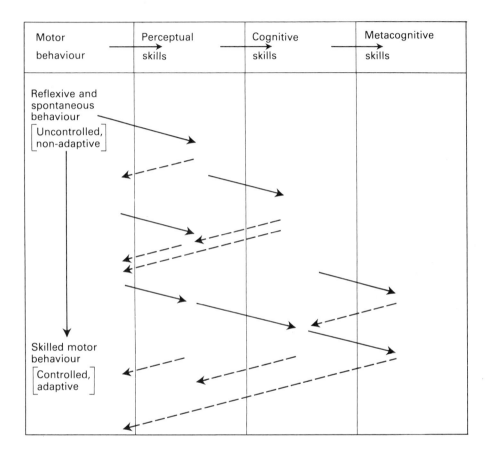

Figure 3.4 *Diagram illustrating a broad view of development in terms of a reciprocal relationship between motor and perceptual/cognitive factors. The acquisition of perceptual and cognitive skills (full arrows in the body of the figure) stems from the motor behaviour and experiences of the child. These skills are in turn employed to gain control over behaviour (dotted arrows).*

development, in turn, complicates the motor picture because motor behaviour depends on the underlying base of perceptual-cognitive skills. One needs to look further than just the motor system to fully understand the psychological characteristics of a physically handicapped child or adult. Referring again to the overall triangular configuration of arrows in Fig. 3.4, the older the individual, the potentially more wide-ranging is the effect of an original physical disability, and points of contrast between the normal and physically handicapped child change and become more and more complex with age.

The third generalisation relates to therapy. If the establishment of relationships is a basic property of perceptual systems, one needs to understand what is being done when we intervene, in the case of a physically handicapped child, in an attempt to 'correct' his movements. As an example, the postures and movement patterns of a cerebral palsied child 'feel right' to him because of his past experiences of moving in, and interacting with his environment. Any attempt to physically intervene or to force a modification to the motor pattern, upsets what is for him the normal relationship between sensory and motor events; the effect is that the 'ideal' pattern of movement being forced on him, in fact, feels wrong. The aim of the therapy is (effectively) to establish a new set of relationships in the entire cognitive-perceptual-motor system, and it is now well established that this is best achieved with active participation by the child, combined with some degree of metacognitive self-control over his thoughts and behaviours. 'Passive' therapy programmes, programmes embarked on without the cooperation of the child or programmes with mentally handicapped patients who do not have the capability to exercise metacognitive control are bound to be of limited effectiveness.

The following chapters review general principles and existing tests that were designed to measure the capabilities of children, and Chapter 7 reports for the first time an attempt to measure capabilities that underlie and determine the motor behaviour of children from the age of five years.

4 ASSESSMENT OF PERCEPTUAL-
MOTOR BEHAVIOUR

A wide variety of tests and methods of assessment has been evolved to measure psychological characteristics and abilities of human beings (e.g. IQ tests, personality tests, etc.; Johnson, 1976). Regardless of the characteristic under examination, all tests share a common feature: they require either a verbal or a motor response on the part of the subject. In the case of preverbal infants, for example, assessment is possible *only* through the observation or measurement of motor behaviour. The limiting effect of this is that in people of all ages, direct measurement of abilities is usually not possible; rather the tester infers a certain underlying characteristic or ability by ascribing a meaning to the subject's behaviour.

Two basic problems spring from the indirect measurement of abilities, one of which is that there is often a lack of agreement among testers on the definitive nature of what is being tested. To take a well-known example: 'intelligence' tested by an IQ test is an assumed capacity of an individual, introduced to account for the wide individual differences seen in performance on certain complex problems (Berger, 1983). Someone scoring highly on a particular test is said to be intelligent, but 'intelligence' has not been defined to everyone's satisfaction. Indeed, the 'intelligence' measured by one test is not necessarily the same as that measured by another test and this lack of agreement on definition of what is measured extends to many other types of psychological characteristics.

The other problem with indirect measurement is that the supposed link between the subject's response and the psychological characteristic of interest can be tenuous and the test result can be open to argument and interpretation. For example, there are problems in concluding something about a child's personality from his drawings (Dileo, 1971). One can imagine how difficult it might be to interpret a drawing when dealing with a physically handicapped child, or a child from an unfamiliar culture.

It might be supposed that at least when perceptual-motor abilities are measured, the tester is on safe ground; he wants to measure the very thing the subject is doing. However, while he may be on *safer* ground, the presently available systems for measuring the perceptual-motor abilities of humans are fraught with problems and inadequacies, which often make the job of interpreting a psychologist's or therapist's report very difficult. The difficulties are compounded when available tests are abandoned in favour of *ad hoc* methods of assessment. Psychologists, clinicians and therapists frequently improvise, or sometimes borrow individual items from available tests, and evolve their own system of assessment — a practice that seems to be more common in the assessment of motor function than, say, cognitive function.

It is the purpose of the present chapter to highlight the roles of standardised testing procedures (not in universal opposition to *ad hoc* procedures, but as favoured alternatives in many situations) and at the same time to point out some of the difficulties associated with test construction. Decisions on exactly what form of test is to be employed must depend on one's motives for assessing a child in the first place, and there is discussion of some of the different functions that tests may serve. It should become clear from a consideration of the content and structure of standardised tests that there is a need for critical scrutiny of the nature of the test items, the measurement of performance and the presentation of results, whenever a standardised test is employed or interpreted. There is no discussion of the statistical procedures necessary for norming of a test and for establishing a test's reliability and validity; the interested reader is referred to 'Standards for Educational and Psychological Tests' published by the American Psychological Association (Nie *et al*, 1975a).

WHY STANDARISED TESTS ARE NEEDED AT ALL

For clinical workers who are accustomed to using their own methods of behavioural assessment, and their own implicit norms in the judgement of behaviour, the value of standardised tests may not be immediately apparent. To understand the need for constructing tests it helps to consider two distinct motives for testing a person and the two contrasting methods of assessment employed. Firstly, one may want to record an individual's competence or behaviour rather than make a comparison with other individuals. Take, for instance, the need to ascertain the degree of independence or self-sufficiency in a physically handicapped child, and the need to find out whether the child is mobile and whether he can carry out self-care and domestic activities. For mobility, a test may list various types of manoeuvres like transferring from a bed to a chair, walking indoors and outdoors, and walking up and down stairs. For self-care the list may include dressing, bathing and grooming, and for domestic activities, preparation of tea, using taps and feeding. A point score on each item will be given, ranging from 1 when the activity is performed without assistance, to 3 when there is a complete inability to contribute in any way to the performance of the activity. The total score over all the items will index the degree of self-sufficiency in a patient (e.g. Benjamin, 1976).

This type of test, in which the basis for reference is a specified set of actions, is called a *criterion-referenced test*. One is not primarily concerned with directly comparing one child with another, even though a comparison may be implied by testing him on items that others can manage. The usefulness of a criterion-referenced test battery depends on the way in which various activities are categorised, and in how representative are the items within a category. The need for such a test has been demonstrated by reports of a large discrepancy between a self-evaluation by patients, and evidence obtained from the application of a test. Some patients underestimate the number of daily activities they can manage (Sheikh *et al*, 1979), a finding that can be of value when decisions are made on management and rehabilitation. However, rigid test standards are not of singular importance here, and more-or-less *ad hoc* procedures can be sufficient, particularly if direct comparisons are not going to be made with other tests or other patients.

The other general motive for testing a child is to evaluate his behaviour with reference to that of a comparable group of children. Take, for instance, the need to ascertain whether a child can catch a ball, or write *as well as* other children of the same age. If the tester does not know exactly how other children behave he may have to rely on the reports of others. If, on the other hand, the tester wants to report results that can be duplicated, compared with or interpreted by other workers, his procedures will have to be painstakingly documented.

In this situation when direct comparisons are being made, there is need for a close agreement between testers on issues such as: what in the behaviour of a child is important to test, the type and nature of test items to be adopted, exactly how to measure performance and what can be inferred from the results of the test. The type of test in which the performance of a child is directly compared to that of other children is called a *norm-referenced test* (e.g. Bruininks, 1978). Rigid test standards are of singular importance and *ad hoc* procedures are less than satisfactory. The fundamental reason for constructing these tests is to avoid the problems arising from everyone having their own procedures, measures and standards that make comparisons difficult or impossible.

TESTS WHICH INCLUDE PERCEPTUAL-MOTOR ITEMS SERVE MANY FUNCTIONS AND ADDRESS BEHAVIOUR AT DIFFERENT LEVELS

The type of test that is selected for an assessment must, of course, depend primarily on one's motive for assessing a child. As an illustration of the variety of possible motives, one may want to screen a large population for a particular class of abnormality, and one chooses an item that is likely to give a quick and easy indication of any problem, to be followed up by a more thorough assessment at a later time; e.g. the use of the Snellen Chart may be used as a measure of visual acuity to screen for possible visual abnormalities. As another illustration, one may wish to examine a particular child in detail to specify as precisely as possible the cause of learning difficulties at school, or to gain measures of behaviour that give an index of his aptitude for learning and so predict, as well as possible, his future achievements. In this case, a carefully selected battery of test items will be needed to assess behaviour in a number of domains.

The type of test that is selected also depends on the level at which one wishes to assess behaviour. There are many different tests that address perceptual-motor behaviour but at different levels, and the choice of particular tests will reflect the interest and concerns of particular psychologists, therapists, developmental paediatricians, educationalists and researchers. It is the purpose of this section to discuss the different levels at which perceptual-motor behaviour can be assessed.

Assessment of practical-functional capabilities

As outlined in the previous section, there are tests concerned with the practical–functional capabilities of an individual that yield information that differs in important ways from verbal reports of such capabilities. As a further illustration of the uses of such tests, take the case of a child entering a residential school for the physically handicapped for the first time. He comes with a detailed medical history, and his psychological characteristics are documented. His parents have been interviewed and they have given details of the sorts of everyday tasks he can manage to do by himself. On entry into school, the child will not have the benefit of the individual attention of members of staff, and the school may wish to have precise and independent information about how much practical assistance this child may require. The school authorities may also wish to record a measure of progress the child may demonstrate as a result of various schemes and methods employed to train the child's motor skills and methods used to teach him to be as self-sufficient as possible in regard to mobility, dressing, feeding, toileting, etc.

A test that is essentially a graded check list of a sample of the myriad of actions that make up our everyday lives will document his present practical capabilities, the areas of specific difficulty and the progress he will show as a result of schooling (e.g. BCP Observation Booklet, 1973). The child is assessed in a framework of what is generally agreed to be socially acceptable patterns of behaviour and levels of self-sufficiency. It may have been quite acceptable and appropriate for the child to have been assisted in feeding and toileting (for example) when he was young and living with his parents, but such dependence on others may be considered undesirable as he grows older, and intolerable as he develops the potential for greater self-sufficiency. Tests of practical–functional capabilities generally reflect the aspirations and expectations of the child's society, and enable a record to be made of any growing independence. These tests fall into the criterion-referenced test category.

Assessment across a number of psychological domains

In another situation, a broad multidimensional assessment of a child's abilities may be required with the aim of determining the pattern and level of development by comparison to established norms. As an illustration, take the case of a child referred to a psychologist working in a child development centre, who has been attending a normal school but is failing to make adequate progress: he is not learning to read, is not grasping the rudiments of mathematics and is unable to cope with the normal demands of dressing for physical education and participating in routine physical exercises. The child does not have a diagnosable medical condition, and the question is whether his present school placement is correct or whether some other form of schooling might more appropriately and beneficially meet his needs. The psychologist wants a broad picture of the child's abilities to form an opinion on his aptitude for learning. He needs an impression of the status of the child in relation to other children of the same age along a number of dimensions to help in making decisions about present school placement, and to predict, as well as possible, the degree of progress that can be expected from the child. To aid making decisions he chooses, perhaps, to assess the child on the Griffiths (1970) mental development scales which give an assessment along six scales: locomotor, personal–social, hearing and speech, eye and hand coordination, performance, and practical reasoning. The test helps to establish whether a child is performing appropriately for his age in any one domain, and also to establish whether the child's abilities are equally well developed across the six domains, i.e. this is a norm-referenced test.

When the developmental status of a child is being broadly assessed, it is common to include motor test items. It is helpful in understanding the reason for this if two general and contrasting classes of handicap are considered. In one, a child demonstrates focal motor disabilities with clear consequences in terms of the difficulties they will cause in the present and future (e.g. the case of a child with spastic hemiplegia and no mental handicap). Such a child may not need a multidimensional assessment that aims at relating motor to other types of behavioural characteristics. In the other type of handicap, a child has motor disabilities that are an integral part of a mosaic of disabilities. The pattern of disabilities and the interrelationship between the various apparently aberrant psychological and motor elements may not be clear. A perceptual-motor deficit may be a prime reason for a retardation in acquiring handwriting skills that lead to secondary behavioural problems like an emotional disturbance or a lack of motivation to learn; e.g. children in normal schools who are intellectually able but are clumsy, sometimes exhibit such secondary problems (Gordon and McKinlay, 1980). On the other hand a general learning disability may manifest as a difficulty in handwriting in the case of an intellectually handicapped child. A broad developmental assessment can aid the understanding of the pattern and inter-relationships of disabilities, and help in the planning of a child's education.

Assessment of specific motor abilities

While it is true to say that a focused assessment in isolation from other considerations might give a distorted picture of a child's capabilities and is not helpful in making broad predictive decisions about education or management, such assessments are called for from time to time. Take, for example, a child in a normal school who has difficulties that seem to be primarily in the motor domain but which are causing anxiety and are affecting his educational and social attainments. He has an interest in learning and acquiring new skills but has unusual difficulties in sports that inhibit an easy social development. A psychologist or physiotherapist may be required to carry out a detailed assessment that will enable a measure of the categories of motor tasks causing the difficulties, a measure of the exact degree of motor impairment in comparison to children of the same age, and an indication of whether the variety of difficulties can be the result of a focal underlying disability. In other words, a differential diagnosis of the particular area of motor impairment is called for, and the child may be assessed on one of the available specific tests of motor behaviour. After isolating and quantifying the areas of difficulty, the tester will have to apply professional judgement as to the likely effect of the difficulty on broader physical and psychological attainments. Such an assessment can be of particular value when conducted along with a broader evaluation of the medical, psychological, physical and educational status of the child.

Differential diagnosis of causes of motor disabilities

There is a progression in the nature of the tests reviewed so far, from broadly functional to specifically motor tests (task-orientated analysis), and the final category of tests completes the progression by enabling the differential diagnosis of underlying behavioural causes or neurological causes of motor problems (process-orientated analysis) to be made. One of the roles of the developmental paediatrician and the specialist psychologist and therapist is to throw light on the cause of failure. It may be abundantly clear that a child has a motor problem which may be more or less focused. The problem is of sufficient magnitude to be of concern to the parent, teacher and child, and has been confirmed by the application of a standard motor test or the use of more qualitative/clinical/*ad hoc* procedures. The question is, why, in the absence of an obvious medical condition is the child failing to achieve a satisfactory standard of performance?

The clinician's approach to diagnosis can be to undertake a very detailed neurological examination of the type proposed by Touwen (1979) which includes a range of motor-type items like the examination of posture and reflexes, and a recording of certain types of involuntary movements. The aim is to detect minor deviations in neural functioning that could account for the motor difficulties experienced by the child. The psychologist's or therapist's approach can be to attempt a fine-grained behavioural analysis. As outlined in Chapters 2 and 3, the performance of motor skills depends on a wide range of perceptual and motor abilities, and the aim may be to determine if the child is failing because he lacks a particular set of subskills or abilities.

It is in this area of differential diagnosis that assessment is still more of an art than a science. Attempts have been made to formulate suitable methods (Ayres, 1972a) but it is fair to say that this type of test is still in the hands of researchers. As will be detailed in later chapters, the utility of a differential diagnostic procedure can only be as good as the theory of motor control and learning on which it is based. Chapter 7 will present the newly formulated Perceptual-Motor Abilities Test, the aim of which is both to assess the perceptual-motor behaviour of children and to diagnose differentially the underlying behavioural causes of motor disability.

THE CONTENT AND STRUCTURE OF PERCEPTUAL-MOTOR TESTS

The test items

Naturalistic items

The choice of items to be used in an assessment will depend, firstly, on the problems and questions that have initiated the assessment. If the aim is to identify the practical capabilities of a child, then the test items will approximate as closely as possible to the everyday types of tasks the child may be required to perform. If, on the other hand, the aim is to quantify precisely the child's abilities or to diagnose differentially the cause of motor difficulties (process-orientated analysis), then specially designed test items will be used.

Specifically designed items

The designing of particular test items introduces a range of problems and difficulties which frequently necessitate compromises. These problems include (a) conceiving of items that measure the abilities in question and are at the same time relevant to everyday behaviour, and (b) the designing of test procedures that take into account the age, temperament or type of handicap of a child. If an item is to measure a specific perceptual-motor ability rather than proficiency, it should be novel and interesting, it should not appear to be too complex or difficult and it should certainly not be intimidating. There are additional problems in structuring the test battery as a whole, problems that vary depending on whether the aim of the assessment is to quantify development accurately or to diagnose differentially the cause of a motor disability, or both. Some of the above issues and problems will be discussed here, while others will be addressed more fully in Chapters 7 and 8.

To illustrate the problems in designing a test item, take as an example the need to measure the tactile-perceptual ability of a child. If a well-designed and controlled method unaffected by motor handicap is wanted, a psychophysical procedure like the Method of Limits (D'Amato, 1970) may be adopted for the measurement of two-point tactile discrimination — one of a number of possible indicators of tactile-perceptual ability. One then has the task of having to give hundreds of trials for this single test item, and of requiring the child to make very difficult perceptual judgements. These two necessities exclude the use of this procedure with young children and certain clinical subjects due to their limited capacity to cooperate and attend for long periods, and to understand instructions.

Another way of indicating the tactile-perceptual ability of a child that involves only a few trials, is to blindfold the child, lightly touch him somewhere on the body, ask him to locate the point that was touched and measure the error in localisation. The advantages of the fewer trials and simpler instruction must now be weighed against the possibility that the child might not understand the need for precision, and the fact that this test item is a more indirect measure of tactile-perceptual ability than was the previous item. Since there is a delay between the application of the stimulus and locating the point, the subject's ability to remember will influence the measure. This procedure for measuring tactile ability is also confounded by the motor capabilities of the child. The test item is virtually useless for indicating the ability in question when there is any physical handicap since the error in localisation will be affected by the child's motor incapacity, as well as by his perceptual ability. The test item is of limited use even if a physical handicap is just suspected. While a positive result in the form of accurate performance will certainly indicate good tactile-perceptual ability, poor performance may be due to a motor and/or a perceptual disability. The general point being made is that compromises in the designing of a test item are sometimes necessary because of the age or handicap of a child. The effect of a compromise is to make the accurate measurement of a particular ability more difficult; greater care is therefore essential in the interpretation of the result.

Another general problem in designing set tasks is the difficulty in utilising available technology. Some children who have poor hand control, even when attempting to watch carefully what they are doing, seem to have a problem in visually tracking a moving object. The question may arise, how to measure the visual tracking ability of a child? The ideal would be to measure eye movement directly and technology has advanced sufficiently to make this possible. But some children are bewildered by unfamiliar surroundings, or are very temperamental and do not like being 'wired-up'. Even if the apparatus is available and can be applied to a child, the eye movements that can be measured are not going to reflect accurately the child's visual-tracking ability if he is under stress and protesting. It may be necessary to compromise and resort to a test item that is more clinical or qualitative, in which the subject's eye movements are simply observed, even though the measure may not be as accurate or as illuminating as the ideal.

An issue behind the above discussion is the distinction between proficiency and ability [see also Chapters 1 and 7, and Wade (1976) for a description of task-orientated and process-orientated test items]. Proficiency can be thought of as reflecting ability *plus* the effects of learning and experience. Alternatively, proficiency can reflect ability *minus* the effect of lack of motivation, feeling of intimidation or failing to understand what is required in a test task. That is, a child's performance can transcend or fall short of the type of behaviour that would accurately reflect his ability (Chess, Korn and Fernandez, 1971). If the aim is to determine the ability of a child to match shapes, a commercially available 'posting box' could be used that allows different plastic shapes to fit through correspondingly shaped holes. It could, however, be argued that the selection of such an apparatus would be unwise because some children may have the toy at home and may have had a lot of prior experience with 'posting' the particular set of shapes; a child's performance could overestimate his basic ability to match shapes. A better test item, less influenced by past experience, would be one employing unfamiliar test shapes, which would be novel for all children.

Test items that are uninteresting, too easy or too difficult can lead to an inaccurate estimate of a child's ability. Items that are uninteresting or obviously too easy can lead to a lackadaisical approach to performance and produce thoughtless errors. On the other hand, items that are too easy can cause a child to look for a trick or a complication that does not exist, leading to an ill-considered approach to performance and the production of needless errors. Children's reactions to items that are too difficult would be worthy of study in their own right. Young children, through past experience or through intuition, have an often surprising perception of what they think they can or cannot achieve. To illustrate this point with a drawing task, it is not unusual for a young child to say, when presented with a diamond to copy and before he even tries the task, 'I can't do that!'. It is the task of the tester to scale the difficulty of a test item to suit the child, or at least to present a difficult item in a challenging way so the child will give it a good try, and his ability will not be underestimated as a result of him feeling defeated even before he has made the attempt.

Finally, test items should not be intimidating. It may not be wise to project a ball to a child with a mechanical ball thrower. The advantages of having control over the speed and trajectory of the ball can be outweighed by a sense of being intimidated; he may be more concerned with ducking, or avoiding being hit by the ball than catching it, leading to an underestimation of catching ability. Likewise, the measurement of sensitivity to whole body tilt is very difficult. Children typically feel unsafe when tilted; they give an early and ill-considered judgement about the direction of tilt simply to stop the tilting, leading to random judgements and an underestimation of ability to perceive whole body tilt. The careful designing of a test item can reduce the above types of testing errors, and enable a valid measurement of a child's ability.

Structure of the test as a whole

As far as the overall structure of a test battery is concerned, if the aim is to quantify precisely perceptual-motor development, individual items must be selected which are graded in the level of difficulty and which will measure the one ability regardless of age. In addition, the judicious formulation of instructions and checks on the child's understanding of the task can be critically important, especially at younger ages when children do not necessarily recognise their own lack of understanding of a task, or at least fail to question an adult when they are unsure about what to do.

In practice, measurement of the one ability regardless of age can be difficult to achieve. Just because there is no obvious external change in a task that is given at different ages, does not necessarily mean the task will be treated in the same way by children of different ages, or that the task will measure the same ability/abilities (see Chapters 3 and 7 for a discussion of developmental changes in processes determining motor behaviour). As an illustration, a young child who cannot predict the motion of a fast moving object will be performing an essentially different task when catching a ball than a child who can behave predictively. The former child does not make fine predictive decisions about where and when to move; rather he makes last minute, chancy decisions, and relies on his ability to use current sensory information to guide his movements and to gather the ball into his arms. An understanding of the perceptual, cognitive and motor abilities underlying and determining motor behaviour is essential for choosing a battery of perceptual-motor items that will measure the underlying abilities and their developmental changes. Such an understanding is crucial if the motor performance of a child is to be explained.

There is a final point to be considered in selecting a test battery with a particular content and structure. If the aim is to diagnose differentially the cause of a motor handicap, then there must be a theoretical underpinning to the selection of test items, with the theory being based on experimental studies of behaviour, and with the items and structure of the test battery reflecting the theory. The importance of this last point is discussed in Chapters 2, 3, 7 and 8.

The measurement of performance

Observational recording

When the test items are tasks associated with everyday living (e.g. 'ties laces into a bow'), measurement can be as straightforward as recording whether the child can complete a set task. The addition of a record of whether the child required any assistance and how long it took to complete the task adds to the assessment. This type of measurement does not present major problems (e.g. Benjamin, 1976).

Pass/fail

If, on the other hand, one wants to describe or quantify the manner in which a task is performed both accurately and objectively, there are several issues and problems that must be considered, and there are a number of different types of measures, each with its advantages and disadvantages (see also Holt, 1975; Keogh, 1973; Neuhauser, 1975). Firstly, there is a variation in the above-mentioned system of recording. For a given ability a series of test items is designed with the items varying in difficulty in the perceptual discrimination or motor control required. The measurement of any one item is simply a pass or a fail, but it is the level of difficulty at which mistakes are made that indicates the child's ability (e.g. Herkowitz, 1978a). Take, for example, a catching task in which a ball is thrown at a progressively faster rate, or progressively smaller balls are thrown. A record of catching successes is made and if there is a point of sudden change from catching to missing, the associated level of task difficulty will indicate a child's catching proficiency. The advantage is clear: the measure is a simple one to make. A major disadvantage, however, is that there is no record of *how* the child performed the task, or of the *kinds* of mistakes that lead to task failure. This is one of the chief criticisms of standard tests of perceptual-motor ability; a single measure on a single test may yield a score for the level of competence but does not necessarily describe the nature of success or the nature of failure. A child with mild cerebral palsy may catch the balls in a standard test item; he passes the test yet it may be clear to anyone observing the child that there is aberrant motor behaviour which remains undocumented with this one score of catching success. Another problem with pass/fail scores is that there is no gradation in the measure of performance. A change in the criterion for pass/fail has a significant effect on the rate of success of a given group of individuals on the one test item. This is a factor that may contribute to variations between published norms on similar test items (see Table I, Frankenburg and Dodds, 1967).

Observational description

A solution to these problems of pass/fail scores is to employ a more descriptive method of measurement in which an observer records in 'long-hand' (with difficulty) or using a standard system of movement notation (e.g. Benesh and McGuiness, 1974) the nature of the movement being observed, or has a check list of commonly occurring aberrant types of behaviour that can be marked where appropriate (e.g. Stott, Moyes and Henderson, 1984). Problems associated with all types of observational methods include clear differences between the abilities of observers (Goodkin and Diller, 1973), and differences between observers of equal ability in what they consider to be aberrant behaviour (the problem of establishing criteria). There are also problems of drift in judgement with the one observer when a task is prolonged and the observer becomes fatigued or loses motivation, or if the observer is hoping for and looking for a certain result.

As an illustration of the problem of establishing criteria, take the example of a therapist who works only with physically handicapped children and who seldom formally observes normal children. There is the possibility that such a therapist will form quite different opinions as to what is clearly aberrant behaviour, compared to a therapist who has periodic experience with normal children (see Boice, 1983, for a review of observational skills). Problems with formal systems of movement notation include the fact that the results of the assessment are not generally intelligible to unskilled personnel because of the specialised nature of the notation. Also, while the assessment yields a detailed record of the pattern of movement, it does not result in a measure of the quality or 'goodness' of the pattern which therefore remains a matter of subjective opinion. The above general problems with observational methods render the reliable comparison between different children, between the performance of the one child on different occasions, and between the assessment of different testers difficult to achieve.

Measurement of speed and/or accuracy

The third way of measuring performance is to quantify it by measuring the speed or accuracy of movement. Measuring speed can be a simple and appropriate measure when the child's task is to move as quickly as possible, like time to run a set distance or time taken to hit a button in a reaction–time task. In other tasks, speed is used as an indirect measure of performance with the child's movements being timed, although the child is not asked to perform the test as quickly as possible; e.g. time taken to complete a pegboard test, time taken to walk a straight line. What the tester might wish to measure is the quality of movement but finds it difficult to define exactly what aspect of movement to measure, or does not have a quick and easy method or the instrumentation for measurement. A possible rationale behind taking time as an indirect measure of accuracy is that the greater the physical handicap, the longer it will take to complete the test.

There can be problems with this kind of indirect measure which may be illustrated by considering a drawing task. A child is required to copy a series of test patterns with pencil on paper. The tester records the time taken to complete each pattern and fast performance is taken to indicate good drawing ability. While there are situations in which this measure can give a reasonable indicator of drawing ability, there are other cases where it fails. For example, a short time will be achieved by a child who cannot detect errors in drawing and therefore does not spend time trying to correct them. A short time will also be recorded in the case of an impulsive child who could possibly detect errors, but does not spend time doing so because of his careless approach to this or any other type of task. In both cases the drawing will be *inaccurate*. On the other hand, a long time score will be gained by a child who succeeds in copying the shape very accurately but takes a lot of time and effort in performing the task.

There is a well-known relationship between the speed of a movement and the degree of accuracy that it is possible to achieve (Meyer, Smith and Wright, 1982). In general, the faster the movement is, the lower the accuracy. The extent to which accuracy is sacrificed for speed in a given task can depend on the age and personality of a subject. Therefore, a measure of time on its own does not give a generally useful measure of the accuracy of movement. As far as is possible, the speed and the accuracy should be measured separately so there is no loss of information about what the child is doing.

Objectively measuring the pattern or quality of a subject's movement (kinematic analysis) is difficult enough with a paper and pencil type task (see Chapter 8), and becomes especially problematic in the case of three-dimensional whole body movements (Grieve *et al*, 1975). It is possible, for example, to record objectively the complex pattern of leg and arm movements involved in gait, although the instrumentation involved, the number of separate measures obtained and the difficulty of interpreting the test results make it a very specialised assessment tool (e.g. Winter, 1976). The level or grain of analysis to be chosen in measuring the quality of movement must depend on the question being asked, and it has to be recognised that there are advantages and disadvantages in having a very fine-grained analysis. A complete analysis of an individual's gait, for example, may include a continuous record of the changing angle of each joint in the body, the electromyographic responses of all the major muscle groups, a record of the pattern of forces exerted by the feet on the ground, and a record of the forward/backward and sideways sway of the body as a whole. This may be very useful as a detailed record of changes in the pattern of locomotion with age or therapy, for detailing what is happening at individual joints, and for objectively comparing different subjects. It is not, however, a generally useful summary or description of an individual's behaviour because there is no way of combining all the separate measures into a global estimate of the pattern of walking in terms of its 'normality' or efficiency. Careful observation by a trained observer may be more practical and may accomplish more despite the problems with observational methods discussed earlier.

The above example of the fine-grained analysis of gait is an extreme example of the difficulties that can arise with the objective measurement of movement quality. The design of practical and objective measures of movement pose less of a problem with simpler types of motor responses.

The test results

Raw measures and profiles

There is no major conceptual problem in presenting the results of a long-hand qualitative description of behaviour because there is not much that can be done beyond organising and summarising the findings, although it is obvious that too much summarising can lead to loss of information. But when an assessment includes many test items and performance is measured objectively with pass/fail, time or accuracy measures, then the question of how to collate, summarise and present the assessment will arise.

The aim of the assessment may be to measure the ability of a child in a number of domains and to compare the child with his peer group in each domain. If there is only one test item for each domain the child's raw score can be considered directly, and collation or summary of the results is not necessary beyond plotting a profile of test results (see Ayres, 1972a, for an example of plotting profiles). If, on the other hand, there is more than one item per domain and if the tester wishes to derive a composite score across the test items for the domain, or even a composite score across domains, then decisions have to be made on how to combine the results of different test items.

Derived scores, composite scores and profiles

Combining measures on different items presents so many problems, and the solutions adopted are often (and by necessity) so arbitrary, that it is useful to begin with a consideration of why a tester should ever want to combine measures across test items. The aim usually is to obtain global indices of performance across broadly defined categories of behaviour, and because each category is broadly defined, there has to be more than one item per behavioural domain. For example, if the aim is to measure how well a child coordinates movements of the upper limbs, there is no single measure on a single test item that will do this in such a way that a child's performance on that one item will indicate his performance on all items and measures involving fine control of arm and hand movements.

One solution to the problem of there being no single representative test of, for example, upper limb coordination, is to take the view that 'upper limb coordination' is not a useful or illuminating category of perceptual-motor behaviour. Different skills involving the same parts of the body demand for their performance different types of motor, perceptual and cognitive abilities in ways that researchers are still working to understand (see Chapters 2, 3 and 7). Because the category is too broad, it would be more illuminating to examine performance on the different tests separately in the light of differences in the underlying component abilities.

Another 'solution' that some workers adopt is to stand by such an operational category of behaviour, acknowledge the fact that no single test will do, test the child on a battery of items all involving upper limb coordination, and then attempt to combine the scores in an overall index of performance. This is where difficulties arise because one cannot simply add the results of different tests. To illustrate, one cannot add the result of how fast a child copies a drawing to how accurately he copies it, nor how accurately he copies to how many balls he catches or how many beads he threads in a given time.

Two general types of solutions are adopted to enable the calculation of composite scores. One solution is to set the difficulty level of the task in advance, set the criteria for pass and fail, and simply add up the pass/fail scores on the different items (see earlier discussion of pass/fail scores). The total score will give an index of the ability to coordinate upper limb movement and each item will contribute an equal weighting to the index (e.g. Griffiths, 1970). The other solution is to measure the child's performance on each test item in terms of speed and/or accuracy, and then to convert the raw measures into point scores. To illustrate, the range in number of finger taps in a rapid tapping task may be zero taps per minute up to 120 taps per minute and this total range can be divided into six equal categories with the child receiving a score of 1 to 6 depending on the category he falls within. Similarly, the range in the number of balls caught out of 18 may be divided into six equal categories and again the child receives a score out of 6. This is done for all the tests within a domain, and adding up the point scores over the test gives an indicator of ability to coordinate movements of the upper limb. Sometimes the tester weights the effect that individual test items have on the total index. This is done by varying the range of point scores for individual items; for example, 0–3 for finger tapping and 0–9 for ball catching if the tester thinks that ball catching is 'more important' than finger tapping, the effect being to favour the child who is a good ball catcher (Bruininks, 1978, employs a weighted point score system).

The general point to be made here is that whenever scores on different test items are combined to obtain composite index scores of a particular behaviour, the questionable assumption is made that the items are sufficiently common in the abilities that determine performance to *permit* the calculation of the behavioural index. In fact, a child's performance on any one test item depends on a number of underlying functions and processes, the precise nature and relative importance of which are different from item to item no matter how similar the items may seem. A composite index calculated from a number of individual test items is a broad and multidimensional measure of behaviour, and is therefore less useful in identifying and quantifying the capabilities of a child than is a consideration of the individual items separately. In addition, the choice of test items making up the index is usually arbitrary, and the calculation of an index from weighted point scores involves another arbitrary set of decisions about the relative importance of the individual test items.

The above discussion relates to combining test results to obtain a score for a particular category of behaviour. There are other examples of test batteries in which test results are combined across domains to obtain measures of even broader categories of behaviour: e.g. a gross motor composite (Bruininks, 1978), an index of motor impairment (Stott, Moyes and Henderson, 1984) and a motor scale (McCarthy, 1972). Performance on individual test items is either measured as pass/fail, or else raw measures of performance are converted to standard or point scores before being added to obtain a composite test result. The problems in combining scores in this way are an extension of, and in some ways, a magnification of the problems outlined in the previous paragraph, especially in terms of the decrease in utility in identifying and quantifying the capabilities of a child (see Holt, 1982, for a similar criticism in relation to general developmental screening tests).

This chapter has reviewed the issues, problems and compromises associated with the designing of individual perceptual-motor test items and of test batteries. The following chapter reviews a range of specific tests that include perceptual-motor items, and the types of solutions adopted by individual workers. The review will focus on the tests' usefulness in measuring and accounting for normal perceptual-motor development, and in diagnosing the nature and causes of perceptual-motor disabilities.

5 CRITICAL REVIEW OF TESTS RELATING TO PERCEPTUAL-MOTOR BEHAVIOUR

SCOPE OF THE REVIEW

Two basic reasons for testing a child on a standard test battery are to measure the developmental status of the child, and to throw light on the pattern of disabilities that is associated with a behavioural disorder (see Chapter 4 for a broader discussion of why standard tests are needed at all). As an example, the developmental paediatrician is often asked to pass judgement on whether a child's motor development is normal, and if it is not, in what way and to what degree is it abnormal. An assessment is not particularly difficult to plan when only a diagnosis is wanted and in a case where the problem is obvious and familiar, as in severe spastic quadriplegia. The clinician may only need to observe the child's attempt at performing a few basic tasks like sitting up, walking or writing to establish the existence of a particular type of disabling motor deficit, albeit not necessarily the degree of deficit. But there are other cases where problems are not clear-cut and difficulties are not easy to pinpoint. The number of cases falling into this grey area bordering on abnormality are far more numerous than cases of clearly defined abnormality. Here, a carefully planned motor assessment by a psychologist (for example) in which the child is directly compared with his peers gives a measure of the child's developmental status and helps the paediatrician to make a diagnosis.

Regardless of the severity of the motor handicap, the clinician may also be asked to give a reason for a motor disability, or to define the effect of a disability on the broader development of, and prognosis for the child, or to give advice on therapy and management. None of these requests pose a particular problem in the case of a familiar pattern of motor handicap for which a diagnosis and prognosis can be confidently given. But in unfamiliar cases, marginal disabilities or when a tailor-made programme of therapy is to be designed, it may be necessary to define the cause and concomitants of a motor disability. For this purpose standard tests may be given to throw light on the pattern of physical, neurological or behavioural disorders and difficulties that will help the clinician give what can sometimes amount to wide-ranging opinions and advice.

The present review will be undertaken with the aim of considering the usefulness of available tests for measuring the development of children's motor skills, and for measuring the attributes of motor disorders. As outlined in Chapters 2 and 3, normal motor control depends on a complex of underlying perceptual, cognitive and motor factors. The measurement of abilities in relation to underlying factors is necessary for defining the reasons for a motor symptom, and for designing a process-orientated programme of therapy. The review relates to tests designed for children within the age range five to 12 years, and not to those tests concerned with plotting the emergence of abilities and skills in the first years of life. The reader is referred to Bayley (1969), Burns and Watter (1974), Frankenburg and Dodds (1967), Gesell and Amatruda (1969) and Milani-Comparetti and Gidoni (1967), for information about early infant development.

There are a number of reasons for choosing the present set of tests for review. The tests are ordered historically and this enables reference to the pioneering work on developmental assessment of Gesell (1941) and Oseretsky (1948) — two sources from which many recent tests were derived — and also enables a consideration of the more recent emergence of process-orientated types of assessment. A number of general developmental tests are reviewed. One thrust of this book is to argue for the assessment of processes determining motor behaviour, through the application of a battery of test items. A discussion of general developmental tests enables a consideration of how previous workers have handled data from a test battery.

The review of each test will be structured in the following way: the specific test manual or book will be reviewed and not the corpus of the author's publications. The original aims of the test battery, the description of its content or list of test items, the measures employed, the collation of the test results and the uses of the test, will be summarised uncritically and, as far as possible in the authors' own terms. The test will then be critically evaluated from the point of view of the authors' stated aim and purpose. The criticisms are often detailed but are useful for pointing out to the non-specialist the difficulties of test construction, and the need for a critical eye when tests and test results are evaluated and interpreted. Finally, the potential usefulness of the test for measuring motor development and for defining the patterns of disabilities associated with, or underlying, a motor disability will be discussed. It is acknowledged that this final topic in the critique may sometimes fall outside the original aim of the test battery. Indeed, many of the present criticisms of individual test items, and criticisms of the modification of data for the calculation of composite scores, are not relevant if one considers the original aim and purpose of a particular test. For example, one criterion of a 'good test item' can be whether the performance of a sample group of children follows a normal distribution, and there may be good statistical reasons for rescaling raw data and for calculating composite scores. While such modifications to raw data distort the detailed picture of a child's functioning, and result in the loss of potentially useful information, test results are not usually taken at face value. Rather, the results are interpreted by the tester, often in conjunction with observations made while the child performed the test, and in conjunction with opinions and data supplied by other specialists. The present book argues for a different emphasis in choice of test items and the design of test batteries, namely, to move away from being motivated primarily by statistical considerations to the construction of tests with items that are specifically designed to orientate the assessment toward basic processes, and to make the interpretation of a child's behaviour more objective. The present purpose is to show how far many of the existing test batteries, when used by themselves, fall short of a diagnostically useful assessment which would give an accurate direction to the design of therapy and management programmes.

The review does not include any detailed discussion of statistical procedures associated with sampling and the establishment of norms, nor is it concerned with questions of reliability and validity except when there seems to be an extreme infringement of minimal test standards. General principles associated with: criteria for selection of test items, nature of test items, type of measurement of performance employed, the calculation of composite scores and collation of test results were reviewed in the previous chapter and will not be discussed in detail. While the present review is not an exhaustive one (there are other tests that fall within the scope of the review but which are not discussed; e.g. Rarick and Dobbins, 1975; Roach and Kephart, 1966), it does cover a range of different types of tests. Finally, while other reviews of test batteries have been published (e.g. Haubenstricker, 1978; Herkowitz, 1978a,b; Wade and Davis, 1983), they differ from the present discussion in both content and purpose since the focal point of these reviews was not the critical evaluation of the diagnostic and therapeutic value of the tests.

GESELL AND ILG (1946): THE CHILD FROM FIVE TO TEN

One of the first comprehensive accounts of child development over the age range five to 10 years was reported by Gesell and Ilg (1946). They conducted a longitudinal-biographical study of, in their terms, the patterning of behaviour in children over the first 10 years of life, and reported the results for the latter five years. The aim was to describe development in a broad and qualitative way, hence clinical or descriptive techniques were employed in the presentation of their findings, rather than rigorous experimental or statistical methods.

A small sample of children (around 50) was examined over the age range five to 10 years. Most of these children were of high average or superior intelligence, and came from homes of middle or high socioeconomic status; they were representative of children from a prosperous American community.

Data on each child at different ages were gathered from psychological examinations, performance, reading readiness and visual skills tests, observations of the child's everyday behaviour, and a wide-ranging interview with the mother concerning the child's behaviour at home and at school. None of the original data was reported by the authors. Rather, the data forms the basis of a broad qualitative description of development in 10 major fields: 1, motor characteristics; 2, personal hygiene; 3, emotional expression; 4, fears and dreams; 5, self and sex; 6, interpersonal relations; 7, play and pastimes; 8, school life; 9, ethical sense; 10, philosophical outlook.

Gesell and Ilg first presented behaviour profiles, devoting a separate chapter to each age level. Each profile is (effectively) a composite character sketch representing behavioural characteristics which are typical of intelligent American children. Following each profile, the authors detail the 'maturity traits' for that age under the above 10 headings. The maturity traits are a cross-sectional description of behaviour, set out as brief informal statements reflecting the everyday happenings of home and school life. In a later section of the book, the material is essentially reorganised to present 'growth gradients' with a separate chapter devoted to the 10 major fields of development; the developmental sequence for one particular maturity trait can be followed across the age levels.

The maturity trait relevant to the present review is 'motor characteristics' which included two subheadings: 'bodily activity' and 'eyes and hands'. These traits relate to how a child's motor coordination changes with age as revealed by body posture, handedness, drawing, the use of eyes and hands, and many other factors. (The division between gross and fine movements was followed in many of the more recent methods of assessing the motor behaviour of children.) To give an indication of the kind of descriptive account that Gesell and Ilg presented, the motor trait for five-year-old and nine-year-old children is given in Table 5.1.

Table 5.1 *A brief description of motor characteristic maturity traits for 5 year olds and 9 year olds, from Gesell and Ilg (1946).*

Eyes and hands

5 years: Coordination has reached a new maturity. He approaches an object directly, prehends it precisely and releases it with dispatch.

Builds with blocks usually on the floor and builds graduated towers or low rambling structures with roads and small enclosures.

Manipulates sand, making roads and houses. Moulds objects with clay.

If cannot do puzzle with precision and dispatch, he will ask for help or abandon it.

Likes to colour within lines, to cut and paste simple things but is not adept.

Makes an outline drawing, usually one on a page, and recognises that it is 'funny'. Likes to copy simple forms.

Paints at an easel or on the floor with large brushes and large sheets of paper. May enjoy making letters in this manner.

Can 'sew' wool through a card by turning it over.

Can manipulate those buttons on clothes which he can see, and can lace his shoes.

Places fingers on piano keys and may experiment with chords.

9 years: Individual variation in skills.

Can hold and swing a hammer well. Saws easily and accurately and uses knee to hold board. Makes finished products.

Garden tools are used and handled appropriately.

Builds complex structures with erector set.

Handwriting is now a tool.

Beginning to sketch in drawing. Drawings are often detailed. Especially likes to draw still life, maps and designs.

Girls can cut out and sew a simple garment and can knit.

Can dress rapidly. Some interest in combing own hair.

Interest in watching games played by others.

Bodily activity

5 years: There is greater ease and control of general bodily activity, and economy of movement.

Posture is predominantly symmetrical and closely knit. May walk with feet pronate.

Control over large muscles is still more advanced than control over small ones.

Plays in one location for longer periods, but changes posture from standing, sitting, squatting.

Likes to climb fences and go from one thing to another. Jumps from table height.

Likes to activate a story. Runs, climbs onto and under chairs and tables.

Throws, including mud and snow and is beginning to use hands more than arms in catching a small ball but frequently fails to catch.

Alternates feet descending stairs and skips alternately.

Attempts to roller skate, jump rope and walk on stilts.

Likes to march to music.

9 years: Works and plays hard. Apt to do one thing until exhausted, such as riding bicycle, running, hiking, sliding or playing ball.

Better control of own speed but shows some timidity of speed of an automobile, of sliding and of fast snow when skiing.

Interest in own strength and in lifting things.

Frequently assumes awkward postures.

Boys like to wrestle and may be interested in boxing lessons.

Great interest in team games and in learning to perform skilfully.

The aim of their book was to impart a 'sense of growth trends' and the purpose was *not* to set up rigid age norms of absolute ability. The maturity traits were not even regarded as models, but rather as 'approximate norms' and as illustrations of the kinds of behaviour which tend to occur at each age. It was suggested that the behaviour traits outlined could be used by parents, teachers, physicians and nurses to 'interpret (a child's) individuality and to consider the maturity level at which he is functioning' (p 5). The growth gradients were intended to show 'the overall developmental sequences of behaviour rather than rigid standards of expectancy' (p 223). They could aid a better understanding of a child, provide reassurance that a child is steadily moving towards higher levels of maturity and enable guidance best suited at any one particular phase of development.

One major strength of Gesell and Ilg's descriptive account of development is that it was based on a relatively rare longitudinal study of a group of children. The usual method employed by developmental psychologists is to study different groups of children at different ages, and to present developmental norms relevant to a 'collective' child together with an account of individuality at each age. Another advantage is that a wide range of different behaviours was examined in the one child. However, these advantages in having detailed information on individual children across five years of development are lost in the collation and summary of results in which a 'collective' child is effectively described and there is no account of individual differences. Other major weaknesses include the absence of any detailed account of the test methods employed, the absence of any measured norms of behaviour (indeed the absence of *measurable* test items), the absence of any justification for the maturity traits that were selected, and the very narrow sample of children studied.

For someone interested in the assessment of the developmental status of a child or possible abnormalities in motor behaviour, this study by Gesell and Ilg is unhelpful because it does not provide guidelines for an assessment, does not present quantitative age expectancies, and, contrary to one of their aims, does not allow for the interpretation of the individual differences that exist between children of the same age. It may, however, be useful as an introductory text to child development for people who have limited everyday experience with closely observing children.

GRIFFITHS (1970): THE ABILITIES OF YOUNG CHILDREN

Griffiths' (1970) approach to the study of child behaviour had much in common with that of Gesell and Ilg (1946). In both cases, a comprehensive account of development was undertaken and observations of everyday behaviour were made. Griffiths, however, made the advance of describing in detail the methodology used for the observational items, as well as for the measurement of children's performance under standard conditions. She gave criteria for pass/fail scoring on the list of items.

Griffiths' aim was to provide a method of assessment that would help in the diagnosis of the mental status in various conditions found among young children. The term 'mental status' was not defined, but she presented six scales of assessment that she claimed would cover virtually the whole range of abilities of children from nought or birth to eight years of age. Table 5.2 lists the six scales and the number of test items within each scale.

Table 5.2 *Summary of the six scales of measurement, and detail of items for three of these scales for 5 year olds and 8 year olds; from Griffiths (1970).*

Scales of measurement	Age (years)							
	I	II	III	IV	V	VI	VII	VIII
	24 items	24 items	6 items	6 items	6 items	6 items	6 items	6 items
A: Locomotor Scale	,,	,,	,,	,,	,,	,,	,,	,,
B: Personal–Social Scale	,,	,,	,,	,,	,,	,,	,,	,,
C: Hearing and Speech Scale	,,	,,	,,	,,	,,	,,	,,	,,
D: Hand and Eye Coordination	,,	,,	,,	,,	,,	,,	,,	,,
E: A Scale of Performance Tests	,,	,,	,,	,,	,,	,,	,,	,,
F: Practical Reasoning	–	–	,,	,,	,,	,,	,,	,,

A: Locomotor

Year V
1 Can run to kick a ball.
2 Walks downstairs: one foot on each step, adult manner.
3 Touches toes with knees straight.
4 Jumps a 6 inch high rope — both feet together.
5 Can climb on and off a bus unaided.
6 Can run upstairs.

Year VIII
1 Runs — downstairs.
2 Can jump off 4+ steps.
3 Rides a bicycle (2-wheeler) in garden short distance.
4 Hopscotch IV. (4 hops — with second foot up).
5 Fast single skipping with rope.
6 Skips well 12+ ordinary double skipping.

D: Hand and Eye Coordination

Year V
1 Copies a cross — good shape and well drawn. Stage II
2 Copies circle — good shape — neatly closed. Stage II
3 Draws a square — recognisable. Stage I
4 Window — recognisable. Stage I
5 House. Stage I
6 Scissors: Can strip edge of paper neatly.

Year VIII
1 Makes 10+ letters.
2 Window. (Stage II)
3 Draws a man. (Stage III)
4 Diamond — good shape — neatly drawn, etc. (Stage B) — (credit as 2
5 items)
6 Makes 24+ letters.

E: Performance

Year V
1 Six-hole board — within 20 seconds.
2 Builds bridge — superior model.
3 Pattern making No. 2 (60 seconds).
4 Builds gate to model.
5 Pattern making No. 2 (40 seconds).
6 Pattern making No. 5 (60 seconds).

Year VIII
1 Pattern making No. 4 — within 30 seconds.
2 Six-hole board — within 10 seconds.
3 Pattern making No. 5 — within 20 seconds.
4 Returns 9 bricks to box+lid — within 15 seconds.
5 Pattern making No. 2 — within 15 seconds.
6 Pattern making No 3 — within 20 seconds.

The test items within each scale were selected partly as a result of years of observing children, and with the aim of including a representative sample of the broad range of skills they naturally acquire as they grow older. However, the major criterion for item selection related to the overall aim of the assessment which was to provide not only a means of establishing whether a child was performing appropriately for his age on any one scale, but also to establish whether his abilities were equally well developed across the six scales. Hence, the items were selected so that the difficulty level of the scales within each age group was equated. The difficulty level was defined as a percentage of children in the normative sample passing the items.

The present review is primarily concerned with methods of assessing motor skills. The relevant scales are: A, Locomotor; D, Hand and Eye Coordination; and E, Performance. It is not practicable to list all the 82 items for the three scales and their pass/fail criteria, but to convey some idea of the content. The items for Year V and Year VIII are listed in Table 5.2. The assessment sometimes involves observing the child performing freely in his natural environment, and at other times the measurement of performance on set tasks under standard conditions. As far as items involving everyday behaviour are concerned, it is not always necessary to actually observe the child attempting the item. Rather, the child can be scored according to information supplied by the parent or child.

The score on each item is a simple pass/fail, the level of difficulty having been set beforehand. The child is effectively credited with half a month for each item passed at Ages I and II, while two months is credited for each item passed at Ages III through to VIII. Testing on a particular scale typically begins somewhat below the child's actual age and progresses upwards until the child has six successive failures. For example, if a child aged IV passes the six items for Age III on the locomotor scale, the six items for Age IV, then two items for Age V before making six successive failures, he is credited with 52 months, and this is said to be his mental age on that scale (note the child is not actually tested on items for Ages I and II but is credited with the months). Hence, each child is assigned a mental age on the basis of a mosaic of small tasks.

In addition to these pass/fail scores, Griffiths also stressed the importance of observing the child performing the test items (a partial solution to the problems of pass/fail scores outlined in Chapter 4). In the items of the locomotor scale it is possible to observe certain weaknesses and disabilities, in the eye/hand coordination scale the hands can be observed for signs of awkwardness, weakness and fumbling, and in the performance scale the examiner can observe skill in manipulation, speed of working and precision. Guidelines for recording observations were not offered, however, and in addition, Griffiths allowed for the use of parents' reports regarding the child's capabilities in performing everyday items. These two factors reduce the objectivity of the observational data, and render them unreliable.

Since the general purpose of the test was to provide a means of 'differential diagnosis of mental status' of children — for discovering whether a child has an all-round mental deficiency or a focal area of retardation — it was recommended that the full test be given as part of a preliminary investigation. Psychologists, medical officers, paediatricians and researchers were suggested as specialists who would find the test useful for measuring the overall mental ability of a child, and defining a child's mental age on each scale. Because the scales had been equated in difficulty it was possible to plot the profile of the six abilities. This would help to answer two questions: (a) How retarded is the child? and (b) In what direction is he failing? The scales can provide the first step in diagnosis, and after the areas of failure were identified, it would be up to the paediatrician or other specialist to discover the *reason* for failure.

Four critical observations of Griffiths' method of assessment can be made. Firstly, while the separate scales were reasonably well equated in terms of difficulty, they include items that share much in common. For example, throwing items are included in the locomotor scale and the hand and eye coordination scale; items involving the placement of bricks are included in the hand and eye coordination scale and the performance scale. In short, the scales are not independent. The inclusion of items of a similar nature into the separate scales reduces the likelihood of achieving the differential assessment of children's abilities that was so central to Griffiths' aim.

Secondly, items within a scale vary greatly at different ages. Within the locomotor scale the following items for Year IV, 'can ride a tricycle', 'marches to music', 'walks a chalk line', have no parallels in Years V and VI. It is clear that the same abilities are not tested at different ages within any one scale, and this is most apparent when comparing items for Year III and above with items for the first two years. That is, a child aged three years who is assessed on all items in a scale up to his own age, and a child aged eight years who is assessed on items in the same scale from five years to eight years, are *in fact* assessed on different types of items. While the items within a scale have been grouped under a common label, and 'months are credited' according to original statistical criteria regardless of the exact nature of the item, the items are not homogeneous in terms of the activity being performed, nor in terms of the underlying abilities which would affect performance.

Thirdly, a number of features of the test design result in a lack of uniformity in the test across the different ages. Items for older children take longer to perform than items for younger children and are therefore more difficult in terms of the length of time a child would have to attend to a test; there is an assumption that older children *should* attend for longer, and the various scales measure this additional unacknowledged 'ability' to attend to, and persist with the performance of a given test. On the other hand, there are more items for younger than for older children in any one scale. Many of these items are not performed but were reported on by the parent, and the width of sampling of behaviour is broader for younger ages. This is contrary to the commonly held view of development discussed in Chapter 3, namely, that the behaviour of children becomes *more* diverse and complex with increasing age. In addition, the '6 item rule' means that for Ages III and above, a child has to fail all six items of an age level for testing to be terminated (two months per item, or a total of 12 months' worth of items). For Ages I and II only one-quarter of the items of an age level has to be failed for testing to cease (fortnight per item, or a total of three months' worth of items). In other words, the scale of assessment for retardation varies with age.

Fourthly, while the test was standardised on children eight years and younger, it was considered adequate for measuring the mental age of handicapped children far beyond the eighth chronological year when the retardation required it. There is an implied assumption in this application of the test, that a 12-year-old physically handicapped child and a seven-year-old 'normal' child (for example) who receive the same score on a particular scale, have the same 'mental age' on that scale. While it has become less acceptable to consider handicapped children as being, simply, underdeveloped 'normal' children, it is still common for mental ages to be calculated and quoted, and there are problems associated with taking 'mental age' at face value.

Three of the six scales were meant to allow for the measurement of children's motor abilities, and for the differential diagnosis of mental status in three motor domains. However, this test is unhelpful for someone wishing to measure motor development because of the odd mixture of items within a scale from year to year. Neither is the test particularly useful for measuring development in different motor domains since the three scales have items of a similar nature and therefore do not measure independent aspects of motor behaviour. The test as a whole may be useful, however, in an *initial* assessment of a child with multiple handicaps, even if it only provides for an opportunity to observe the child's attempt at a wide variety of different tasks.

McCARTHY (1972): McCARTHY'S SCALES OF CHILDREN'S ABILITIES

Like Gesell and Ilg (1946) and Griffiths (1970), McCarthy (1972) had a broad interest in child development. Her scales were designed to measure the 'general intellectual level' as well as the strengths and weaknesses in different abilities in children from $2\frac{1}{2}$ to $8\frac{1}{2}$ years of age. Her approach was different to the previous authors in that her system of assessment included *only* a series of set tasks to be performed under standard conditions; there was no provision for observing the child performing everyday activities. Furthermore, while pass/fail scores were given on some items, on other items a graded point score was given, the score depending on the excellence of a child's performance.

Eighteen tests, each with a number of items relating to language, numerical concepts, motor coordination and other skills generally considered to reflect cognitive and motor abilities were grouped into five scales, namely, Verbal, Perceptual-Performance, Quantitative, Memory and Motor. Test results on three scales (Verbal, Perceptual-Performance, Quantitative) could be combined to form a sixth scale to gain a measure of a child's General Cognitive Ability. A summary of the 18 tests and the six scales is presented in Table 5.3.

According to McCarthy, decisions on the choice of particular test items and their grouping into scales were primarily made on the basis of her own extensive teaching and clinical experience in developmental psychology and her many years of training and supervising test examiners. A factor analysis on part of the normative data gave some measure of support for her grouping of tests into the six scales, but the composition of the scales was largely decided on the basis of 'intuitive and functional considerations' (p 2).

McCarthy claimed the test provides a means for determining the general intellectual level of young children, as well as their strengths and weaknesses in important abilities. The application of her test battery should lead to a better understanding of both normal children and those with learning disabilities. She suggested that a child be assessed on the full battery of tests so that a profile of abilities can be established. The Verbal scale was said to assess the child's ability to express himself verbally, and also to assess the maturity of his verbal concepts. Tests making up the Perceptual-Performance scale required no verbal response and assessed the child's reasoning ability through the manipulation of objects. Tests in the Quantitative scale assessed the facility with numbers and understanding of quantitative words. The above three scales combined made up the General Cognitive Scale. Each of the tests in the Memory scale assessed the child's short-term memory for auditory, visual, verbal and numerical information. Tests in the Motor scale assessed the child's coordination as he performed a variety of gross and fine motor skills.

The most relevant scales to the present review are the Performance and Motor scales. However, because scales termed General Cognitive and Memory have the potential for throwing light on causes of motor disabilities, the 18 tests making up the six scales are briefly described in Table 5.4.

The method of allocating point scores for the separate items is complicated, and it varies from item to item. For some items there is only one correct answer, and a child is given a 1 for pass and a 0 for fail (e.g. 'Number Questions'). For other items the point score is graded from (for example) 2 for good performance, 1 for partial success and 0 for fail, with the criteria for the three possible scores rigidly defined (e.g. 'Leg Coordination'). The procedure for allotting point scores to some of the items is very complicated. For example, a child can receive a point score of 0–20 for 'Draw-a-Child' depending on a large number of set criteria.

Table 5.3 *The grouping of tasks into six scales of measurement from McCarthy (1972).*

	Test tasks	Number of items	Verbal	Perceptual performance	Quantitative	General cognitive	Memory	Motor
								Scales
1.	Block Building	4		P		GC		
2.	Puzzle Solving	6		P		GC		
3.	Pictorial Memory	6	V			GC	M	
4.	Word Knowledge	19	V			GC		
5.	Number Questions	12			Q	GC		
6.	Tapping Sequence	8		P		GC	M	
7.	Verbal Memory	7	V			GC	M	
8.	Right–Left Orientation	9		P		GC		
9.	Leg-Coordination	6						MOT
10.	Arm-Coordination	6						MOT
11.	Imitative Action	4						MOT
12.	Draw-a-Design	9		P		GC		MOT
13.	Draw-a-Child	1		P		GC		MOT
14.	Numerical Memory	11			Q	GC	M	
15.	Verbal Fluency	4	V			GC		
16.	Counting and Sorting	9			Q	GC		
17.	Opposite Analogies	9	V			GC		
18.	Conceptual Grouping	9		P		GC		

Table 5.4   *A brief description of 18 tasks from McCarthy (1972).*

	Test tasks	Description
1.	Block Building	Copy four structures built by the examiner out of one inch cubes.
2.	Puzzle Solving	Assemble a series of puzzles that form pictures.
3.	Pictorial Memory	Recall the names of pictures.
4.	Word Knowledge	Name pictures and give the meaning of words.
5.	Number Questions	Answer questions on number information.
6.	Tapping Sequence	Initiate sequences of notes on a xylophone.
7.	Verbal Memory	Repeat words and sentences and retell a story.
8.	Right–Left Orientation	Identify right and left on own body and on a picture.
9.	Leg Coordination	Walk, stand on one foot, skip.
10.	Arm Coordination	Bounce, catch, throw.
11.	Imitative Action	Copy actions of an examiner.
12.	Draw-a-Design	Copy designs of varying difficulty.
13.	Draw-a-Child	Draw a boy or a girl.
14.	Numerical Memory	Repeat sequences of digits.
15.	Verbal Fluency	Quickly think of words falling into certain categories.
16.	Counting and Sorting	Count, and understand quantitative words.
17.	Opposite Analogies	Think of opposite key words.
18.	Conceptual Grouping	Classify groups of blocks.

As outlined in Chapter 4, there are severe problems in combining scores on different tests to obtain a composite score. Griffiths (1970) 'solved' the problem by setting the difficulty level for each item, and scoring the child as either pass or fail. The number of items within a scale that are passed are simply added to obtain the 'mental age', with each item carrying equal weight within a scale.

McCarthy had a somewhat different approach. For a start, the individual items and therefore the 18 tests making up the total battery vary in their possible point scores. In the Motor Scale the maximum possible score for 'Imitative Action' is 4, while the maximum possible score for 'Arm Coordination' is 28. Rather than simply adding the raw scores to obtain a total for a particular scale, the scores on some tests are first weighted and then added. The raw score weights for each test are based on two factors: (a) the author's judgement of the relative importance of the individual test; and (b) the size of the standard deviation of the raw scores on the test for the normative sample. 'Tests with small standard deviations of raw scores received greater weights when it was desired to increase their relative contribution to the composite score' (p 20). For example, in the Performance scale the raw score on 'Puzzle Solving' is multiplied by $\frac{1}{2}$ before being added into the composite score, while the raw score on 'Opposite Analogies' is first multiplied by 2. The overall effect of this graded-weighted point score system is that the tests within a scale do not contribute equally to the composite score. In the case of the motor scale, the order of 'importance' of the six tests and their respective maximum possible scores (in brackets) is: 'Arm Coordination' (28), 'Draw-a-Child' (20), 'Draw-a-Design' (19), 'Leg Coordination' (13) and 'Imitative Action' (4). There is no obvious rationale to this particular ordering.

The sum of a child's weighted raw scores on all tests comprising a scale is the composite raw score for that scale. The maximum possible composite score varies from scale to scale because of the graded-weighted point score system. This posed a further problem for McCarthy because she wanted to allow for a direct comparison between scores on different scales (in much the same way as Griffiths, 1970). To facilitate such a direct comparison the scores on the separate scales had to be equated. This is achieved by the use of tables which rescale the composite scores to a standard distribution with a fixed mean and standard deviation, and convert the composite scores to 'scale index' scores. For the General Cognitive Scale the mean is 100 and the standard deviation 16. For all other scales the mean is 50 and standard deviation is 10. The result of all this modification of data is the plotting of a profile of the child's abilities according to the six scales. Finally, another table can be consulted to convert the scale index of the General Cognitive Scale to a mental age for the child.

Three critical observations of McCarthy's method of assessment can be made. Firstly, just like the Griffiths (1970) scales, the six scales of the present test are not independent. Some tests in the Memory and Motor scales are also included in the Verbal, Perceptual-Performance and Quantitative scales. This calls into question the usefulness of the battery for differentially assessing areas of strengths and weaknesses of young children.

Secondly, the complicated system of allocation of point scores, weighting of raw scores, computation of composite scores and derivation of scale index scores makes it difficult to see exactly what a scale is measuring. The final test result is so far removed from the child's actual performance on a test item, that the 'ability' being assessed by a particular scale is no more than a broad and amorphous characteristic of the child. This lack of definition in what is being measured by a scale index score cannot be offset by a consideration of a child's performance on an individual test item because, as McCarthy pointed out, many of the separate tests are not sufficiently reliable by themselves to permit a meaningful evaluation of performance.

Thirdly, to quote McCarthy, 'Many mentally retarded children have multiple handicaps of varying degrees of severity and in a wide variety of pathological syndromes, so it may not be possible to administer the entire battery to them' (p 27). It would seem that the test is of limited usefulness in throwing light on the pattern of disabilities in a child with a learning problem.

Two of the scales related specifically to the measurement of the child's Motor and Perceptual-Performance abilities, and could therefore be useful for assessing motor development. The fact that the test items are the same for all children regardless of age is a solution to one of the difficulties found in Griffiths' test in which the items vary with the age of the child. However, McCarthy pointed out that items in the Motor scale are really only useful for children up to six years of age. This not only limits the range of ages over which motor development can be assessed by this test, but the limitation also means that a full test profile can only be obtained on children six years and younger, i.e. below the age when the learning difficulties that were of such interest to McCarthy become clearly apparent at school. It was McCarthy's view that motor ability is developmentally most important at earlier ages. This is not an opinion that many developmental psychologists would share. Furthermore, the 'motor ability' that is assessed by the Motor scale is too ill-defined to be of particular help in understanding motor development and its abnormalities.

A test battery that includes, along with a Motor scale, a Perceptual-Performance, Memory and General Cognitive scale, could be useful in coming to an understanding of the pattern of disabilities associated with a particular motor disorder. However, if one is assessing a child who has poor hand control and therefore a low score on the Performance scale, the chances are that he will also score poorly on the General Cognitive scale because the two scales share many common items. On the other hand, items in the Memory scale are largely irrelevant to the motor behaviour assessed by the Perceptual-Performance and Motor scales. The test battery is made up of heterogeneous test items and the relationship between these items within a scale and across scales is ill-defined. The battery is of limited use for understanding the interrelationship between disabilities. Indeed, this shortcoming was highlighted by McCarthy who pointed out that when testing a child with a physical impairment, the examiner should try to administer all *but* the Motor scale.

If one accepts the ill-defined nature of McCarthy's ability scales, and if the measurement problems apparent in the test are not considered to be serious, the test could be useful in the initial assessment of a child up to six years of age with a learning disability, providing the suspected mental handicap is not too great, and providing there is no physical impairment.

STOTT, MOYES AND HENDERSON (1972, 1984): TEST OF MOTOR IMPAIRMENT

A review of the original test published in 1972 will be followed by an account of the changes made in the 1984 revision together with a discussion of the advantages of this new form of the test. Two objectives will be achieved by this approach. Firstly, many workers who have access to the old test may want to decide whether a change to the revised version is warranted. Secondly, it will be possible to show how a test may undergo sensitive revision in the light of current thinking on the development and assessment of perceptual-motor behaviour.

While the test battery designed by Stott, Moyes and Henderson (1972) has a title specifically related to motor behaviour, their primary interest was broader than the immediate measurement of motor impairment. The authors were concerned with theoretical uncertainties surrounding the origin of behavioural disturbances and learning disabilities in children. The underlying causes of the wide-ranging problems that fall under such headings is far from clear, though some kind of fundamental neural dysfunction seemed plausible.

Where other authors, interested in learning disabilities, have opted for an assessment of a wide range of capabilities (e.g. Griffiths, 1970; McCarthy, 1972), the approach adopted by Stott *et al* focused on motor behaviour as, in their terms, an index of neural dysfunction. It was argued that efficient and smoothly working neural control mechanisms are needed for the monitoring of an ever-changing environment, and for the necessary continuous adjustments underlying motor behaviour. Hence, a neural dysfunction would affect motor responses. They proposed objective measures of motor impairment for use as evidence of broad neural dysfunction, which in turn could be linked to behavioural disturbances and learning disabilities.

In designing the test battery, the aim was to minimise every cause for failure at motor control *except* that of neural dysfunction. Two such unwanted variables were perception and cognition. The authors argued that any test involving a significant perceptual variable would not accurately measure neurological dysfunction because perceptual discrimination depends on motivational, temperamental and experiential variables (implying that motor responses need not). Accordingly, they wanted to avoid test items that would involve fine perceptual discriminations. With regard to the cognitive variable, they wanted to avoid tasks that looked difficult or frightening to a child. They argued that a child may avoid trying hard on a test item just because it appears complex, and they stressed the importance of ensuring that the child fully understood the task and was willing to cope with its demands.

Other general factors which were considered in the choice of test items were the effect of cultural influences, sex differences and physical strength: none of the tasks should be influenced by such variables. Finally, they stressed the importance of choosing biologically natural tasks. In avoiding tasks that were affected by differences in prior experience, the authors considered it was easy to go to the opposite extreme and devise activities that were far removed from real life or were in conflict with the natural mechanisms determining motor coordination.

A test battery originally designed by Oseretsky (1948) was a basis for the content and form of the Test of Motor Impairment, and about a third of the test items came from the older battery. There are a total of 45 items grouped under five categories of motor function: (1) control and balance of the body while immobile, (2) control and coordination of the upper limbs, (3) control and coordination of the body while in motion, (4) manual dexterity with the emphasis on speed and (5) tasks which emphasised simultaneous movement and precision.

The objective was to detect minor degrees of failure in motor coordination. Many of the items are timed and the difficulty level of each item is set at a point where failure according to rigidly defined performance criteria has been a handicap to a child in his everyday life. In practical terms this meant setting a difficulty level at which 15% of the general population of children at a given age would fail. A simple 0 (pass) or 2 (fail) is given for each test. A score of 1 (partial failure) is given if a child fails a test with one hand or foot but not the other. The test battery was designed for children in the age range five to 13+ years, and is summarised in Table 5.5.

Table 5.5 *A summary of tasks in five categories, for nine ages from Stott, Moyes and Henderson (1972).*

Age (years)	Category				
	1	2	3	4	5
Sub-5	Heel–toe balance 10 s	Bridge of rods	Jump and clap	Pinboard 18–20 s	Simultaneous match sticks 10 s
5	Toe balance 10 s	Bouncing, two-hand catch 4 catches	High jump over string at knee height	Posting coins 18–20 s	Simultaneous counters 12 s
6	One leg balance 15 s	Bouncing, one-hand catch 4–8 catches	Hopping forward	Threading beads 25 s	Circle trace
7	One leg balance, arms raised 20 s	Spiral of holes 23–28 s	Heel–toe walk	Pegboard 17–21 s	Finger-tip touching
8	Stork balance 20 s	Catching off wall 4 catches	Sideways jumping	Lacing board 16 s	Bead-on-board balance
9	Board balance I 10 s	Catching one hand 3–6 catches	Jump and clap twice	Nine-hole board 14–15 s	Simultaneous pegs 16 s
10	Board balance II 14 s	Guiding ball among tees	Jump with one foot landing	Match boxes 48 s	Simultaneous squares 16.5 s
11+	Two-board balance 10 s	Hitting a target	Sideways hopping	Piercing holes 30 s	Simultaneous pegs and squares 15 s
13+	One-foot toe balance 10 s	Ring and coat hanger	Jumping within circles	Track rotating	Simultaneous piercing 15 s

The test was for the detection of impairment of motor function and testing begins at the child's own age level. He is given the five appropriate items and receives a score of 0, 1 or 2 on each item. A well-coordinated child scores 0, and total failure results in a score of 10. If he fails any item (score of 2), he is tested on all five items at the age level below. Testing continues until he passes all five items within an age level. If at the end of testing the child scores a total of 6 or above, regardless of the age level of the failed items, he is deemed to be showing definite signs of motor impairment.

In one major respect, this test battery is similar to that of Griffiths (1970) and McCarthy (1972) in that motor behaviour is broadly assessed and there is no provision for the separate assessment of proficiency at different types of motor behaviour. The child has to fail at least three items across any of the categories up to and including his age level to be declared motor impaired. In a validation study, Henderson and Hall (1982) showed that the battery does seem to be useful for identifying children with subtle motor problems. They asked school teachers to identify children who had poor motor coordination for their age, *and* whose lack of coordination was significantly affecting school progress. These children performed significantly worse on the test than the control group of children who had no motor coordination problems, a finding which supports the validity of the test.

With regard to their original aim of designing a test battery that would give an index of neural dysfunction, the authors studied the relationship between motor impairment and maladjust-ment. Behaviour disturbance was assessed by the Bristol Social Adjustment Guides and results showed an overall increase in the mean maladjustment scores with increasing motor impair-ment. Whether maladjustment was the cause of the motor difficulties, or *vice versa*, was not of central concern. Rather, the finding was quoted as support for the argument that there was a common factor in the relationship between motor impairment and maladjustment and this connecting factor may well be some form of general neural dysfunction.

Regardless of whether one follows Stott, Moyes and Henderson's suggestion and uses the test to detect motor impairment, or whether the test is used to obtain a behavioural index of neural dysfunction rather than employing neurological types of tests for this purpose, two critical observations can be made. It would seem that some of the test items fail the authors' criterion of not placing any demands on the perceptual or cognitive abilities of a child, while other items are sensitive to physical strength. As illustrations, the balancing tasks surely demand the accurate perception of vestibular, kinaesthetic and visual information relating to movement of the body. Catching tasks demand the accurate perception and cognition of the speed and trajectory of the approaching ball (see Chapter 3). Bead threading, paper piercing and track rotating demand a certain degree of visual-perceptual acuity and kinaesthetic sensitivity. Failure on any one of these tasks can be caused by a perceptual/cognitive deficit as much as a motor deficit. On the other hand, their aim in wanting to limit perceptual and cognitive demands seems pointless. Neural dysfunction can affect a subject's perceptual and cognitive abilities as much as his motor control. Motivation, temperament and experience — the three factors that were considered to be undesirably associated with a child's perceptual performance — can surely also affect a child's motor performance. As far as physical strength is concerned, the hopping and jumping tasks depend on the strength of the muscles in the legs. Failure can result from peripheral muscular weakness as much as from central neural dysfunction.

Secondly, it is not possible to quantify the degree of motor impairment. In calculating the test index, all items carry an equal weighting regardless of their age level relative to the child's chronological age. In other words, all items failed at the child's age earn an impairment score of

2. But items failed below the child's age, while being indicative of much greater impairment, also earn an impairment score of 2. The total score on the test does not reflect the level at which items are failed, and therefore does not indicate the magnitude of motor impairment.

A test battery that assesses a number of different categories of motor behaviour is potentially useful for measuring motor development in a number of domains. However, two characteristics of the present test disallow the measurement of motor development. Firstly, test items within some of the categories and across different age levels are of a heterogeneous nature. For example, items in Category 2 are meant to measure the control and coordination of the upper limbs. However, the specific demands made by each item vary greatly. Items for ages 5, 6, 8 and 9 involve catching a moving object and therefore demand perceptual prediction and motor anticipation on the part of the child, together with an accurate timing of the motor response. Items for ages sub-5, 7, 10, 11–12 and 13+ in the same category require the precise placement of the limbs in relation to a static object, and the timing of the motor response is therefore not as critical. Indeed, the items for ages 7, 10 and 11–12 seem to have more in common with items in Category 4 which are meant to measure manual dexterity with an emphasis on speed. A similar heterogeneity of test items is apparent in Category 5 which is meant to include tasks that emphasise simultaneous movements and precision. Some of the items (ages sub-5, 5, 9, 10, 11–12 and 13+) demand simultaneous use of the two hands while the child is seated. Another item (age 8) requires movement of the whole body together with a balancing task, while items for ages 6 and 7 have little in common with other items in this category. Finally, a type of task demanding an accurate movement of the upper limb within visually defined error limits is scattered across three categories: 'ring and coathanger' in Category 2, 'track rotating' in Category 4 and 'circle tracing' in Category 5. The heterogeneity among items within a category and across age levels does not facilitate the measurement of development of different aspects of motor behaviour.

The second limiting characteristic of the present battery is that it specifically aims at testing motor impairment, not motor excellence, and the method of test administration and scoring was designed to identify the child whose motor capabilities are well below the average for his age. Accordingly, there is no possibility of assessing a child with above average or exceptional motor skills, and therefore no way of evaluating the full range of individual differences within an age level.

The heterogeneity among test items within a category discussed above also rules out the use of the test in identifying a specific area of motor impairment — information that would be of value in understanding the reasons for an overall disability. If a child fails an item at his own age level, the long form of the test requires him to be tested on all items at the younger age to see if he can perform the lower items in the same category, as well as the items in the other categories. It would have been valuable to have the same capabilities assessed at the lower level, but one cannot be sure that the test accomplishes this. It is, therefore, difficult to understand the significance of a pass or fail score on the items below the child's age level, and the test does not help to clarify the pattern of a child's disabilities.

Disregarding the above problems, the test is nonetheless useful for identifying children whose motor functioning, broadly 'defined', falls below a specified level for their age.

The Henderson revision (Stott, Moyes and Henderson, 1984)

The Henderson revision of the Stott, Moyes and Henderson test incorporates significant changes that solve some of the problems with the earlier test. It is still a test of motor impairment with the aim of identifying and describing educationally significant impairments of motor function. However, the revision places great emphasis on observing children performing the test items, and in so doing partly avoids the problems associated with pass/fail test scores (see Chapter 4). It enables the tester to gain some insight into the nature of the motor handicap, and an indication of a child's capacity for improvement in motor function. There is less emphasis on the use of the test as an indicator of neural dysfunction.

The revision involves changes in two major respects. Firstly, there is a re-structuring of the test. Some of the original items were deleted, new items were designed, and there is a regrouping of the items into fewer and broader age bands and a larger number of motor categories. The overall effect is a significant reduction in the heterogeneity of test items within a category. The eight categories of motor function are: (1) manual dexterity 1 (speed and sureness of each hand separately), (2) manual dexterity 2 (coordination of the two hands for the performance of a single operation), (3) manual dexterity 3 (hand–eye coordination using the preferred hand), (4) static balance, (5) ball skills 1 (catching), (6) ball skills 2 (throwing), (7) dynamic balance 1 (making spatially precise movements in slow motion), (8) dynamic balance 2 (making movements that are less spatially precise but demanding control of momentum). The eight categories and their associated test items are largely determined by the nature of the items in the original test battery, rather than from a consideration of factors or abilities that may underlie motor behaviour; 'the test should sample a broad range of motor skills such as are required by a child in everyday life' (p 16). As in the old version of the test, the difficulty level of each item is set at a point where failure, according to rigidly defined performance criteria, is a handicap to a child in his everyday life. A simple 0 (pass), 1 (partial failure), 2 (failure) score is given on each item. There are separate criteria for failure for the two ages within any one age band. The test battery is summarised in Table 5.6. The asterisked items are new.

The second major change to the test battery was aimed at providing a means for understanding the nature of a motor failure. While a child may perform poorly because of an intrinsic motor disability, poor performance may also result from such non-specific factors as the child's attitude and temperament. It was argued that one way of gaining an insight into the nature of a child's failure is to apply specified observational procedures during the performance of the standard test items. Three aids to observation are provided in the new test to avoid weaknesses inherent in the unstructured recording of observations (Chapter 4). The Concurrent Observations Checklist offers a means for the exact task-by-task analysis of the child's failure, by drawing the tester's attention to common faults observed in the performance of children whose motor functioning is poor. The Faults of Coping Style Checklist is provided to record the way in which a child addressed a task. This aids in identifying non-motor causes for failure like lack of attention and concentration, timidity, impulsivity, nervousness, tenseness, oversensitivity to failure, poor motivation, and a variety of negative and uncooperative attitudes. The Faults of Motor Control Checklist enables the tester to pinpoint sources of impairment such as awkwardness or immaturity of motor patterns, inaccurate timing or spatial adaptation, sequential confusion, poorly established laterality, extreme muscular tension, poor eye-movement control or defect of vision.

The test was seen to serve four main functions, the first being that of a normative test. For this purpose the child is tested on just the eight items from his own age band. In the event of failure the total score is compared to the norms for his age. The second function of the test is that of 'clinical exploration'. The child who fails at his own age band is tested at lower levels until he

Table 5.6 *A summary of tasks in eight categories, for four age bands from Stott, Moyes and Henderson (1984): The Henderson revision.*

Age band	1	2	3	4	Category 5	6	7	8
1 (Age 5–6)	Posting coins *	Threading beads	Flower trail *	One leg balance	Catching a bean bag *	Rolling a ball into a goal *	Walking, head-raised *	High jump over string at knee height
2 (Age 7–8)	Pegboard	Lacing board	Flower trail *	Stork balance	Bouncing one-hand catch	Throwing bean bag *	Heel–toe walking	Jumping in squares *
3 (Age 9–10)	Shifting pegs in rows *	Threading nuts on bolt *	Flower trail *	One board balance	Catching off wall, two hands	Throwing bean bag *	Balancing ball while walking *	Hopping in squares *
4 (Age 11+)	Piercing holes *	Cutting out elephant *	Flower trail *	Two board balance	Catching off wall, one hand	Hitting a target	Walking backwards *	Jump and clap

'Flower trail' is a paper and pencil tracing task.
*Denotes new items.

passes all eight items of an age band. The profile of failures would help in the assessment of the degree and nature of the motor difficulty. The third function is that of providing a measure of the capacity for improvement. Some children fail a motor test not because of an intrinsic motor impairment — the child's motor capabilities may be normal — but as a result of poor performance stemming from non-participation and lack of previous experience. The child is asked to repeat those tasks he has difficulty with to see if a correction of a particular fault can be achieved. By using the test in the second and third ways described above, and by interpreting the outcome of the various checklists, a fourth main function is served; that of providing information to a teacher or therapist for the design of a remedial or therapy programme.

As with the old test, the revision is not useful as a method of assessing normal motor development. The test aims at detecting motor impairment and there are no standards for assessing a child with above average or superior motor skills, and therefore no way of evaluating the full range of individual differences within an age level.

The revision is a significant advance on the initial test. It provides a useful means of measuring motor impairment, and enables the collection of some basic information for the design of remedial programmes.

GUBBAY (1975): STANDARDISED TEST OF MOTOR PROFICIENCY

Gubbay (1975) was concerned with the development of tests for the rapid identification of mild degrees of motor impairment or clumsiness in children. He pointed out that abnormal clumsiness could arise from virtually any disturbance of the nervous system, and also from disorders of the peripheral neuromuscular and joint apparatus. A large number of defects were catalogued with motor coordination as one of the presenting symptoms. Motor problems are very often accompanied by definite physical and neurological signs like muscular wasting, abnormal posture, low muscular tone, abnormal reflexes, obvious defects in sensation or abnormal EEG. In such cases it can be relatively easy to arrive at a diagnosis and to understand the underlying causes of a child's motor deficit.

There is, however, a category of motor disorders that defies neurological definition or diagnosis. Gubbay claimed that between 3% and 10% of children in regular schools have motor problems that can relate to fine movements of the hand in writing and drawing, and/or gross movements of the body as in gymnastics or sports. Very often the problems that children in regular schools face in trying to cope with everyday demands go unrecognised, although the perceptive school teacher can readily identify the child whose progress is being hindered by a motor disability (see Henderson and Hall, 1982). Failure to identify the problem often leads to severe emotional and social disorders when the child fails to 'keep up', is rejected by his peers for being useless at games, or starts to lose self-confidence and develops feelings of inferiority (Chapter 1). The so-called clumsy child can suffer far more severely from such secondary disorders than children with frank and definitely diagnosed motor problems (e.g. cerebral palsy) whose disabilities are sensitively managed by the clinician, school teacher and parent, and are acknowledged by his peers. Gubbay suggested that the school population should be screened for an early identification of unskilled children who could otherwise develop secondary problems because of a lack of appreciation of their motor difficulties by teachers and parents.

It was argued that clumsy children suffer from some kind of minimal cerebral dysfunction; minimal in the sense that there are few or no definite neurological signs. In discussions reminiscent of Stott, Moyes and Henderson (1972), Gubbay considered a possible link between the three factors of: motor impairment, behaviour and learning difficulties, and some kind of underlying neurological dysfunction. And like Stott *et al* (1972), he proposed a behavioural test of this dysfunction, albeit one that was short enough to be useful as a routine screening device.

Gubbay presented a battery of eight test items that satisfied the following four criteria: (a) ease of administration, (b) speed of administration (less than five minutes total), (c) independent identification of children who had been assessed subjectively by teachers as having motor problems, and (d) accessible and easily understood norms. The test items are in three broad categories comprising facial and lingual praxis, trunk and leg praxis, and manual praxis (see Table 5.7).

Table 5.7   *A brief description of eight test items from Gubbay (1975).*

Item	Test
1	Whistle through pouted lips.
2	Skip forward five steps.
3	Roll ball with foot.
4	Throw, clap hands and then catch a tennis ball.
5	Tie one shoelace with double bow (single knot).
6	Thread ten beads.
7	Pierce 20 pinholes.
8	Posting box.

Items 1 and 2 are scored as either pass or fail. For items 3, 5 and 8 the number of seconds taken to complete the task is recorded, up to a maximum of 60 seconds beyond which a fail is recorded. Item 4 has a graded point score of 0 to 4 depending on the number of claps up to a maximum of four claps. For items 6 and 7 the number of seconds taken to complete the task is recorded with no upper time limit. Tables are presented detailing the 5th, 10th, 50th, 90th and 95th percentiles for ages 8, 9, 10, 11 and 12 years on the eight test items. The test items are administered in the same way to all children regardless of age. A child is regarded as having failed an individual item if he falls below the 10th percentile for his age. As an illustration, the 10th percentiles for an eight year old on the eight items are: 1, cannot whistle; 2, cannot make five skips; 3, takes 26 seconds or more to roll a ball with his foot around the matchboxes; 4, cannot manage two claps while catching a ball; 5, cannot tie a shoelace; 6, takes 44 seconds to thread 10 beads; 7, takes 39 seconds to make 20 holes; 8, takes 25 seconds to perform the posting box. Failure on one or two items is not considered significant. A child is deemed clumsy if he falls below the 10th percentile on any three or more test items.

At first inspection this short battery of tests seems to be more attractive than that proposed by Stott *et al* (1972). Both tests aim to identify mild motor disabilities and they share some common types of items, the basis for a diagnosis of impairment/clumsiness is failure on a mixture of test items, and the criteria for failure are set to identify the lowest 15% and 10% (respectively) of the regular school population. Gubbay's test has the advantage that a tester has to familiarise himself with only eight test items, while the Stott *et al* (1972) test has 45 items. Furthermore, Gubbay's test takes approximately half the time to administer.

However, closer examination of the validation data reported by Gubbay indicates the test to be of little use in identifying children with mild motor impairment. From data presented in his

Tables 4.13, 4.14 and 4.15 it is apparent that 68% of children identified as clumsy on the screening test were not thought by their teachers to have below average handwriting, 54% were not thought to have a low sporting ability and 61% were not thought to be clumsy. In other words, while the test was certainly quick and easy to administer, it fails Gubbay's third criterion for selection of test items, namely, that the battery should accurately identify children who had been assessed subjectively by teachers as having motor problems.

The test items are the same for children of all ages, and 'norms' were reported for superior and inferior performance. The test, however, is not useful for measuring perceptual-motor development because the battery was designed to be a brief screening test, there is a very limited range of test items, and the measurement of performance on some of these items is not finely graded. The test has no potential for throwing light on disabilities underlying motor problems experienced by clumsy children.

BRUININKS (1978): BRUININKS–OSERETSKY TEST OF MOTOR PROFICIENCY

A comprehensive system for assessing motor behaviour was proposed by Bruininks (1978). It shares features in common with many of the earlier systems of assessment, but has the potential for a finer grained objective analysis of motor proficiency than was hitherto possible. The items demand performance on set tasks and there is no formal provision for observational recordings of behaviour. In common with Griffiths (1970) and McCarthy (1972), Bruininks aimed at measuring a profile of proficiencies but in the present case a profile relating only to motor behaviour. Like McCarthy (1972) and Gubbay (1975) the same items are given to all age levels, and children are given a graded score.

Bruininks designed his test battery for the assessment of motor functioning of children from $4\frac{1}{2}$ to $14\frac{1}{2}$ years of age. Many of the 46 test items were drawn from the original 'Oseretsky Tests of Motor Proficiency' and were chosen and designed with a number of criteria in mind. The items should, in Bruininks' terms, (1) permit the broadest sampling of motor behaviour, (2) represent significant aspects of motor development at each age, (3) assess the abilities of mildly and moderately handicapped children, (4) measure motor skills relevant to everyday tasks, (5) primarily assess proficiency of movement and motor performance, as opposed to perceptual skills, (6) require minimal verbal comprehension and memory, (7) yield a wide enough range of scores to discriminate between children of various abilities, (8) require inexpensive and portable equipment, (9) be easy to administer, (10) not be physically threatening or frightening for children, and (11) permit simple and objective scoring procedures.

The 46 separate items are grouped into eight subtests that enable the examiner to obtain a comprehensive index of motor proficiency, as well as separate measures of gross and fine skills. The eight subtests are as follows: (1) running speed and agility, (2) balance, (3) bilateral coordination, (4) strength, (5) upper limb coordination, (6) response speed, (7) visual-motor control, (8) upper limb speed and dexterity. Scores on subtests 1 to 4 are used to obtain a Gross Motor Composite score, scores on subtests 6 to 8 a Fine Motor Composite, and scores on all subtests give an index of general motor proficiency (Battery Composite). Table 5.8 presents an outline of the content and form of the test battery.

Table 5.8 *A summary of test items and their grouping into eight subtests from Bruininks (1978).*

	Subtests							
	1	2	3	4	5	6	7	8
Test items	1 Running speed and agility	1 Standing on preferred leg on floor Eyes open 10 s	1 Tapping feet while making circles with fingers	1 Standing broad jump	1 Two-hand bouncing and catching	1 Stopping a moving 'speed stick' from sliding down the wall	1 Cutting out circle	1 Placing pennies in a box
		2 Standing on preferred leg on balance beam Eyes open 10 s	2 Tapping foot and finger on same side	2 Sit-ups	2 Preferred hand bouncing and catching		2 Drawing line through crooked path	2 Placing pennies in two boxes with both hands
		3 As above Eyes closed	3 Tapping foot and finger on opposite sides	3 Push-ups	3 Catching a tossed ball with both hands		3 Drawing line through straight path	3 Sorting shape cards
		4 Walking forward on line	4 Jumping with arms and legs on same side synchronised		4 Catching with preferred hand		4 Drawing line through curved path	4 String beads
		5 Walking forward on balance beam	5 As above but opposite sides synchronised		5 Throwing a ball at a target		5 Copying circle	5 Displacing pegs
		6 Walking heel–toe on line	6 Jump up and clap hands		6 Touching a moving ball		6 Copying triangle	6 Drawing vertical lines
		7 Walking heel–toe on balance beam	7 Jump up and touch heels		7 Touching nose with index finger, eyes closed		7 Copying diamond	7 Making dots in circles
		8 Stepping over stick on balance beam	8 Draw lines and crosses simultaneously		8 Touching thumb to finger tips, eyes closed		8 Copying overlapping pencils	8 Making dots
					9 Pivoting thumb and index finger			

The scoring procedure is complicated. Firstly, raw scores are given for each test item and are expressed in one of four ways depending on the nature of the item: (a) time taken to complete a task, (b) number of units completed in a fixed time, (c) number of errors made, (d) a pass/fail record based on fixed performance criteria. Like all other methods of assessment reviewed, the items were never intended to be given and interpreted individually. Rather, the aim is to obtain composite indices of fine, gross and general motor proficiency. As discussed in Chapter 4 and in the review of the McCarthy scales (1972), there are inherent problems in combining raw scores obtained on a number of different items into an overall index of proficiency. Bruininks handled the problem in a similar way to McCarthy (1972) by converting raw scores to point scores. For this second step there is a point score conversion scale for each item. The design of each scale 'satisfied' three criteria: (a) a range of point scores was selected which was sufficient to discrimi-nate between different levels of performance as shown by the raw scores, (b) a maximum point score for each scale was selected to give more points (more weight) to items judged to be more important within a subtest, and (c) the scales were constructed to spread the raw scores from the normative sample evenly through the range of allotted points. The weighted point scores are added to obtain a total for each of the eight subtests.

The possible range of subtest totals varies depending on the number of items within a subtest (one for subtest 1, nine for subtest 5), and the maximum point scores for the individual items (one for 'stepping over response stick', 17 for 'stopping a speed stick'). For subtest 1 the range of possible totals is from 0 to 15, while for subtest 8 the range is from 0 to 72. The third step involves rescaling the summed point scores for each of the subtests so that they contribute an *equal* weighting to the composite scores. Age-appropriate tables are provided to convert the variably ranged subtest totals to a standard range of 1 to 36. These standard scores are then summed to obtain a Gross Motor Composite, a Fine Motor Composite or a Battery Composite.

The possible range of the three composite scores varies depending on how many subtests are contained within each composite. To enable a direct comparison between the three composite scores the fourth step involves yet another rescaling of the test results to a common scale. Finally, an additional set of tables enables the conversion of subtest total point scores to 'age-equivalent scores', to obtain a profile of the child's performance across the eight subtests.

In summary, to obtain composite scores of a child's gross, fine and general motor proficiency, the test results are weighted and rescaled three times. Firstly, the raw scores on each item are weighted and rescaled according to somewhat arbitrary criteria in the allocation of point scores. Secondly, each subtest is rescaled (and effectively weighted) to ensure that all the subtests contribute equally to the Gross Motor, Fine Motor and Battery Composite scores. Thirdly, the composite scores are rescaled to enable a direct comparison to be made between them, and an assessment of whether a child's gross motor proficiency is better or worse than his fine motor proficiency.

The test was intended to provide educators, clinicians and researchers with information relevant to a child's motor skills that would assist in developing and evaluating motor training programmes, and in evaluating serious motor dysfunctions and developmental handicaps. Recommended uses for the test included: (a) making decisions about educational placement, (b) the assessment of gross and fine motor skills by physical education teachers and occupational therapists, (c) identifying students with deficiencies in motor skills who would benefit from motor training programmes, and then evaluating their progress, (d) screening children for an early identification of physical and other problems, and (e) the use of the test by neurologists and paediatricians would enable the clinician to make differential diagnoses of various developmental problems of children, and would enable them to study the motor dysfunctions of children. The author gave the following guidelines for interpreting the results of the test. In the evaluation of the subtest profile of scores, a difference of at least 5–6 standard score units between subtests is needed before a difference is considered significant. In the evaluation of differences between composite scores, a difference of 10 standard score units between the gross and fine motor composite is needed before a difference is considered significant.

Two critical observations can be made regarding the content and form of this test. Firstly, a number of test items fail the authors' own criteria for item selection. For example, test items should 'represent significant aspects of motor development at each age'. It is difficult to see how 'tapping feet alternatively while making circles with fingers', 'drawing lines and crosses simultaneously', and 'pivoting thumb and index finger' satisfy this criterion. While it is true that each of these items shows a developmental trend, showing a trend does not necessarily establish the usefulness of an item in throwing light on motor development, or in elucidating the nature and cause of a motor disability.

The criterion used to 'primarily assess proficiency of movement and motor performance, as opposed to perceptual skills' was also infringed. All balancing items demand accurate perception of kinaesthetic information. All items demanding eye–hand coordination also demand accurate visual and kinaesthetic perception. In short, it is possible to fail most of the items as a result of a lack in perceptual skills as much as a lack in motor skills. As a final example, tests should 'yield a wide enough range of scores to discriminate between children of various abilities'. Eight of the items are in fact scored as either pass or fail. Six out of the eight items in the bilateral coordination subtest are scored in this way, which raises the question of the usefulness of this subtest in finely discriminating between children.

The second critical observation relates to the calculation of composite scores. All test designers who aim at obtaining an index of proficiency based on performance on many test items face one basic problem — how to combine the separate scores in the calculation of the index. Whatever the precise method, the test designer must make single-minded and idiosyncratic decisions about the weight that each item contributes to the overall assessment, perhaps also taking into account statistical considerations. The decisions made by Bruininks when he rescaled the raw test scores to obtain point scores, and rescaled the subtest totals to obtain standard scores illustrates this point, and it is not difficult to find areas of argument. For example, why should 'standing on preferred leg on balance beam with eyes closed' contribute more to the balance subtest score than 'walking forward on a walking line'? On the basis of one of his criteria, i.e. tests should 'measure motor skills relevant to everyday tasks', the reverse weighting would be more logical. Why should 'drawing lines and crosses simultaneously' contribute more to the bilateral coordination subtest score than 'tapping foot and finger on same side synchronously'? Both items seem equally irrelevant to everyday tasks and should contribute an equal weighting (!). In the rescaling of subtest totals, why should the 'bilateral coordination' subtest (just 'declared' irrelevant) and the 'balance' subtest contribute an equal weighting to the Gross Motor Composite? Should the 'response speed' subtest (one item) and the 'upper-limb speed and dexterity' subtest (eight items) contribute equal weighting to the Fine Motor Composite? There are no acceptable answers to these questions, and decisions made by Bruininks were arbitrary, and therefore of doubtful validity.

It was said at the outset that this test had the potential for a fine-grained objective analysis of motor proficiency. Certain characteristics favour its use for the measurement of normal motor development: the same items are given to children regardless of their age, upper and lower norms are presented, norms for individual subtests are given that enabled the calculation of 'age equivalence' in different areas of motor behaviour, as well as overall composite scores that enable measurement of the full range of proficiency from superior to impaired. However, the separate test items were never intended to be given and interpreted individually. This is one of the major weaknesses of the test. In these times of a heightened awareness of the numerous and the inter-connected nature of factors and abilities underlying the performance of any one motor skill, it is not unfair to call a test designer capricious who 'muddies the pool' by giving norms based on composite test scores without allowing for the analysis of individual tasks. The failure to allow for an evaluation of performance on any one test item significantly compromises the use of the test for the first three purposes proposed by Bruininks.

The test provides for the evaluation of subtest scores, and gross and fine motor composite scores. Yet the interpretation of differences between subtests (and differences in the broad motor capabilities they imply) is compromised by the sharing of items of a similar nature — the subtests were not independent. For example, the items 'jumping up and clapping hands' and 'jumping up and touching heels with hands' of the bilateral coordination subtest, also belong in the strength subtest. 'Drawing lines and crosses simultaneously' of the bilateral coordination subtest also belong to the upper-limb speed and dexterity subtest. 'Pivoting thumb and index finger' of the upper limb coordination subtest belong to the visual-motor control subtest. The test is there-fore best used for assessing the gross, fine and overall motor proficiency of a child, allowing for the fact that these categories of behaviour are broad and amorphous.

As far as the study of abnormalities of motor behaviour is concerned, the test is useful for measuring a mild to moderate, though ill-defined, motor deficit. The test by itself cannot be used for arriving at a differential diagnosis of developmental problems (the fifth recommended use listed earlier) and is not useful for differentially diagnosing underlying causes of a confirmed motor disorder.

AYRES (1972a): SOUTHERN CALIFORNIA SENSORY INTEGRATION TESTS

A feature in common among all methods of assessment reviewed so far is that they did not aim to establish objectively the cause for inadequate performance of a test item [note: Stott, Moyes and Henderson (1984), published observational guidelines for this purpose]. The tests can at best describe motor behaviour, or measure the overall level of motor proficiency (normal or abnormal). They cannot account for the processes underlying normal motor developmental changes, nor can the tests account for the underlying causes of a motor impairment (see Chapters 2, 3 and 7). There are, however, other methods of assessment that seem to have the potential for elucidating mechanisms underlying and determining motor behaviour.

Ayres (1972a) aimed at an understanding of perceptual-motor and related deficits, in children who have learning and behaviour disorders. While she claimed to be interested in general learning and behaviour disorders, her main interest centred on disorders of motor behaviour. She proposed a battery of 17 test items for use with children aged four to eight years. The criteria for selection and design of these items was not described. She recommended that any one child be tested on all 17 items, and the pattern of results (the test profile) would assist in differentiating four types of sensory integrative dysfunctions underlying a disorder in behaviour. Table 5.9 summarises the test items.

Table 5.9 *A summary of 17 test items from Ayres (1972a).*

Item		Description
1.	Space visualisation	Fitting shapes into a 'form board'.
2.	Figure-ground perception	Selecting patterns 'embedded' in a test plate.
3.	Position in space	Choosing a given picture from a set of pictures that differed slightly in placement of details.
4.	Design copying	Copying pictures onto a grid of dots.
5.	Motor accuracy	Tracing over a large test figure.
6.	Kinaesthesia	Actively relocating a position from memory – without vision.
7.	Manual form perception	Perceiving the shape of an object held in the hand.
8.	Finger identification	Locating a finger that had just been touched.
9.	Graphaesthesia	Reproducing a design from memory that had been drawn on the hand.
10.	Localisation of tactile stimuli	Locating a point on the body that had been touched — without vision.
11.	Double tactile stimulation	Locating two points on the body that had been touched simultaneously.
12.	Imitation of postures	Imitating 12 standard postures.
13.	Crossing midline of body	Imitating actions which crossed the midline.
14.	Bilateral motor coordination	Rhythmic tapping of hands on thighs.
15.	Right–left discrimination	Identifying right and left sides of body.
16.	Standing balance: eyes open	Standing on one foot.
17.	Standing balance: eyes closed	Standing on one foot.

The scoring procedures for many of the test items are very complicated, but they fall into four main categories: (a) length of time that a particular activity is maintained, (b) number of errors made on a set of pass/fail items, (c) point scores on the basis of complicated criteria for the accuracy of performance, (d) combined speed/accuracy measures in which penalty points were subtracted for slow performance, from error or accuracy scores (see Chapter 4 for a discussion of speed/accuracy scores). The raw score obtained on each test is converted to a standard score by reference to tables. The standard score is the number of standard deviations from the normative mean according to the normative data obtained in a standardisation study of children in the Los Angeles area. The standard scores for each of the 17 test items is marked on a diagram of a normal distribution. This test profile is subsequently examined and 'diagnoses' made.

The following descriptions of what each item is said to measure were taken directly from the manual to give an accurate account of Ayres' standpoint. 'Space visualisation' is intended to require perception of stimuli composed largely of spatial elements, including mental manipulation of space or space visualisation. 'Figure-ground perception' assists in determining deficits in visual perception and requires selection of a foreground figure from a rival background. 'Position in space' was designed to measure the perception of the same form in different orientations. 'Design copying' measures a combination of visual perception of a geometric design and the capacity of the brain to direct the hand in duplicating the design – it taps several neural systems. 'Motor accuracy' is another test that employs a motor response in connection with a visual stimulus, but it emphasises the motor aspect; it measures the degree of, and changes in, sensorimotor integration in upper extremities of individuals with nervous system dysfunction. 'Kinaesthesia' is intended to measure the capacity to perceive joint position and movement. 'Manual form perception' is based on classic methods of testing stereognosis and involves identifying the two-dimensional visual counterpart of a geometric form held in the hand. 'Finger

Table 5.10   *The grouping of test items relevant to the diagnosis of four sensory integrative disorders from Ayres (1972a). For example, if a child is found to be deficient on items 1, 2, 3, 4, 6, 7 and 8 he is said to be suffering from a disorder in form and space perception.*

	Disorders			
Item	Form and space perception	Praxis	Postural and bilateral integration	Tactile defensiveness
1	X			
2	X	X		X
3	X			
4	X	X		
5		X		
6	X	X	X	
7	X	X		
8		X		
9	X	X		
10		X		X
11		X		X
12		X		
13			X	
14		X	X	
15			X	
16			X	
17			X	

identification' was included for the examination of sensory integration of individuals with dysfunction. A description of what 'graphaesthesia' measures is not given. 'Localisation of tactile stimuli' was said to detect mild to severe deficits in tactile perception, depending on the age of the child. 'Double tactile stimulation' is a test of a certain type of attention. In the remaining five tests an attempt is made to evaluate some of the higher levels of sensory integration, based on assimilation of sensation from several sensory modalities and requires greater central nervous system processing than in simple somatosensory perception. 'Imitation of postures' requires motor planning or programming a skilled or non-habitual motor act. 'Crossing midline of body' is a test of sensory integration. 'Bilateral motor coordination' measures motor planning and integration of function of the two sides of the body: it has a sensorimotor rather than a cognitive basis. 'Right–left discrimination' measures the ability to discriminate right from left on self and another person. The 'standing balance' items measure the ability to balance with and without vision.

Ayres placed great weight on obtaining and interpreting constellations of test scores. Dysfunction was operationally defined as a 'meaningful cluster of test scores that fall a standard deviation or more below age expectations or below other meaningful test score clusters in the same child' (p 5). On the basis of a factor analysis study, she claimed the profile of scores on the test battery could assist in differentiating four types of sensory integrative disorders or dysfunctions: (a) form and space perception, (b) praxis, (c) postural and bilateral integration and (d) tactile defensiveness — each with particular disordered neural systems. Table 5.10 shows the four principal groupings of items. Defective performance on any one cluster would lead to one of the above diagnoses. Other groupings of items are also possible, and these could be used to describe other types of dysfunction.

It is not unfair to say that Ayres' description of the four sensory integrative disorders is obscure, and it is difficult to describe the type of learning and behaviour disorders that were expected in a child with a diagnosed dysfunction in sensory integration. She alleged that children with very broad types of learning difficulties are frequently diagnosed to have disorders in form and space perception. Children with difficulties in planning and executing skilled and non-habitual motor tasks have disorders in praxis. Children with learning problems, especially in reading, are found to have disorders in postural and bilateral integration, while tactile defensiveness is found in children who were hyperactive, distractable, and possibly apraxic. Ayres (1972b) proposed four programmes of therapy to correct the sensory integrative dysfunctions, and alleviate the associated learning and behaviour disorders.

Four critical observations can be made in relation to Ayres' system of assessment. The first concerns the choice of test items and the descriptions of what they measured. Ayres' aim was to measure disorders of sensory integration, and while 'sensory integration' was not defined, even from an intuitive understanding of the term there are doubts regarding the validity of many of the test items. Firstly, she presented certain items in a way that strongly implied the testing of a sensory function and claimed that skilled motor responses were required only when there was an intention to evaluate motor functioning. Three examples of test items which do not conform to this principle can be given.

1. The 'test for kinaesthesia' (Item 6) did not unequivocally measure 'the capacity to perceive joint position and movement' since it demanded remembering a location and performing an accurate movement, i.e. good performance would indicate good kinaesthesia, but poor performance could just as easily be due to poor memory or poor motor control, as poor kinaesthesia.
2. The 'test for graphaesthesia' (Item 9) implied a test of the sense of touch, but this item was designed in such a way that performance also depends on memory and fine hand control.
3. All test items in the battery demand a motor response from the child albeit not always a finely graded one.

A number of items, while not demanding an accurate motor response, impose penalty points for slow performance. Items 1, 3 and 7 have such penalty points and along with Items 6 and 9 (discussed above) are used to diagnose a disorder in form and space perception. A physically handicapped child performing poorly on these items can be incorrectly judged to have a disorder in 'form and space perception' when in fact his motor incapacities are the primary cause for failure. Secondly, Ayres presented no theory, system or taxonomy as a basis for her selection of the particular set of test items. On the other hand, while many of the items conformed to an intuitive understanding of a 'test of sensory integration', it is difficult to see what sensory integrative function some items are supposed to be measuring; e.g. 'finger identification' and 'crossing midline of body'.

The second critical observation relates to the diagnosis and definition of the four sensory integrative disorders. There were no clear arguments or evidence to corroborate the grouping of items (shown in Table 5.10) that were used to diagnose the ill-defined disorders. The grouping seems to be largely a function of an unexplained factor analysis study, and Ayres' intuition and clinical experience. Nonetheless, some of the groupings of items seems reasonable albeit not on the basis of Ayres' description of what the items measure. For example, items 4, 5, 6, 9, 10, 12 and 14 all demand an accurate motor response from the child and it would not be unexpected for a child with a motor disability to score poorly, and therefore not unreasonable to diagnose that child as having a disorder in praxis. But then any test of motor function could achieve such a diagnosis when praxis is defined as the 'doing or performance of an action' (Dorland's Medical Dictionary, 1965). On the other hand, as argued in the previous paragraph, performance on the group of items used to diagnose a disorder in space and form perception can be affected by disorders in praxis, and the validity of such a diagnosis would therefore be questionable in the case of a child with even the mildest motor disability.

The third observation relates to the proposed links between the four sensory integrative disorders and different types of learning disabilities. The nature of, and reasons for the proposed links are particularly difficult to comprehend when both the sensory integrative disorders and the groups of learning disabilities are themselves poorly defined. An apt example of an unexplained and obscure relationship between an integrative disorder and a learning disability is the suggested link between a disorder in postural and bilateral integration and reading problems.

Finally, Ayres implied that each sensory integrative disorder is associated with a particular disordered neural system, and her programmes of therapy that were aimed at correcting the integrative disorder would also correct the neural disorder. For a clearly argued criticism of this approach to therapy see Cratty (1981).

It is judicial to end this section with a defence of one element of Ayres' work. More than anyone else in the field of assessment of handicapped children and the design of therapy programmes, she has been a patron of the senses and their role in normal and abnormal motor behaviour. This is no minor point, considering the contrast between the wealth of attention that has been lavished on cataloguing, describing and measuring the overt manifestations of motor development and physical handicaps, and the paucity of work attempting to elucidate the perceptual (and motor) processes and mechanisms underlying and determining motor behaviour.

TOUWEN (1979): EXAMINATION OF THE CHILD WITH MINOR NEUROLOGICAL DYSFUNCTION

Ayres (1972a) proposed tests of perceptual-motor behaviour for the explanation of underlying causes of learning and behaviour disorders. Touwen (1979) was also interested in diagnosing the causes of behavioural disorders but his approach as a clinician differed from that of all test designers whose work has been reviewed so far. He explained that children are often referred for a full neurological examination 'because of complaints by parents or teachers about behavioural and/or learning difficulties which have no apparent neurological cause, and who have no other disorder which would offer an obvious neurological clue' (pp 1-2). He designed, as one part of the total developmental assessment of a child from three to 12 years of age, a detailed examination, the purpose of which is to reveal a possible minor neurological dysfunction that could be an 'organic basis' for the aberrant behaviour. While the neurologist can be faced with a wide range of behaviour and learning disorders in children, the examination relates mostly to the motor system, presumably because it alone is responsible for all manifestations of behaviour. The test items involve little or no voluntary participation on the part of the child, and in cases where the child is required to perform a movement, the movement is very rudimentary. The basic approach is to eliminate, as far as possible, perceptual, cognitive, intellectual and volitional

Table 5.11 *A brief description of the neurological test proforma from Touwen (1979).*

Category	Types of items
1. Assessment of sitting	Examination for spontaneous motility; involuntary movements; resting posture; reaction to push; visual tracking of moving object.
2. Examination of the motor system	Muscle power; resistance to passive movement; range of movement; kicking.
3. Examination of reflexes	Tendon, plantar and other reflexes.
4. Assessment of standing	Similar to 1. as well as a test of proprioception that was confounded by motor ability.
5. Test for involuntary movement	Arms outstretched, finger spreading, tongue protruding, with maximal effort.
6. Tests for coordination and associated movements	Including rapid pronation/supination of hand; finger–nose, finger-touching, finger-opposition tests; standing with eyes closed; reaction to push.
7. Assessment of walking	Including posture; gait; walking a line; walking on toes; walking on heels; one leg standing; hopping.
8. Assessment of the trunk	Inspection of back and spine; skin reflexes.
9. Assessment of lying	Including inspection of back; resting postures.
10. Assessment of the head	Including observing facial muscles; eye movement; hearing; vision; tongue movement; pharyngeal arches.
11. General data	Including physical measures; hand, foot, eye preference; clinical tests of touch, pain, temperature and kinaesthetic sensation.

factors that influence behaviour, and examine the basic integrity of the motor, and to a lesser extent, the sensory system. A highly abbreviated examination proforma is shown in Table 5.11.

Responses to the various tests are first assessed by observing the child, who is then allotted a point score according to given criteria. The absence of a response is recorded as 0 or 1, and a strong response is recorded as 3. In addition, a note is made of the 'optimal response': when a response is normally present the optimal score is usually 2, and when it is normally absent the score is 0. A single non-optimal result is not considered significant. Rather, the number of such findings are counted and this 'optimality score' gives a means of identifying the overall integrity of the central nervous system.

Deciding on the cut-off point between an optimal response and a frankly abnormal pathological response is difficult, and the description of the examination included no statement about 'normative values'. Indeed, Touwen questioned the value of general population norms. He said that every examiner has to find his own norms, and his book simply suggested a method or procedure.

In an argument reminiscent of Ayres (1972a), Touwen said that clusters of neurological signs can be used to diagnose a number of clinical entities. There are seven main points in the following critical discussion of these diagnostic categories.

1. The majority of items involve testing each side of the body separately. 'Hemisyndrome' or lateralisation syndrome can be diagnosed if a combination of neurological signs form a specific unilateral pattern. The signs can vary from very severe to very mild. The most severe examples are called hemiplegic or hemiparesis, while mild forms not interfering with everyday activities are not significant. A hemisyndrome could originate from pre- or perinatal brain damage, or could be acquired in infancy or childhood.

2. The test for involuntary movements and other tests can be used to diagnose a variety of forms of dyskinesia including: choreoathetosis, chorea, athetoid cerebral palsy, dystonia, choreiform movements, athetotiform movements and tremor. The appearance of these disordered patterns of movement was poorly described. Choreoathetosis was said to occur with lesions of the striatum and basal ganglia. Athetotiform and choreiform dyskinesia were said to be due to 'instability of motor units' (p 110), a term that has an indeterminate physiological meaning.

3. Some of the items listed under 'tests for coordination and associated movements' and 'assessment of walking' are used to diagnose 'associated movements'. These movements were described by Touwen as accompanying voluntary or involuntary movements in young children, generally in contralateral and symmetrical parts of the body. The prevalence of associated movements was said to decrease with age and their disappearance was thought to be a sign of the functional maturation of the nervous system. Their persistence was taken as a sign of impaired neurological functioning, due to a retardation of nervous development. The validity of this link between associated movements and neurological immaturity and impairment is, however, open to question. Associated movements can be seen in otherwise skilled older children and adults. They need not interfere with normal function; indeed, too much emphasis on suppressing associated movements can lead to a disruption of skilled behaviour. It is, therefore, difficult to infer from their presence anything about the neurological status of a child. Their value as diagnostic signs of neural abnormality is further reduced by Touwen's statement that associated movements may be part of a wide range of other syndromes, the examples of hemisyndrome, dyskinesia and motor retardation being given. If this is the case then how useful are they in making a differential diagnosis of the cause of a behaviour or learning disability?

4. 'Developmental retardation' is diagnosed when mental retardation is found together with a failure to develop certain behavioural skills such as building a tower of bricks, drawing a circle inside a square, or speaking sentences. However, a criterion on which this assessment system was based was the exclusion of perceptual, cognitive, intellectual and volitional factors from the test items, and hence the diagnosis of 'developmental retardation' cannot be made within the confines of Touwen's assessment.

5. Tests for coordination and associated movements are used to make a diagnosis of 'difficulty in coordination, clumsiness or awkwardness'. It will be recalled that the basic aim of the present system of assessment was to reveal a possible neurological dysfunction that could be an 'organic basis' for aberrant behaviour. It seems incongruous that this diagnostic category was included since the examination of voluntary movement had no priority in the assessment. The items chosen have limited diagnostic potential and accomplish no more than the other behavioural tests reviewed earlier, i.e. they simply confirm the existence of a motor deficit. As Touwen pointed out, brain structures that may be involved with motor coordination include the vestibular system, reticular formation, cerebellum and the parietal lobes. The present test battery does not permit a differential diagnosis in terms of the area of the brain responsible for a given disability.

6. 'Sensory disturbances' are listed as a diagnostic category. However, except for vision and hearing Touwen found it difficult to devise tests of sensory functioning. Even the very detailed analysis of the visual system may not 'bear fruit' because, as he pointed out, there is no direct relationship between the possible visual system disorders that could be detected and behavioural and learning difficulties.

7. Touwen acknowledged a considerable overlap between the above six diagnostic categories, and a considerable difficulty in interpreting any given set of individual signs. He suggested the drawing up of a neurological profile when minor signs cannot be arranged into any pattern which allows for a definite diagnosis. He grouped all the tests in the proforma into the following 10 subsystems: (1) sensorimotor apparatus, (2) posture, (3) balance of trunk, (4) coordination of the extremities, (5) fine manipulative ability, (6) dyskinesia, (7) gross motor functions, (8) quality of motility, (9) associated movements and (10) visual system. These subsystems are not independent, and the grouping of tests is determined partly by practical considerations and partly by neurological considerations, and is partly arbitrary. Plotting the profile of the number of 'optimality scores' in the 10 subsystems was said to serve two purposes: (a) it enables the examiner to arrange his findings into an easily 'digestible' form, and (b) groups of children can be distinguished, and an attempt can be made to establish relationships between test findings and other objective evaluations of the child's behavioural condition.

In a similar way to Stott, Moyes and Henderson (1972) and Ayres (1972a), Touwen drew attention to the fact that abnormal behaviours must ultimately have a neural basis. All three systems of assessment have as a basic aim the measurement, illustration or diagnosis of neural impairment, and the authors propose motor tests, 'sensory-integrative' tests and neurological tests (respectively) for this purpose. However, the assessments fail to diagnose neural bases for behavioural disorders, or to pinpoint malfunctioning parts of the central nervous system. This is perhaps not surprising when the current view of brain functioning is considered. The idea that categories of behaviour or psychological processes can be anatomically localised within the brain is not supported by evidence suggesting that the nervous system functions as an integrated and unified whole. Perceptual-motor behaviour in particular involves most of the central nervous system (see Chapter 2) and it is unlikely that an arbitrary set of test items will reveal a malfunctioning part of that system.

The practical problem of pinpointing brain dysfunction with neurological tests or by measuring behaviour was highlighted by Touwen. The absence of a neurological sign is no proof of the perfect integrity of the brain, and the presence of isolated signs is not necessarily significant. On the other hand, the presence of 'significant' neurological signs does not automatically imply a causal relationship with the manifested behavioural disorder (Fig 5.1). It is possible to have apparently normal behaviour in the presence of clear neurological abnormalities. Conversely, it is possible to have very abnormal behaviour and a complete absence of any neurological abnormality. Differences in behaviour between children who sustain apparently similar brain injuries can be due to differences that existed prior to damage, differences in neural adjustments after injury and differences in specific environmental conditions. In short, the relationship between neurological dysfunction and behavioural disorders is variable and strongly influenced by many poorly understood factors. A child's behaviour can fall short of or transcend the 'functional status' of the central nervous system especially as revealed by a neurological examination. A traditional diagnosis linking behavioural disorder with neural impairment is not always possible and is particularly difficult in cases of children with behavioural and learning difficulties — exactly those children for which Touwen's assessment was designed.

Besides this difficulty in arriving at a diagnosis, two other critical observations can be made. The first is the absence of norms for the tests, and the suggestion that every examiner must try to

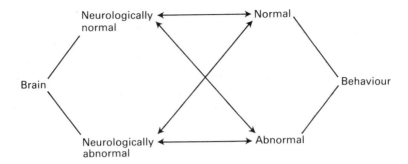

Figure 5.1   *There is no simple relationship between the presence or absence of neurological abnormalities and the presence or absence of abnormal behaviour. The double-headed arrows indicate that all combinations can be found among children.*

find his own norms. This absence of norms results in two related problems. It is difficult to establish consistent norms for tests when the assessment depends primarily on observation rather than measurement. Neurologists are generally examining actual or suspected cases of abnormality and they often have neither the opportunity nor the time to develop well-defined, albeit implicit, observational norms. While accurate and valid clinical judgements are not especially difficult to make when abnormalities are severe, in the borderline cases for which this examination was designed the absence of objective measures and established norms must be considered a disadvantage.

Secondly, there are no formal tests of perception other than visual and auditory acuity, and only a limited range of tests of voluntary motor behaviour. Touwen justified these omissions by questioning the usefulness of tests that can be failed for a wide variety of reasons, and added that it is difficult to pinpoint a cause of failure on a perceptual-motor type of test. Yet many of his tests have wide-ranging possible behavioural and neurological causes for failure. On the other hand, perceptual abilities and the ability to perform skilled motor tasks are relevant to everyday behaviour and their evaluation should be considered in any system of assessment aimed at illuminating underlying causes for behaviour and learning difficulties.

OVERVIEW

In this chapter eight test batteries concerned with the assessment of perceptual-motor behaviour were reviewed. Table 5.12 summarises the aim, motor content, problems and uses of these tests.

While some of the tests satisfactorily fulfil the author's stated aim and purpose, two issues emerge from this review which foreshadow the chapters to follow. Firstly, in none of the tests was the choice of test items, the measurement of performance or the grouping of items into categories and scales governed by a theory of behaviour or at least a task taxonomy. At best the items were chosen to cover as 'broad a range of behaviour as possible', and groupings or categories were decided on the basis of face validity or practical considerations. The lack of an experimentally based rationale for the choice, measurement and grouping of test items greatly restricts the usefulness of the tests in defining the pattern of disabilities that are associated with or underlie a motor disability — a point to be taken up in Chapters 7 and 8.

Secondly, in none of the tests is the formal measurement of perceptual abilities undertaken. When perceptual items are included they are either limited to a basic assessment of visual and auditory acuity, or else they are confounded by memory or the motor ability of the child, thus preventing the measurement of perceptual abilities in handicapped children. Indeed, there is an apparent uncertainty as to what constitutes a test of perception and how perceptual tests differ from perceptual-motor tests. In the following chapter a perceptual test of kinaesthetic sensitivity will be reviewed which will demonstrate how perceptual and motor factors can be disentangled.

Table 5.12 *Overall summary of aims, content, uses and problems of test batteries reviewed in this chapter.*

	Gesell and Ilg (1946)	Griffiths (1970)	McCarthy (1972)	Stott, Moyes and Henderson (1972)	Henderson revision (1984)	Gubbay (1975)	Bruininks (1978)	Ayres (1972a)	Touwen (1979)
Overall aim of the test battery	Description of development in broad, qualitative terms; developmental sequence	Measurement of development in broad terms	Measurement of general intellectual level as well as strengths and weaknesses	Measurement of motor impairment as index of neural dysfunction	Measurement of motor impairment	Rapid identification of mild motor impairment	Measurement of motor proficiency	Diagnosis of causes of learning and behaviour disorders	Diagnosis of causes of learning and behaviour disorders
Age range (years)	5–10	0–8	$2\frac{1}{2}$–6 ($8\frac{1}{2}$)	5–13+	5–11+	8–12	$4\frac{1}{2}$–$14\frac{1}{2}$	4–8	3–12
Content or list of test items	Table 5.1 Everyday activities	Table 5.2 Everyday activities and set tasks	Tables 5.3 and 5.4 Set tasks	Table 5.5 Set tasks	Table 5.6 Set tasks	Table 5.7 Set tasks	Table 5.8 Set tasks	Tables 5.9 and 5.10 Set tasks	Table 5.11 Set tasks
Measurements	Descriptive techniques	Observation; pass/fail on fixed criteria	Graded point scores on fixed criteria	Pass/fail on fixed criteria	Pass/fail on fixed criteria; observation guidelines	Pass/fail; point scores; timed	Pass/fail; timed; no. of errors; no. of units completed	Pass/fail; timed; no. of errors; no. of units; combined speed/accuracy	Graded point scores on observations
Collation or summary of test results	Behaviour profiles Maturity traits Growth gradients	Profiles. Mental age on each scale and on total	Point scores → composite scores. Profile. Mental age	Number of items failed at or below age level	Number of items failed at or below age level	Number of items performed at below the 10th percentile level for age	Raw scores → point scores. Point scores → standard scores. Standard scores → composite scores. Age equivalents. Profile	Raw scores → standard scores. Profile	Observation → point scores. Profile

	Provide reassurance. Enable guidance	Differential diagnosis of mental status	Measurement of general intellectual level and pattern of abilities	Measurement of motor impairment	Measurement of motor impairment, the pattern of impairment, the capacity for improvement, guidelines for therapists	Identification of clumsiness	Measurement of motor development and motor impairment	Measurement of sensory-integrative disorders	Defining neurological basis for learning and behaviour disorders
Claimed uses for the test	*(see header above)*								
General problems with the test	Methodology not described. Norms not presented. No measurable test items	Scales not independent. Items vary with age. ? mental age	Scales not independent. ? abilities	Items vary with age. ? item selection ? test items have equal weighting regardless of age level		Does not identify clumsy children	? item selection ? composite scores. Subtests not independent	? item selection, ? sensory integration. ? learning disabilities. ? diagnosis/ therapy relationship	No norms. ? differential diagnosis
Potential usefulness for measuring motor development	None	None	Same tasks for different ages but limited age range, and task types. ? abilities	None. Not a test of motor excellence	Not a test of motor excellence	None	Limited broad and amorphous behavioural measure	Limited. ? task description	None
Potential usefulness for defining pattern of disabilities associated with motor disability	None	Limited. ? mental age	Limited. Cannot give all scales to handicapped children	None	Check lists and guidelines for understanding the cause of motor impairment	None	None	None	Limited. ? differential diagnosis
Usefulness of the test, not necessarily conforming to the stated aim of the test	Introduction to child development for parents and students	Observation in initial assessment of a child with multiple handicaps	Uncertain	Identifying motor impairment from mild to severe	Identification and understanding of motor impairment	Uncertain	Measuring normal motor proficiency, and mild to moderate handicap. Amorphous behavioural measure	Uncertain	Clinical. Neurological signs in moderate to severe handicap

→ = Conversion or rescaling of scores.

? = Problem with, or uncertain nature of, a particular factor.

6 CONSTRUCTION OF A KINAESTHETIC SENSITIVITY TEST

WHY THE KINAESTHETIC SENSITIVITY TEST IS NEEDED

Kinaesthesis, the sense of movement and position, is essential to the learning and performance of all skilled motor acts (Chapter 2). Efficiency of motor performance depends on both the control of the muscles and the use of information generated by the kinaesthetic receptors. A well-performed motor act depends on the integrity of both motor and sensory processes. In the assessment and management of motor disorders, the differentiation of possible sensory and motor defects is of practical importance. One would not train an extremely myopic child to play long-distance ball games without first correcting the visual defect: indeed, if the visual defect is corrected with suitable spectacles, any difficulty with ball games may disappear. The same logic applies to the child suffering from kinaesthetic insensitivity. If as a result of assessment a child is found to be deficient in kinaesthetic perception, correction of the sensory deficit would lead to improved motor performance (Chapter 8).

The integrity of, or impairment in the visual, auditory and tactile systems can be established using routine clinical tests, but a clinically useful kinaesthetic test has not been available. Considering the fundamental role this modality plays in motor behaviour, a well-established test of kinaesthesis, providing developmental norms, could be expected to be in use yet such a test has not been available.

The need for a kinaesthetic test was well recognised by the 1950s. Scott (1955) cites a number of kinaesthesis, providing developmental norms, could be expected to be in use, yet such a test 'Measurement of kinaesthesis' she wrote:

> An attempt at definition and identity which is essential as a starting point in measurement is impossible because the facts are lacking. It represents a challenging type of investigation, but in analogy in a situation of trying to lift one's self by the boots without even the boot straps to grasp. (p 324)

Indeed, she did not measure kinaesthesis in isolation but used 26 motor items in the test, and relied on correlational statistics to arrive, indirectly, at a measure of kinaesthetic processing. This approach is unsatisfactory. It could be compared with a test of visual acuity where the patient is tested on reading performance. Undoubtedly, visual acuity is necessary in reading, but it is not the only factor which contributes to the ability to read, nor can the clinician derive a quantitative measure of visual acuity from a test of reading skill.

Some selected aspects of the kinaesthetic system, such as position discrimination in the elbow joint (Cleghorn and Darcus, 1952), kinaesthetic scales of apparent force perception (Stevens and Mack, 1959), perceptual scales of arm movements (Hoff, 1971), and estimation of weight (McCloskey, 1974) have been investigated. The experimental techniques were, in the main, unsuitable for testing children, and consequently were not used to establish developmental norms, or as diagnostic tools. Rather than attempting to adapt some of the experimental techniques to fit the clinical demands, clinicians designed kinaesthetic tests in which motor and other factors contaminated the kinaesthetic measures.

In this chapter the effectiveness of combining research and applied interests is demonstrated by describing the construction and application of the Kinaesthetic Sensitivity Test. The successful separation of perceptual function from motor involvement makes it possible, for the first time, to define the course of kinaesthetic development and to present the test as a useful diagnostic tool in determining kinaesthetic dysfunction. The chapter includes a detailed account of the construction of the Kinaesthetic Sensitivity Test in order to illustrate the steps involved in the construction of a perceptual test and to offer an opportunity for evaluation of the test and the theoretical and practical implications resulting from its use.

The purpose in constructing the present test is threefold: (a) to establish developmental norms for kinaesthesis, (b) to distinguish sensory from motor disorders, and thus (c) to facilitate diagnosis of kinaesthetic dysfunction.

PHYSIOLOGICAL BACKGROUND

There are four classes of stretch receptors contributing to the sense of kinaesthesis; namely, joint receptors, tendon organs, muscle spindles and skin receptors (Matthews, 1972; McCloskey, 1978).

Movement of a limb or the body cannot occur without kinaesthetic receptor activity. If a joint is passively flexed, the receptors on the extensor side are stretched and their firing rate increases, while the receptors on the flexor side are unloaded. This change in receptor activity is the basis for the detection of the angle of the joint, and the speed of the movement. If a joint is actively flexed, the receptors on the extensor side are stimulated in essentially the same way as in the passive situation. However, the muscle spindles (through gamma efferent activity), tendon organs and joint receptors on the flexor side are now loaded owing to the active muscular contraction. Hence in the active situation, the receptors around a joint can detect the angle of the joint, the speed of movement, the force of muscular contraction and the degree of resistance to movement (e.g. the weight being lifted).

The input from the kinaesthetic receptors has two broad functions. It enters into a reflexive modulation of motoneurone activity via short (spinal) and long (brainstem, cerebellar and cortical) reflex arcs. It also provides a source of information about movement. The activity generated by the four classes of kinaesthetic receptors leads to the global perception of movement and position.

PSYCHOLOGICAL BACKGROUND

Kinaesthesis in motor control and learning

The control of skilled motor behaviour has been described in terms of closed-loop theories (Chapter 2; Pew, 1974a). These theories emphasise the interaction between perceptual, motor and cognitive factors in motor control. An integral part of all closed-loop models is the sensory feedback loop. Kinaesthesis, a component of the feedback loop, is important in all stages of the performance and learning of a skilled act. It supplies positional information which is used in the initiation of a movement. Following initiation and while the movement is in progress, an evaluation of the movement can begin on the basis of kinaesthetic information, and errors in the movement can be detected. The detection of errors can lead to reprogramming of the movement and subsequent error correction. Kinaesthetic memory traces are stored and are utilised in subsequent movements, providing the basis for motor learning.

Kinaesthetic input accompanies all movements and is important in all skills. The importance of other sensory channels depends on the task to be performed. For example, in ball games, vision, and in playing musical instruments, audition, provide valuable information, while in ballet and gymnastics kinaesthesis must be relied on.

Motor control in the absence of kinaesthesis

Deafferentation research indicates that input from kinaesthetic receptors is critically important for fine motor control. When the limb of a monkey is deafferented by dorsal rhizotomy (thus removing sensory input originating from receptors in the limb) fine control is lost (Taub, 1977). The monkey will tend to neglect the deafferented limb, although it can be taught to use it. Normal fine control cannot be reacquired, however, not even when the animal visually monitors his movements.

Reliance on kinaesthesis in motor learning

It was demonstrated in studies carried out by the present authors that when subjects practise a skill they develop an increased dependence on kinaesthetic information for subsequent performance of that skill. Subjects were required to practise writing letters of the alphabet with only kinaesthetic information to guide the movement. When kinaesthetic information was subsequently eliminated with the ischaemic nerve block (Bairstow and Laszlo, 1976; Laszlo and Bairstow, 1971b) their performance was depressed further than that of the group which had no practice prior to deafferentation (Laszlo and Bairstow, 1971a). The more practice a subject was given with kinaesthetic feedback, the greater was the depression in performance under conditions of deafferentation (Laszlo, Bairstow and Baker, 1979). It was argued that practising a motor skill with kinaesthetic feedback leads to the development of kinaesthetic memory traces and an associated dependence on kinaesthetic feedback for performance of the skill.

Kinaesthesis and motor development

It was pointed out in Chapter 3 that studies of motor development have been largely restricted to the description of the emergence of motor skills. Relatively little attention has been paid to investigating underlying processes. It is important to establish why a child becomes faster and more accurate in his motor behaviour as he grows older. A variety of factors which might underlie and enable the expression of progressively higher levels of motor skill were discussed previously. The development of perceptual abilities may be one of the significant factors contributing to increased motor efficiency. The test of kinaesthetic perception here described may clarify the relationship between kinaesthetic and motor development.

Tests of kinaesthesis

The tests of kinaesthetic ability that have been used in the past have not measured kinaesthesis directly. The clinical test of kinaesthesis (Slinger and Horsley, 1906) requires the blindfolded subject to point his hands towards each other as accurately as possible. The disparity in position of the two hands is observed (not measured) and is taken as an estimate of the error in the subject's kinaesthetic perception. In the test of kinaesthesis proposed by Ayres (1972a), the subject's hand is placed on a point on the table surface, then moved back to a starting position. The subject then has to locate the point from memory by moving his hand, and the error in localisation is recorded. Both of these tests involve a motor response and errors in performance could be due to motor dysfunction as much as to insensitivity to the kinaesthetic input. This confounding of kinaesthetic ability and motor control is especially problematic in children with physical handicap. Memory is an additional confounding variable in the Ayres test (Chapter 5).

In the present test the use of passive movement eliminated reliance on motor control. Furthermore, memory for kinaesthesis is introduced as a test variable in one task and eliminated in the other. The test incorporates two tasks. In everyday life many movements must be performed with precision, and they demand good kinaesthetic acuity. The first task was designed to measure this acuity. Kinaesthetic perception and the storage of kinaesthetic memory traces underlie learning of skilled movements; the second task measures these factors.

APPLICATIONS OF THE TEST

The test was designed to be applicable in research, as a diagnostic tool, and to assist with the training of kinaesthetic perceptual ability.

Research psychologists working in the field of motor control and skilled motor behaviour can, with the aid of the test, investigate the relationship between perceptual and motor factors in the performance and acquisition of various skills. The test may assist in establishing the effect of individual differences in kinaesthetic sensitivity on motor ability.

Diagnostically, the test will enable the clinical and educational psychologist and the physiotherapist and occupational therapist to separate average from below average kinaesthetic function. A child or adult who has difficulty in controlling his movements, or in learning motor skills (e.g. clumsy children) may have a number of possible causes for the disability. It is routine to check a child's vision and audition, and the test here described makes it possible to examine kinaesthetic function routinely as well. This is necessary if management of the child is to be focused on the locus of the disorder rather than relying on general, non-specific training (Chapters 7 and 8).

DESCRIPTION OF THE TEST ITEMS

Test of kinaesthetic acuity

This test required the subject to discriminate the heights of two inclined runways shown in Fig. 6.1(a). The overall length of the apparatus was 31 cm. The two runways were hinged to a baseboard at the end nearest to the subject. The angle of the runways could be independently set over the range 0° to 22° from the horizontal. The subject's two hands were placed around two pegs resting on the starting platforms. The masking box covered the subject's arms and the apparatus to exclude vision (Fig. 6.1b). The subject's two hands were moved concurrently up the two runways by the experimenter. The runways varied in their verticle angle, and the subject

Figure 6.1 *Apparatus for the Kinaesthetic Acuity Test.   (a) Runway.*

was required to discriminate between the height of the runways, by indicating which hand was moved higher.

The psychophysical method of constant stimuli was employed (D'Amato, 1970). The standard setting of 12° angle was arbitrarily chosen, and one of the runways was always set at this angle. The other runway was set at one of four settings: 7°, 9°, 15° or 17°. During the development of the test, the subject's difference limen was calculated. Difference limen is a psychophysical term; it is a measure of the fine limits to discrimination and is derived by statistical means. In practical terms, and in the present context, the difference limen represents the minimum difference between the angle of the runways the subjects could correctly and reliably detect as a difference in angle. It is the critical difference below which the runway with the higher angle could not be reliably selected.

Test of kinaesthetic perception and memory of movement patterns

This test required the subject to restore a displayed pattern to the orientation the pattern had when previously traced. The apparatus is shown in Fig. 6.2. The overall dimensions of the apparatus were 28 cm × 28 cm × 2 cm. A central perspex disc was mounted on a wooden base. The disc could be rotated like a gramophone turntable, and its position could be measured from

(b) Marking box.

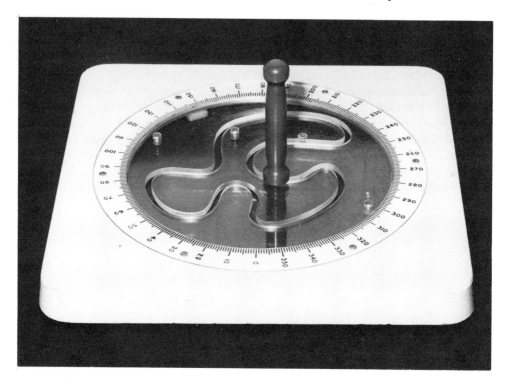

Figure 6.2   *Apparatus for the Kinaesthetic Perception and Memory Test.*

a scale in degrees displayed on the wooden base. A set of 12 arbitrary, curved, closed patterns had been cut into perspex. These stencil patterns could be placed individually on the rotatable disc. With the masking box to exclude vision, a stencil was placed on the rotatable disc, and the stylus which was held by the subject was guided around the stencil for two circuits. The subject's hand was removed from the apparatus, the pattern was rotated clockwise or anticlockwise and the masking box was removed. The subject was asked to reorientate the pattern back into the position it was in when he was tracing it.

The position of a landmark on the stencil was set for the original position of the pattern. The position of the landmark after the subject reorientated the pattern was then recorded. The absolute error in degrees between the original position and the subject's reorientated position was the error score. The rationale for the test was as follows: the more accurately the subject perceived the kinaesthetic information generated by the movement around the pattern and the clearer his memory of the perceived information, the lower would be his reorientation error.

DEVELOPMENT OF THE TEST

The test was developed in two stages. In the first stage (Laszlo and Bairstow, 1980) the subjects were 180 volunteers from the University of Western Australia and from a primary school in the

Perth (Western Australia) metropolitan area. There were eight groups of children over the age range five to 12 years, and a group of adults with a mean age of 22 years, with 20 subjects (10 males and 10 females) in each group. All subjects with a medical history of developmental abnormality and/or motor disorder were excluded from the study. In both tasks, subjects moved actively; i.e. they actively pushed wheeled toys up the sloping runways and actively moved the stylus around the stencil patterns. In Table 6.1 the group results for the kinaesthetic acuity task are presented. A significant developmental trend was demonstrated. It was shown that with increasing age the ability to discriminate kinaesthetically between arm position and movement improved. Kinaesthetic acuity varied for subjects within age groups, e.g. some five year olds performed at adult level.

Table 6.1 *Kinaesthetic acuity: accuracy of discrimination of movement and position of the upper limbs. The arms were moved actively and the difference limen was calculated. Modified from Laszlo and Bairstow (1980).*

Age (years)	5	6	7	8	9	10	11	12	M̄ 22 (adult)
Mean	19.0	13.4	7.8	4.7	3.6	6.1	5.2	3.5	3.0
Standard deviation	17.6	10.9	9.2	3.5	2.3	5.0	3.4	3.3	3.0
Range: Best	1.8	2.7	2.1	1.3	1.1	1.1	1.6	.9	1.0
Worst	52.0	35.5	42.2	16.5	8.6	20.6	15.0	12.6	13.5

In Table 6.2 the group results for the kinaesthetic perception and memory task are presented. A significant developmental trend and individual differences within age groups were demonstrated in this task as well; e.g. the best five year old performed at better than average adult level. A low positive correlation was found between performances of the two tasks.

Table 6.2 *Kinaesthetic perception and memory: accuracy of perception and memory of the orientation of complex movement patterns. The arm was moved actively and the error in memory for orientation was measured in degrees. Modified from Laszlo and Bairstow (1980).*

Age (years)	5	6	7	8	9	10	11	12	M̄ 22 (adult)
Mean	78.1	75.7	75.5	64.1	60.9	58.9	62.9	58.3	36.0
Standard deviation	19.2	20.1	13.9	17.6	15.6	19.9	14.4	19.7	19.0
Range: Best	38.2	33.9	44.5	39.6	37.7	20.4	36.9	24.6	11.1
Worst	112.7	116.3	93.2	93.4	92.0	99.1	87.3	86.1	80.8

The major change of using passive movements instead of active movements in both tasks was introduced in the second stage (Bairstow and Laszlo, 1981). In the acuity task the subject's arms were pulled up the runways by the experimenter and in the pattern perception and memory task the experimenter guided the subject's hand round the stencil patterns. While in the first study the subject's movements were fully constrained by the apparatus, some motor control was still necessary in performing the tasks. Thus the subject's perceptual ability may have been underestimated if he had to attend to the control of his limb movements. In passive movement the necessity for motor control is eliminated and does not confound the perceptual measure. The separation of perceptual from motor factors is especially valuable when testing subjects with severe motor difficulty.

A further change was introduced in the kinaesthetic acuity task for the five and six year old children. These children were tested on larger runway separations than the older age groups, i.e. 7° and 4° angle differences were used rather than the 5° and 3° angles given to the older groups (settings were: 12° constant stimulus, 5°, 8°, 16° and 19° for the variable setting). In this way the task was made easier for the two youngest groups to avoid guessing (Davis, 1974) in children, many of whom have low kinaesthetic acuity and a short attention span. Furthermore, the number of trials in the acuity task was reduced from 60 to 32.

Table 6.3 presents the group results for the kinaesthetic acuity task. Developmental trends similar to those of the previous study were demonstrated. There was no significant difference between the active and passive movement conditions.

Table 6.3 *Kinaesthetic acuity: accuracy of discrimination of movement and position of the upper limbs. The arms were moved passively and the difference limen was calculated. Modified from Bairstow and Laszlo (1981).*

Age (years)	5	6	7	8	9	10	11	12
Mean	19.2	17.6	11.2	6.8	8.0	7.3	5.9	3.0
Standard deviation	17.3	17.1	15.4	10.1	11.2	9.4	7.1	6.2
Range: Best	2.3	1.9	1.7	1.1	.9	1.0	.9	.7
Worst	50.0	50.0	50.0	50.0	50.0	50.0	33.7	6.7

A further change to the pattern perception and memory task was that the five and six year old groups were tested on four patterns only. The four patterns were chosen from the previous study because they were the easiest for the two youngest groups. Here again, task difficulty and length of testing was adapted to the sample's predicted kinaesthetic processing ability and attention span. From age seven years on, the 12 patterns were retained.

Table 6.4 presents the group results for the kinaesthetic perception and memory task. The five and six year olds did not differ from each other, or from subjects in the previous (active) study. There was a significant improvement with age from seven to 12 years and performance was significantly better for the passive compared to the active condition. The lower error scores in the passive condition in this task compared to active conditions show that even in normal subjects the need to control the movements places an attentional demand on the subject which seems to interfere with the perception and storage of the kinaesthetic input. This interference effect would be more pronounced in the physically handicapped child.

Table 6.4 *Kinaesthetic perception and memory: accuracy of perception and memory of the orientation of complex movement patterns. The arm was moved passively and the error in memory for orientation was measured in degrees. Modified from Bairstow and Laszlo (1981).*

Age (years)	5	6	7	8	9	10	11	12
Mean	54.3	64.3	63.8	60.0	56.5	58.3	50.5	46.3
Standard deviation	22.5	27.1	14.9	15.7	18.0	13.6	15.1	12.2
Range: Best	8.5	24.0	36.1	28.7	22.1	40.8	24.8	25.2
Worst	91.8	117.5	88.4	93.2	94.6	89.7	77.9	79.9

FINAL MODIFICATIONS AND NORMATIVE DATA

Modification to scoring of the kinaesthetic acuity task

In the first two stages of test construction the method of constant stimuli was employed, and the difference limen was calculated for each subject. It was found, however, that the relationship between the number of correct responses and the difference limen was not linear (see Fig. 6.3). It seemed unreasonable to give more weight to changes in the success rate at levels of performance closer to random performance (random responding is defined as 16 out of 32 correct responses) compared to levels close to perfect performance. Accordingly it was decided to adopt the method of constant stimuli, but to record the number of correct responses in preference to calculating the subject's difference limen.

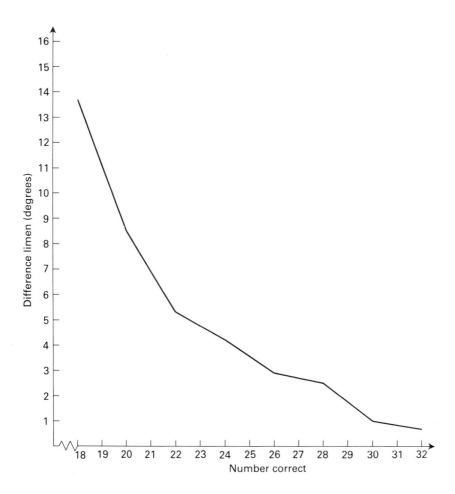

Figure 6.3 *Non-linear relationship between the number of correct responses and the difference limen measure.*

Modification to kinaesthetic perception and memory task

The major modification to the kinaesthetic perception and memory task relates to the choice of patterns. On examination of individual patterns, some were shown to be unsuitable as test items. One of these, the most complex of the range, proved to be too difficult even for adults. Subjects reorientated this pattern randomly. Two bilaterally symmetrical patterns yield bimodal error distributions. Subjects either set the patterns correctly or inverted them. In kinaesthetic terms, a small error in perception could lead to a maximum error in discrimination. These three patterns were consequently eliminated from the test. Sets of patterns were chosen for each age group which gave the highest reliability coefficient. The norms presented below relate to the results gained from these selected sets of patterns. The nine patterns retained in the test are shown in Fig. 6.4.

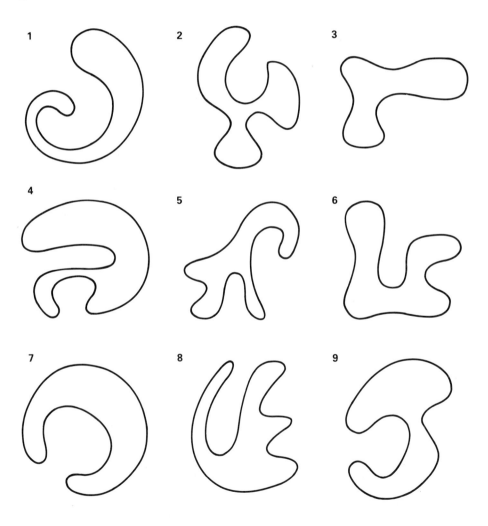

Figure 6.4 *Patterns used in the perception and memory task.*

The normative sample

The normative sample included children from primary schools of the Perth metropolitan area and rural areas of Western Australia, and multiracial urban schools of London; the adult sample included university students from the University of Western Australia and the University of Waterloo, Canada (Bairstow and Laszlo, 1981).

No sex differences have been demonstrated nor were there significant differences between right- and left-handed subjects. It has been shown that performance on the test did not vary as a function of the source of subjects. Hence the data has been pooled across sex, handedness and source.

The normative data

The normative data for the kinaesthetic acuity task, and the kinaesthetic perception and memory task are presented in Tables 6.5 and 6.6 respectively.

Table 6.5 *Kinaesthetic acuity: the normative data.*

Age (years)		5	6	7	8	9	10	11	12	$\bar{M}$ 22 (adult)
Mean number correct out of 32		20	21	21	22	23	23	24	25	27
Standard deviation		4.0	4.8	3.7	3.4	3.8	4.1	3.8	3.4	3.4
Percentiles	10	–	–	–	16	17	18	18	20	22
	15	–	–	16	18	18	18	18	21	22
	25	16	16	17	19	19	20	20	22	24
	50	18	20	20	21	22	22	23	25	26
	75	22	24	23	24	24	26	26	27	28
	85	23	26	24	25	26	28	27	27	29
	90	24	27	25	25	28	29	28	28	30

Table 6.6 *Kinaesthetic perception and memory: the normative data.*

Age (years)		5	6	7	8	9	10	11	12	$\bar{M}$ 22 (adult)
Mean error (degrees)		59.7	65.8	60.9	57.1	52.7	50.2	45.6	42.1	24.6
Standard deviation		27.2	26.9	25.9	26.3	20.5	23.1	19.3	20.0	12.4
Percentiles	10	–	–	–	–	88	81	75	68	40
	15	–	–	–	90	78	71	69	60	37
	25	79	85	74	69	66	63	63	55	32
	50	60	67	58	55	53	49	40	40	21
	75	42	47	45	38	37	37	28	26	14
	85	34	42	36	33	33	33	24	21	12
	90	30	36	29	30	31	27	21	16	11

RELIABILITY OF THE TEST

Hoyt's reliability coefficients (r) (Helmstadter, 1964) were calculated for each task and each age group. For the kinaesthetic acuity task r values were: 5 years, r=0.59; 6 years, r=0.69; 7 years, r=0.52; 8 years, r=0.38; 9 years, r=0.54; 10 years, r=0.65; 11 years, r=0.65; 12 years, r=0.57; adults, r=0.83; for kinaesthetic perception and memory: r=0.38, 0.38, 0.16, 0.61, 0.46, 0.80, 0.59, 0.95, 0.97 respectively. While some of these reliability coefficients are low, Helmstadter (1964) is reassuring when he states (p 85):

> In some instances a reliability which is far from perfect may be the best yet, or much better than impressionistic judgement, or simply ignoring the trait because no measuring device is available.

This statement is fully relevant to the measurement of kinaesthesis.

Consideration was given to increasing the test length in order to bring reliability within the normally acceptable range. This was however rejected because a fine differentiation between performance scores is not required. The test has been demonstrated to separate subjects with poor kinaesthetic ability from those with adequate to good kinaesthetic ability. Certainly the evaluation of kinaesthetic ability in five-, six- and seven-year-old children must be restricted to gross differences in performance scores.

VALIDITY OF THE TEST

Content validity

The test of kinaesthetic acuity tests one aspect of kinaesthesis, namely the ability to discriminate between the relative positions and movements of the upper limbs. The movements are linear, parallel to the sagittal plane, they are of the same length and the arms are moved at the same velocity and vary only in terms of the angle from the horizontal and the height of the final position. They involve abduction/adduction of the wrist, flexion/extension of the elbow and flexion/extension at the shoulder. Hence, the test is directly relevant to only a small class of all possible movements of the upper limb. It is concerned with spatial discrimination and is not relevant to other dimensions of kinaesthesis such as perception of velocity or the force generated by muscular activity. The task was designed to excite kinaesthetic receptors. It activates muscle spindles, tendon organs, joint receptors, and stretch receptors in the skin overlying the joints. The task has been constructed to eliminate the systematic participation of all receptors, other than kinaesthetic receptors. Thus the kinaesthetic cues are isolated and the subject is forced to base his judgement on these cues alone in discriminating between the positions and movements of the two upper limbs.

The test of kinaesthetic perception and memory, the pattern reorientation task, is also restricted to the processing of specific aspects of kinaesthetic information. The movements which the subject's preferred hand and arm are guided through are strictly defined. They are two-dimensional, curved closed movement patterns performed in the horizontal plane. They involve flexion/extension of the elbow and shoulder, and are closely related to large drawing and writing movements. As in the acuity task, the movements excite all classes of receptors relevant to kinaesthesis and eliminate systematic activation of the receptors of other modalities. Thus the subject is forced to rely on kinaesthetic information alone in the performance of the pattern reorientation task. The task is concerned with perceiving directional changes in arm movement and memorising the perceived spatial configuration of the movement pattern.

There are difficulties in designing a direct measure of perception and memory of kinaesthetic information. The measure of pattern reorientation was chosen for the following reasons: (a) it allows for a fine measure of kinaesthetic perception and memory; (b) it is an objective measure; (c) it yields a wide range of scores; and (d) it is quick and easy to record during test administration. The reorientation response can be performed without the demand for fine motor control and it can be adapted to children with severe motor disability (i.e. the tester can rotate the pattern). The rationale underlying the reorientation task is that the more accurately the subject perceives the movement pattern, the more accurate his memory is of the pattern, and the more accurately will he place the pattern into its original orientation.

A possible objection to visual reorientation as a measure of kinaesthetic function is that it involves a cross-modal judgement. Kinaesthetic–kinaesthetic reorientation has been considered and, indeed, it has been used when testing blind subjects. In a pilot study sighted adults were tested under both intra- and intermodal conditions. The scores of kinaesthetic and visual reorientation did not differ significantly. However, practical considerations favour the intermodal response mode as kinaesthetic matching is extremely time-consuming. Furthermore, the subject with motor disability would be unable to find his way repeatedly round the patterns when attempting to establish kinaesthetically the correct orientation of the patterns.

The correlation coefficient between the two tasks was $r = 0.20$. This low positive correlation indicates that the two tasks measure different aspects of kinaesthetic function.

Construct validity

In both tasks of the test specific movements of the upper limbs are used to generate the kinaesthetic information. The question arises of whether the measure of kinaesthetic function, as tested, can be considered a general index of the subject's kinaesthetic sensitivity. It has been found that young adults who practise ballet dancing and gymnastics perform the test of kinaesthetic perception and memory significantly better than other adults who participate in various other forms of sport [$t(40)$, 3.35, $P < 0.01$] (Bairstow and Laszlo, 1981). Kinaesthesis is of singular importance in ballet and gymnastics. The performer must rely on kinaesthesis alone to monitor his movements and postures since the postures and movements of the limbs and the body as a whole cannot be visually monitored. It should be noted that the specific movements involved in the test are never used during dancing or gymnastics. The superior performance of the dancers and gymnasts compared to others on the pattern reorientation task strongly indicates that the test measures a general kinaesthetic ability.

Motor and kinaesthetic development tend to parallel each other, at least from five years of age. While a cause and effect relationship cannot be assumed, results found with the test indicate a strong relationship between kinaesthetic ability and fine motor control. At the age of six years a significant positive correlation was found between drawing ability and kinaesthetic acuity

($r_s = 0.77$), and between writing ability and kinaesthetic perception and memory ($r_s = 0.68$) (Bairstow and Laszlo, 1981).

A group of 16 children who were described as clumsy and poorly coordinated were given the Kinaesthetic Sensitivity Test. These children, who were aged between seven and 15 years, had been referred to developmental paediatricians for a full developmental and/or neurological assessment because they had difficulty with fine manual skills (e.g. handwriting) or gross skills (e.g. they had failed to acquire sports skills that should have been easy for their age). On the basis of the paediatric assessment the motor difficulty was confirmed but a specific diagnosis could not be made. Seventy per cent of these children performed below the 25th percentile for their age on the kinaesthetic acuity task. Fifty per cent performed below the 25th percentile for their age on the kinaesthetic perception and memory task. Thirty-eight per cent performed below the 25th percentile on both tasks. It is suggested that kinaesthetic deficiency in clumsy children could be one of the causes of clumsiness.

All the above findings show a close relationship between kinaesthetic ability and motor control and indicate that kinaesthesis is an important source of information in skilled behaviour. The present test provides the means for measuring kinaesthetic ability and thereby assists in elucidating the interrelationship between motor and perceptual skills. It is not implied that kinaesthesis is the only factor in the control of motor behaviour, but that it does have a primary role in the performance of motor tasks.

INTERPRETATION OF TEST RESULTS AND THE RELATIONSHIP TO MOTOR PERFORMANCE

Interpretation of results on the two kinaesthetic sensitivity tasks

A child who scores at or above the mean of his age group on kinaesthetic acuity can be said to have a normal kinaesthetic apparatus and that the information provided by the kinaesthetic receptors is used in simple discrimination tasks. It is analogous to finding normal visual acuity. The acuity score, however, tells us nothing about the more complex processes of perceiving and memorising kinaesthetic information generated by complex movement patterns. To turn to vision as an example again, normal visual acuity does not necessarily lead to depth perception or recognition of visual shapes. The kinaesthetic perception and memory task gives an indication of higher kinaesthetic processes. A child who gains scores that conform to the mean or above mean performance for his age on the pattern reorientation can be said to be able to interpret the kinaesthetic information and to store it for future use in a meaningful and adequate manner.

Deviations from the norm can be determined from the percentile distributions provided in Tables 6.5 and 6.6 for all age groups in the kinaesthetic acuity task, and from eight years of age in the kinaesthetic perception and memory task. The low reliability coefficients found for the five-, six- and seven-year-old children on the pattern reorientation task lessens the precision with which the young child's kinaesthetic processing ability can be evaluated. Such low test reliability for the five- to seven-year-old children is not unusual and is possibly due to two factors: (a) kinaesthetic sensitivity is developing rapidly, hence considerable variance occurs in performance; and (b) the attention span of the five to seven year olds is short. However, it is safe to assume that a five year old who scores highly on the kinaesthetic perception and memory task can process this kinaesthetic information since high scores are unlikely to occur by chance.

The child who gains low scores, on the other hand, could be either kinaesthetically deficient or inattentive or both. It may be argued that attention will fluctuate more when the kinaesthetic signal generated by the movement is not clearly perceived by the child, compared to the subject where the signal is clearly discernible from the background of total sensory input. Thus the kinaesthetically less able child will be influenced more by attention fluctuation than his able peer. The same logic applies to adherence to instructions. If the child can perceive the kinaesthetic information relevant to the pattern, and if he can store this information in memory, he will follow instructions. If, however, the information is not perceived the child will formulate an idiosyncratic system to solve the problem presented by the task; e.g. he will always twist the patterns by 90°. Thus the child whose kinaesthetic processing ability is low may gain even lower scores than his ability would warrant.

It was shown that the correlation between the two tasks is low; i.e. children can score highly on one of the tasks, while performing poorly on the other. The child with high acuity scores, but low perception and memory scores is able to feel discrete limb position and movement, but he is unable to form an integrated picture of the sequentially generated kinaesthetic information and/or to store that information and to retrieve it when needed. On the other hand, there are children who gain high scores on kinaesthetic processing and memory, yet show low acuity. In the pattern reorientation task, some of the directional changes in the movements around each pattern were greater than 5° or even 8°. Thus, even with low acuity some pattern features could be discriminated. This means that the child who is aware of kinaesthetic input and who can process and store that input may reorientate the relatively large patterns correctly, working on the distinct features of the patterns, but that smaller changes in direction, such as occur in hand-writing, will not be perceived.

Kinaesthetic sensitivity and motor function

Kinaesthetic processing is an integral part of motor function and hence the level of kinaesthetic ability of the subject is of paramount importance when assessing general motor ability. In the clinical setting, the Kinaesthetic Sensitivity Test should be used in conjunction with a general developmental and/or neurological assessment in arriving at a diagnosis of possible underlying causes for motor disability. In the educational setting the Test can be used in isolation in an assessment of the kinaesthetic ability of children experiencing difficulties with the learning and control of motor skills.

If a child gains high kinaesthetic scores and has no difficulty in the skilled motor tasks demanded of him by the school, in sports, and in everyday activities, the child is obviously 'normal' as far as skilled perceptual-motor behaviour is concerned. In the case of the child who is performing adequately in motor tasks but poorly on the kinaesthetic test, the tester could suggest one of two possible courses of action. He could consider that while kinaesthetic development is retarded, the child should be allowed to develop at his own pace since he has obviously found some compensatory mechanisms to counterbalance the lack of kinaesthetic information processing; or it could be suggested that the child be trained in the kinaesthetic task or tasks in which he was found to be deficient. The latter course of action is possibly beneficial for the child. Compensation for the low level of kinaesthetic function usually involves heightened monitoring of other information channels such as vision and/or hearing. These modalities are normally used as supportive information channels additional to kinaesthesis. Solely relying on these less efficient information sources places a high attention demand on the child during the performance of a motor act and limits the accuracy, the rate of acquisition and the enjoyment in motor skills. Kinaesthetic training could accelerate motor development in these cases. In any case, by the time the child reaches the age of 12 years he needs to process finely detailed kinaesthetic information to achieve the accuracy in motor control expected of him (see Chapter 7 for further discussion of perceptual-motor development and the processes underlying age-related improvement).

The child who shows high kinaesthetic awareness but has difficulty in controlling his movements (provided other sensory modalities are functioning normally) might have difficulties in some aspect of motor programming (for further details see Chapter 7).

In physically handicapped children large individual differences were found in kinaesthetic sensitivity. Children suffering from cerebral palsy, spina bifida, progressive neuromuscular diseases and clumsiness were included in the sample. One 15-year-old boy suffering from a progressive neuromuscular disease of unknown aetiology showed the most advanced kinaesthetic sensitivity and indeed was known to use the minimal muscle power still available to him in an astoundingly efficient manner. Some of the cerebral palsy and spina bifida children showed normal kinaesthetic ability for their age. There were, however, a number of children who were markedly retarded in their kinaesthetic sensitivity. Of special interest for the present argument are the spina bifida children. While there was no neurological reason for their upper limbs to be affected, they were extremely clumsy in manual skills and their kinaesthetic test scores proved to be very low. Training these children in kinaesthetic awareness could alleviate the motor difficulty experienced by them in the use of their upper limbs.

The class of 'clumsy' children can again be mentioned. Some of these children are found in regular schools and are identified by teachers and educational psychologists as having difficulties with fine manual skills and/or gross skills. Others are identified by paediatricians who confirm the motor difficulty following a full developmental and/or neurological assessment, but fail to arrive at a more specific diagnosis.

Many of these clumsy children perform below average on the Kinaesthetic Sensitivity Test. It is very difficult to perform and learn the skill of printing and writing when the position and movements of the hand cannot be accurately felt. Failure to detect deficits in kinaesthetic sensitivity results in the child being labelled as clumsy. Such a label may cause withdrawal from motor activity. A decrease in the amount of activity leads to a decrease in the generation of kin-aesthetic information, and a consequent decrease in processing kinaesthetic input, further retarding the child's development of kinaesthetic awareness. The Kinaesthetic Sensitivity Test enables diagnosis of the specific difficulty, and training in kinaesthetic awareness eliminates the difficulty in motor control. With the aid of the test, kinaesthetic readiness (Chapter 8) necessary for the performance and learning of fine manual skills can be established.

7 CONSTRUCTION OF A PERCEPTUAL-MOTOR ABILITIES TEST

WHY A PERCEPTUAL-MOTOR ABILITIES TEST IS NEEDED

This chapter presents the rationale, method, results and some applications of a recently constructed diagnostic perceptual-motor abilities test. It is not meant as a test manual, but the chapter is included both to illustrate the problems which are encountered in attempting to construct a test based on a process-orientated theoretical framework, and to describe the encouraging results achieved. The test manual can only be prepared when the testing programme with the clinical sample has been completed.

Tests constructed to demonstrate developmental trends in motor behaviour can include a large variety of tasks in order to show age-related improvement in skilled performance. There are a range of skills in a child's motor repertoire from which the test items can be selected for inclusion into a task-orientated test battery. The items chosen may reflect the test constructor's personal preference for tasks which reflect everyday skills, or ones which are easy to administer, or are easily scored.

An example might illustrate the limitations of choosing an everyday skill as a test item. The tying of shoelaces is such an item, included in a number of test batteries (Chapter 5). This skill improves systematically with age. Most five year olds find this task very difficult and many cannot tie a bow at all. In the six to seven-year age groups bows are tied, albeit the bow is usually asymmetrical, or incomplete, and the task is performed slowly. In later years, the double bow is tied symmetrically, and quickly by most, but not all, children. There are two possible performance measures which one might record: the accuracy of the performance expressed as symmetry of the two sides of the bow, and the time score for completion of the task. The tester could decide on recording both scores. Using a large sample of children of different ages a developmental trend would be demonstrated for both accuracy and time scores. If a more sophisticated approach was preferred, macrame knots could be substituted for shoelace bows, again using accuracy and time scores. Improvement with age would be demonstrated with this task also. If normative data for the item is available, the performance of the child can be compared with that of his own age group. That is, one would be able to state whether the child could perform the prescribed task at below average, average, or above average level for his age. But the administration of this test item would not help in the understanding of problems nor

:o the knowledge of the child's perceptual-motor functioning beyond that which
ied from reports from parents or teachers.

the number of tasks included in the test would lead to a larger number of scores,
.... ..ould describe the child's achievement level compared to the level expected for his age.
When test items are chosen arbitrarily, and when the selection is governed by the test
constructor's idiosyncratic interest or by the task's obvious relationship to skills relevant to
everyday function, the test results can only provide a measure of the child's performance on
individual tasks. The results cannot explain performance on tasks not included in the test
battery, nor can they give an indication of the perceptual-motor abilities or potentials of the child
(see Chapter 4).

Normal developmental trends established for specific skills are often used by clinicians and
therapists to compare the performance of a child with motor disability with the performance
expected of normal children. Many clinicians and therapists also rely on their own judgement,
observing children as they perform more or less everyday tasks (Holt, 1977). That is, the task-
orientated approach has often been adopted. Most tests, as discussed in Chapter 5, rely to a
greater or lesser extent on a task-orientated approach, rather than a process-orientated approach.
While the former aims at measuring performance levels on individual tasks, the latter aims at
assessing perceptual-motor abilities and describing development in terms of basic processes.

Gelman (1978), discussing cognitive development, argues that test items measuring task
performance alone are less useful than tests which indicate underlying abilities or capacities. In
the former, the test merely gives a measure of what the child can or cannot do, and in the latter
the reason for any difficulty can be established. The same logic is valid in the motor domain.
Holt (1977) states that: 'There is no satisfactory test for clumsiness or for motor skills' (p 201).
This is not unexpected in view of the many factors affecting motor development. Tests of motor
proficiency are available, 'which help to identify a clumsy child but do not untangle the various
factors involved' (p 201).

In the next section, the process-orientated Perceptual-Motor Abilities Test will be described,
detailing the considerations which governed the choice of test items to be included in the test
battery.

THE RATIONALE ON WHICH THE PERCEPTUAL-MOTOR ABILITIES TEST IS BASED

Motor development is often described as a smooth, predictable progression from the unskilled to
the skilled level, with specific skills emerging in an orderly sequence (Chapter 3, and Bairstow,
1983). Individual differences are found in all tasks, at all age levels — children develop skills at
different ages, often in a different order, and to different degrees. Individual differences persist
into adulthood. Performance level on one task is a poor predictor of performance in other tasks.
Performance on gross motor skills does not correlate with performance in manual skills, and
even within these categories a child's level of performance will vary from task to task. A child
might be a strong swimmer, yet show little aptitude in ball games. The neatest writer in a class
might not be talented in sewing. Thus, in describing a child's general motor efficiency one is
faced with the near impossible task of comparing a good swimmer with a neat writer, a weak ball

player with a talented painter. A large number of skills is needed to adequately describe a child's motor profile, when a task-based analysis is employed, yet the reason for the particular motor profile may not be clear.

Rather than concentrating on individual tasks, one might consider the underlying perceptual-motor abilities responsible for skilled performance. Both Clark (1978) and Wade (1976) emphasise the need to focus attention on the underlying reasons for observed developmental changes rather than being satisfied with the descriptive level. The process-orientated approach would enable us to choose tasks in a rational way and to describe an individual's overall perceptual-motor standing in terms of abilities. Measurement of the relatively few abilities underlying the large number of tasks that we perform would not only be economical in terms of testing time, but would also give a test result which explains and predicts performance on a large number of tasks. That is, if a child is deficient in a specific perceptual or motor ability, tasks which rely on that ability would be performed poorly. However, tasks which are relatively independent of the deficient process would be performed adequately (see Fig. 1.1). Causal diagnosis of motor deficiency would then be possible, facilitating the design of management programmes directed at correcting diagnosed deficiencies.

The process-orientated approach is advocated by Keele and Hawkins (1982). They argue that the study of individual differences in motor behaviour should incorporate an attempt to isolate constituent processes and that test tasks should be selected to reflect these processes. Process–task relationships, according to Keele and Hawkins (1982) and Fleishman (1966), are best established through factor-analytical techniques. Additionally, Fleishman argues that motor skill research should proceed in two distinct steps. Firstly, the proposed theoretical structure should be investigated by a series of experiments. Each experiment should be concerned with one specific aspect of the theory, leading to acceptance, or where necessary, alterations of the theory. Secondly, if the theory is to be applied to test individual differences the relationship between the theoretical processes and test items should be established. Factor analysis is the most suitable statistical method here. This method, based on multiple correlations between tasks, yields a number of factors. Within each factor the tasks most strongly related to each other are grouped together. The factor structure should reflect the theoretical processes if the theoretical framework is sound, and if the tasks are selected according to valid criteria.

In Chapter 2 a closed-loop model was described. Some of the experimental evidence which led to the acceptance of this model, and the research relevant to the component processes, was discussed as well. Each component process of the closed-loop system contributes to the acquisition and/or performance of perceptual-motor skills. Children might differ in the rate of development of these processes, and in the final efficiency reached in each process. This uneven development might contribute to, or even be primarily responsible for, the uneven performance of motor tasks observed in any one individual and for the differences found between individuals.

In constructing the Perceptual-Motor Abilities Test, tasks were selected with the aim of addressing perceptual-motor processes, and consequently measuring underlying fundamental abilities, rather than performance on particular motor skills. However, within the framework of a closed-loop system complete isolation of single processes is not possible. Due to the nature of closed-loop systems the processes are not independent from each other, but instead they interact. It follows that any test item will reflect more than a single process. The criteria used in task selection must take this process interdependence into account. Accordingly, the tasks included in the test might depend predominantly on one single factor or a combination of factors.

Within this limitation in the process-orientated approach, the choice of test tasks was governed by theoretical principles rather than intuitive opinions as to what a task involves. An example might best illustrate the latter point. Free drawing and tracing are both paper-pencil skills which bear a strong superficial resemblance, while ball roll aiming tasks and whole body balance appear to be unrelated to each other and to paper-pencil skills. When considering the underlying processes responsible for the successful performance of these tasks, free drawing and ball aiming tasks form one group, while tracing and balance form the other. In free drawing, as in the aiming task, planning of the movement is of paramount importance, while in tracing and balance, efficient processing of kinaesthetic and visual information, and consequent error corrective programming are the decisive factors.

The two approaches to motor skill testing, task- and process-orientated, can now be compared in terms of their relative theoretical and practical values. Task-orientated tests do not depend on a theoretical backing in contrast to process-orientated tests. It is the theoretical framework on which the latter approach is based which leads to a systematic and justifiable item selection, and enables experimental verification of the test and a diagnostic interpretation of the results.

The cause of individual differences can be explored with the aid of the process-orientated testing approach, rather than just measuring strengths and weaknesses in particular tasks. This advantage is important in relation to the understanding of normal developmental trends. Once the order and rate at which the perceptual-motor factors develop is known, educational programmes could be evaluated in order to avoid the introduction of skills into the curricula before the child has developed the necessary abilities (see Chapter 8 on kinaesthetic readiness and handwriting). Remedial teaching of individual children should also improve following process-orientated testing. Rather than training the child in the specific skill at which he is performing badly, an attempt could be made to alleviate the weakness found in an underlying perceptual or motor factor. Improvement here could lead to better performance in all skills dependent on the specific factor.

Causal diagnosis in motor dysfunction is made possible by the use of the process-orientated testing procedure. To illustrate the advantages of this testing method when it is applied in the diagnostic situation, a brief description of a possible example might be useful. An eight-year-old boy is referred to the clinician by the parents and educational psychologist because he seems to be clumsy at a number of motor skills, such as drawing, dressing himself and playing ball games. The clinician, after establishing that the child shows no neurological abnormalities, tests him on a task-orientated test battery. Items included in the battery are drawing, tying shoelaces, catching balls, balancing, whistling and bead threading (e.g. Gubbay, 1975). The boy gains below-average scores on the first two items and whistling, but reaches average performance level on the remaining items. The clinician comes to the conclusion that the child is somewhat clumsy. This diagnosis concurs well with the observation made by the parents and educational psychologist, but fails to explain the reasons for the failure or to produce a solution to the problem the child is experiencing. On the other hand, if the boy could be tested on a process-orientated test, the test scores could indicate, for example, that he is below average at tasks which demand planning and spatial programming ability. A training schedule could then be designed to enhance his planning and spatial programming abilities. The schedule would first introduce him to selected tasks which, though demanding spatial programming, do not overtax his ability. The difficulty level and spatial programming demands of the task could be gradually increased as performance improves.

In the task-orientated test situation the boy performed adequately on the ball catching task, yet it was said that he was weak at ball games. This apparent contradiction could be resolved if factors determining performance were assessed. Catching a ball when standing in a set position is a task with few demands other than positioning hands and arms to receive the ball thrown by the clinician. During a ball game, on the other hand, the player must plan his game strategy, taking into account the other players and environmental conditions, run towards the ball and catch it. That is, in the test situation only spatial programming of a relatively simple movement is necessary, while during the game the child must formulate a plan of action and accordingly generate a complex sequence of spatio-temporal programmes to intercept and catch the ball. The findings of a process-orientated test would show that the boy was deficient in planning and spatial programming, thus the difference found between the two ball catching situations is readily explained.

In summary, the advantages of the process-orientated approach over the task-orientated approach can be listed: it facilitates the systematic choice of tasks; it leads to systematic explanation of developmental trends and individual differences; and it enables the clinician to provide a causal diagnosis of motor dysfunction.

It may seem from the previous discussion that the present authors see no role for a task-orientated system of assessment. This is not the case. If, for example, one wishes to assess a child's handwriting, the best test item for this purpose is one involving handwriting. If, on the other hand, one wants to understand the reasons for a handwriting problem a battery of tests that has only handwriting items will not identify the possible perceptual-motor factors responsible for the problem — only specifically designed tests, which address basic processes, will accomplish this objective. The rest of this chapter describes a research project aimed at the construction and application of a process-orientated test battery.

PERCEPTUAL AND MOTOR FACTORS TO BE EXAMINED IN THE PERCEPTUAL-MOTOR ABILITIES TEST

The functional integrity of both perceptual and motor systems is necessary for adequate performance of skilled tasks. There is unequivocal anatomical and neurophysiological evidence to support the contention that the sensory and motor systems are integrated in cortical and subcortical areas of the brain (Brooks, 1979; Fetz and Cheney, 1980; Fromm and Evarts, 1982; Godschalk *et al*, 1981; Macpherson *et al*, 1982). The neurophysiological findings of sensory–motor interaction are reflected in the closed-loop model presented in Chapter 2. Both anatomical and functional considerations lead to the conclusion that motor behaviour cannot be examined in isolation, but must always be considered in conjunction with perceptual processes, i.e. as perceptual-motor behaviour.

However, in most of the motor tests, reviewed in Chapter 5, emphasis was placed on the measurement of motor function and only in some of the tests was the attempt made to measure perceptual function, though even here perceptual and motor performance was not separated — the perceptual scores were always contaminated by motor demands. The close association between perceptual and motor systems does not exclude the possibility of testing perceptual functions alone, unconfounded by motor involvement (Chapters 6 and 8).

In the Perceptual-Motor Abilities Test the emphasis is placed on assessing the perception of kinaesthetic information, a concomitant of all movements. In regard to the other relevant sensory systems, only one specific aspect of visual perception is included, i.e. visual velocity discrimination. Clinically, both visual and auditory acuity tests are well known, and the integrity of the tactile system is routinely investigated in neurological examinations.

Vision provides information about the external environment and the relationship between environment and movement. Thus, a child suffering from a visual defect might manifest clumsy motor behaviour, even though his motor control system might not be defective. Even moderate myopia can severely disrupt motor function, and if undetected might lead to the mistaken diagnosis of clumsiness. A myopic child, placed at the back of a classroom might find accurate copying of the letters of the alphabet an impossible task, not because of motor difficulties, but through difficulties of clearly seeing the model letters displayed on the blackboard. In the playing field his ball skills would be significantly impaired. Being short-sighted, he would see the ball later than a child whose vision is unimpaired. Thus, he would not have sufficient time to effectively plan the catching movement, generate the motor programme and execute the ball catch.

Diagnosis of possible hearing loss is equally important since misunderstanding of verbal instructions might severely impair effective motor performance both in the classroom and on the playing field. Thus, even mild, partial hearing loss might, if undetected, lead to the mistaken label of clumsiness.

While the Perceptual-Motor Abilities Test does not include visual and auditory examinations, the necessity of the examination of these modalities cannot be stressed too strongly.

It was indicated in Chapter 6 that developmental trends for kinaesthetic function have not been established, i.e. independently of motor function, prior to the introduction of the Kinaesthetic Sensitivity Test. Yet kinaesthetic information is essential in skilled motor behaviour. The two tasks described in the Kinaesthetic Sensitivity Test have been included in the Perceptual-Motor Abilities Test, giving a measure of kinaesthetic acuity, and kinaesthetic perception and memory.

In the present test battery two additional kinaesthetic tasks are also included. The first of these relates to the perception of static postural information, in contrast to the combined position and movement-generated information measured in the Kinaesthetic Sensitivity Test. The ability of the child to perceive the position of his limbs is examined here. This ability is necessary in both locomotive skills, and in the preparatory postural adjustments which precede all skilled movements.

Besides information about the body and limbs, and the extent, direction and force of movements, kinaesthesis provides information about the velocity of movements as well. In many everyday tasks temporal constraints are imposed on the performance of the skill and it is essential to perceive the velocity of the movement in order to control it. Information about movement velocity and the velocity of moving objects is given both by kinaesthesis and vision. With the aid of these modalities moving objects can be either intercepted or avoided. In many situations visual and kinaesthetic velocity information needs to be matched. For instance, when catching a ball, the velocity at which the ball approaches is visually observed, while the velocity of the movement to catch the ball is kinaesthetically monitored. Hence both visual and kinaesthetic velocity discrimination are measured in the test battery and a cross-modal, visual–kinaesthetic velocity discrimination task is also included.

The motor tasks selected for inclusion in the test battery are grouped according to the planning and programming demands that they place on the subject. Before a skilled movement is started, a plan of the movement must be formulated, followed by the generation of the motor programme which is to correspond with the chosen plan. Planning is most important in tasks where the subject is free to select one specific strategy from many possible strategies with which the task could be performed. The plan might include decisions of the starting point of the movement, the posture which should be adopted, the course the movement should take, and the velocity and force of its execution. The fewer the environmental constraints which are imposed by the task, the greater will be the scope of planning. For example, there is a wide scope for formulating a plan in free drawing, whereas there is much less, if any, in tracing, and there is more scope in catching a ball during a game than catching a ball tossed directly at the waiting child.

There are three aspects of a movement that can be controlled: direction, velocity and force. Accordingly, three motor programming parameters can be distinguished: spatial, temporal and force. These programming parameters have been shown to have corresponding neural control mechanisms (Brooks, 1981; Desmedt and Godaux, 1979; Evarts *et al*, 1983; Freund, 1983). In most tasks all three parameters need to be controlled, although they can be controlled independently from each other. A movement to a set location might be made in a straight line or through a complex, curved route, it can be fast or slow, and it can be executed with light or heavy pressure. It is the task itself that defines the specific way in which the three parameters should be combined.

Tasks are included in the Perceptual-Motor Abilities Test which can be grouped according to dominant underlying programming parameters. Additionally, tasks are used in which a set combination of two programming parameters are combined, to gain a wider representation of programming ability than would be possible by employing single factor tasks alone.

GENERAL CONSIDERATIONS GOVERNING THE CHOICE OF TASKS IN THE TEST

The choice of tasks to be used in the test battery is governed primarily by theoretical considerations. There are, however, a number of general principles of test administration which must also be taken into account.

It was decided that as far as possible novel tasks should be used, rather than tasks which the child might have practised outside the testing situation. Care was taken, however, to choose tasks which represent types of skills expected of children in their everyday lives. There are two reasons for the decision to use novel tasks. Firstly, the test aims at measuring perceptual-motor abilities, not learning. With extended practice on one specific task the child may reach an inflated level of performance in that task, without improvement of related tasks. The enhanced scores gained on the specific task would not reflect the level of development in the underlying perceptual-motor process. For instance, frequent repetition in drawing a small square might result in producing acceptable small squares but fail to improve the drawing of large squares or other geometric figures. Planning and spatial programming ability would remain at a lower developmental level than the small square drawing score would indicate.

The second consideration relates to motivational factors. Expectancy of failure would be experienced by the child when confronted with a task he knows he cannot do well. The child might feel embarrassed at being asked to attempt the task. An effective way of coping is to give up trying and display carelessness or boredom because he finds it easier to be labelled careless rather than clumsy. The process-orientated test approach circumvents this problem, firstly by presenting the child with a novel task, thus avoiding possible expectations of failure, and secondly by measuring ability rather than assessing previous experience.

Every test item included in the test battery should be applicable across the entire age range for which the test has been designed. Developmental trends in perceptual-motor abilities cannot be defined if different tasks are used at different ages. It is not possible to directly compare bead threading scores at one age with pegboard scores at another age since it is likely that the two tasks rely on different perceptual-motor processes. The tasks should be interesting for children from five to 12 years of age and should not be too difficult for the youngest, nor too easy for the oldest children.

Objective scoring is important when aiming at comparisons between individuals, across age groups and between normal and disabled children. Observational scores are often influenced by the tester's experience and sometimes by his bias (Chapter 4). A tester or therapist used to the functional level of severely disabled children might underestimate the extent of mild handicap and, conversely, if routinely working with normal children might overestimate the severity of relatively mild handicap. An objective scoring procedure effectively guards against this type of bias.

Finally, some additional points can be listed: tasks, whenever possible, should be presented as a game; need for complex instructions should be avoided; the tasks should not appear threatening to the child nor should they expose him to undue failure which he is aware of.

THE SAMPLE USED

All the children and adults tested were living in Perth, Western Australia. The children were drawn from six metropolitan primary schools, the adults were students of the University of Western Australia.

Table 7.1 summarises the information relevant to sampling.

Table 7.1 *Description of sample.*

Ages (years)*	School year	No. tested	No. of females	No. of males
5.5–6.5	1	100	44	56
6.5–7.5	2	100	50	50
7.5–8.5	3	100	49	51
8.5–9.5	4	23	14	9
9.5–10.5	5	28	15	13
10.5–11.5	6	100	41	59
11.5–12.5	7	20	8	12
$\overline{M}$ 23.1	Adults	20	10	10

*These ages will be referred to in the text by using midpoints, e.g. 5.5–6.5 will be called 6.

The grouping of the sample was according to school years rather than chronological age, and hence some overlap in chronological age occurs between groups. However, Table 7.1 presents the age range of the children tested in each class.

The number of children tested in the seven groups was uneven. The numbers in Years 4, 5 and 7 reflect one class size for each age.

The number of males and females could not be equated since all the children from a class whose parents gave their consent to their child's participation in the project were tested.

Both right- and left-handed children were included in the samples. In all tasks performed with one hand, the child used his preferred hand.

DESCRIPTION OF THE TASKS AND SOME OBSERVATIONS ON HOW THEY WERE PERFORMED BY THE VARIOUS AGE GROUPS

The tasks are grouped according to the underlying factor or factors on which they primarily depend.*

Motor tasks

Planning and spatio-temporal programming

(i) Ward game — aiming at a moving target. The game was played on a modified billiard table (Laszlo *et al*, 1980). At one end of the table, nine 5 cm flaps were hinged to a rail. The nine flap

Figure 7.1   *Ward game: Emil, aged 10 years.*

*Exact dimensions and measurements will be given in the test manual for the test equipment.

target assembly moved from side to side at a constant speed (59 cm/s). Fig. 7.1 shows the apparatus. The child's task was to roll 20 billiard balls, one at a time, aiming for the middle flap. Hitting the middle flap scored 1, and the two adjacent flaps scored 2. This error score was increased in single steps to 5 for the outer flaps, and 6 was scored for a ball which missed the target entirely.

Performance on the Ward game depends, to a large extent, on the adequate planning of the task strategy. Planning is involved in selecting an appropriate posture, ball grip and roll style. Following the general plan, the spatio-temporal programme is formulated to define when and where the ball should be rolled.

Children at different ages performed this task using a variety of performance styles. The six- and seven-year-old children tended to roll the balls in a haphazard manner. Ball grip was changed from trial to trial. Occasionally they even attempted to bounce the billiard balls, rather than rolling them. There seemed to be scant regard for the target: balls were rolled sometimes straight down the middle and at other times towards the edge of the table. By the ages of eight and nine a consistent, target-orientated performance style seemed to emerge. Most children, at this age, showed consistent, stereotyped ball rolling movements throughout the 20 trials, regardless of whether the response was successful or not. Children in the three oldest groups exhibited consistent ball grip, but varied the spacing and timing of the ball roll from trial to trial. Their performance appeared purposeful and flexible.

Spatio-temporal programming

(ii) Video game — manual target interception task. The child was seated in front of a television screen which was mounted horizontally. The screen lit up at the commencement of each five-target trial block. The child was told that a black square would appear on the green screen when the tester hit a key on the computer keyboard. The square always travelled in a straight line. The child held the light pen on the marked starting position, and when the square appeared, attempted to cross over it with the pen. The computer registered 'hits' and 'misses' (Fig. 7.2).

Three target sizes and three velocities were used, and each target presentation was designated as one trial. Following familiarisation trials two conditions were administered. In Condition 1, 45 trials were given where the target appeared at different points on the far edge of the screen, travelling directly towards the child. In the last 45 trials, Condition 2, the target moved diagonally across the screen with starting points from three edges of the screen. The target was not presented from the edge nearest to the child.

In the familiarisation trials the three target sizes and velocities were systematically introduced. The scores gained from these trials are not included in the data analysis. In the two experimental conditions first 15 large, then 15 medium and lastly 15 small targets were presented. Within each target size block, five slow (7.4 cm/s), five medium (19 cm/s) and five fast (30.5 cm/s) velocities were given. The maximum error score a child could receive was 90.

The successful performance of this task depends primarily on spatio-temporal programming parameters. The movement of the child's hand holding the light pen must be related to the direction and velocity of the movement of the target to achieve a 'hit'.

Besides recording the 'hits' and 'misses' the entire course of the aiming movements could also be plotted. Fig. 7.3 gives these sample plots, representing three age groups. These plots were chosen as representative examples of the functional style of children at three different age levels.

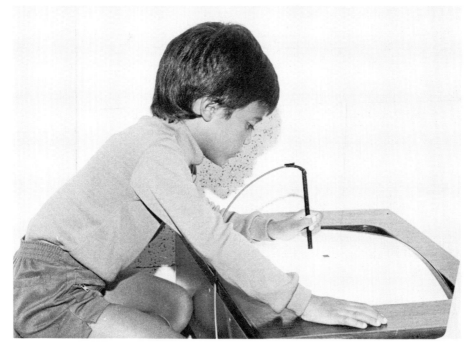

Figure 7.2   *Video game: Damon, aged seven years.*

Two motor programming parameters are represented by the plotted movement curves. Firstly, spatial programming is represented by the overall shape of the plotted movement curves, and secondly, error corrective programming is reflected by sudden, well-defined directional changes in the movement curves.

The aiming movements of the youngest child were placed close to each other, mostly at the lower half of the screen, regardless of where the target was travelling or of target velocity. It seemed that the child programmed his movements independently from the movement of the target. The movement curves were smooth and no evidence of error corrective programming was shown. The movements were often terminated by unnecessary directional changes which were independent of target trajectory.

The records for nine year olds did not differ markedly in appearance from those of six year olds except that the movements were terminated smoothly. There was no discernible evidence of error corrective programming.

The movement curves recorded during the oldest child's (12 years) performance appeared widely spaced across the screen, in all three velocity conditions. This wide placement indicated that each movement programme was generated in accordance with the specific target trajectory and velocity, aiming for a predicted interception point between target and light pen. Directional changes in the aiming movements could be observed, often just before the point of interception between arm and target movements showing evidence of error corrective programming.

Regarding the speed of the aiming movements, it was noted that the youngest children moved across the screen at great speed, in all trials, regardless of target velocity. The older children varied the speed of their movements according to the velocity of the target movement.

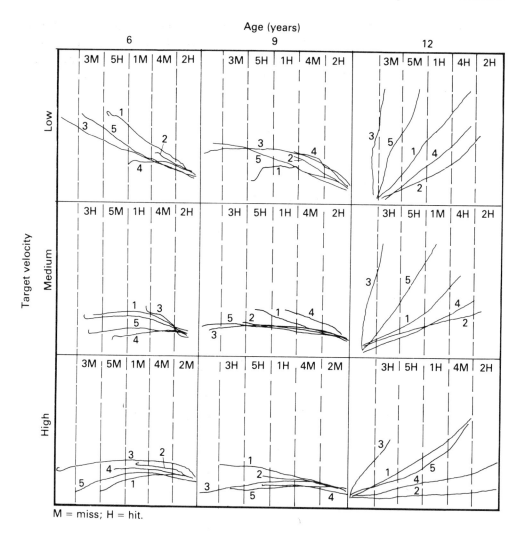

Figure 7.3 *Video game: condition 1 — medium target speed. For each child, 15 trials of Condition 1, medium target size, at the three target velocities are shown.*

(iii) Ball catching - whole body, target interception task. The child was asked to catch a ball rolled towards him down a chute (length 52.5 cm). The chute could be set at five different angles (15°, 20°, 25°, 30°, 35°) from the horizontal, and four balls of graduated size were used (Fig. 7.4). Over the five chute settings and four ball sizes the ball roll velocity was linear. The series of trials was started with the lowest chute setting and largest ball, followed by the other three balls in order of decreasing size. The chute was set at the next, steeper angle, and the balls again rolled in order of decreasing size. This procedure was repeated for all five chute settings. The child was told to stand behind the starting line which was three metres from the end of the chute. He was

to run forward as soon as the ball started rolling down the chute, and was to catch the ball before it hit the ground. Misses were recorded as errors. If one of the four balls was not caught at any of the chute settings, the four ball series was repeated. If eight consecutive balls were missed at any one chute setting, the task was terminated and misses were recorded for the aborted trials. Thus, the maximum error score a child could get was 40.

Figure 7.4   *Ball catching: Damon, aged seven years.*

As in the previous task, efficient spatio-temporal programming was necessary to perform this task successfully. The child had to move to the right place, arriving at the appropriate time to catch the ball. While in the video game only arm movements needed to be programmed, for ball catching whole body movements were required.

Six- and seven-year-old children performed this task badly. They often missed the ball, running forward after the ball hit the ground, or taking up the wrong position, usually too close to the chute. Many of the children held their arms and hands in an inappropriate position for receiving the ball. Sometimes the children seemed to register surprise when the ball landed between their arms or hands, and let the ball slip out of their grip. Low performance level on this task does not conform with normative scores for these age groups recorded in the various motor test manuals. In tests of ball catching ability, described in these manuals, the child plays the role of passive receiver, with the tester performing the active movement, i.e. the child stands still and waits for the ball to land in his hands. In the present task the child is the active participant, having to programme his movements to intercept and catch the ball as it falls.

   This ball catching skill improved markedly by the age of eight. The child anticipated the arrival of the ball by well-timed, accurately positioned preparatory movements and efficient catching grip. The task called for a stereotyped response pattern which was well within the child's programming ability.

   By nine years of age performance appeared effortless, and was practically error free.

Planning and spatial programming

(iv) Ball handling — manual dexterity. Two small plastic buckets were placed, side by side on a low table, in front of the child. The child could see into the buckets. The bucket near the child's preferred hand contained 18 balls, three balls in each of six size categories. Ball sizes varied from

Figure 7.5   *Ball handling: Damon, aged seven years.*

cricket balls to small marbles. The child was asked to transfer the balls into the second, empty bucket, one at a time, and as fast as possible, with his preferred hand (Fig. 7.5). Time taken for the completion of the task was recorded. Planning of the task strategy relates primarily to the order in which the balls are to be picked up. Efficient spatial programming assures the secure and speedy grasp of the ball, and the smooth transfer of the ball from one bucket to the other.

Age-related performance differences separated the two youngest age groups from the eight year olds, while performance style remained unchanged thereafter. The slow performance recorded for the six and seven year old children could be observed to be caused by the lack of a

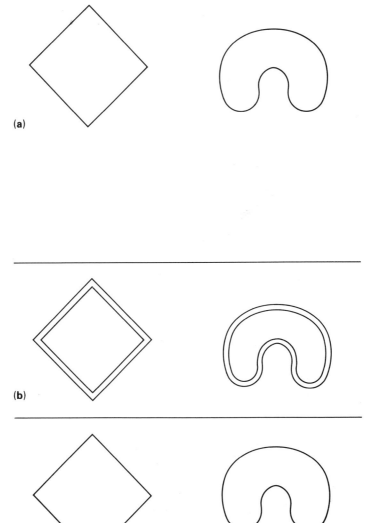

Figure 7.6 *Drawing and tracing test sheet.*

well-planned task strategy. They would reach into the bucket, stir the balls around, and after considerable delay pick up a ball apparently chosen at random. The older children, in contrast, showed a more systematic approach to the task. They aimed, with some precision, for the ball lying uppermost. Further improvement in the time score might be attributed to increased precision of the aiming movements.

All the children tested could grasp the balls securely. Thus, the efficiency of the grasping movement by itself could only be a minor factor in the time taken to perform this task.

(v) Drawing. Line drawings of a diamond and a horseshoe figure were placed in front of the child (Fig. 7.6a). He was asked to copy first the diamond, then the horseshoe. He was told to copy the figures accurately in shape and size, without hurrying.

The error in accuracy of the copied figures was measured by calculating the area discrepancy between the model figures and the child's drawings. Time taken to complete each figure was also recorded, without the child's knowledge. In formulating the plan of action in free drawing, decisions about the starting point and the direction of the movement must be made. Adequate spatial programming is necessary to control the movement extent, location and placements of angles and curves of the figures.

Changes in drawing style, characteristic of the various age groups, could be observed in this copying task.

Many of the children aged six and seven hesitated before starting a figure and needed encouragement to make an attempt at copying. In the drawing of the diamond the first side and angle were relatively well defined, but as the child progressed each successive angle became further distorted. Some children could not achieve closure of the figure. The child often expressed dissatisfaction with his drawing. Given the opportunity to repeat the drawing, he replicated his first attempt without improving it (Fig. 7.7). The child was aware of the difference between the model figure and his own drawing but was unable to make the necessary corrective changes in his drawing movements to improve it. These replications were not scored. The copied horseshoe shape was often asymmetrical and frequently unrelated to the original figure (e.g. see Fig. 7.8). When asked where he went wrong he gave a general answer such as 'too skinny' or 'too fat'.

The time scores did not reliably represent the speed of performance. The children tended to stop drawing, look around the room or start a conversation. Observational data indicated that as the figure progressed, drawing speed declined. This was especially noticeable just prior to attempts at closure of the figure.

Eight and nine year old children, on the other hand, started drawing without hesitation. Some of them progressively decreased the speed of their drawing as the figure neared completion. Closure was always achieved. At the later age groups the task was performed efficiently and with assurance.

At all ages large individual differences could be observed.

Spatial programming

(vi) Drawing between lines. The diamond and horseshoe figures were outlined by parallel lines, 3 mm apart. These models were given to the children (Fig. 7.6b), and they were asked to draw a line between the printed lines.

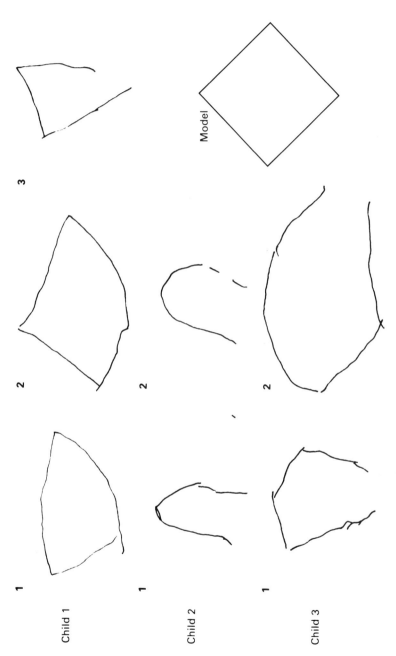

Figure 7.7 *Repeated drawing attempts of the diamond by three five-year-old children.*

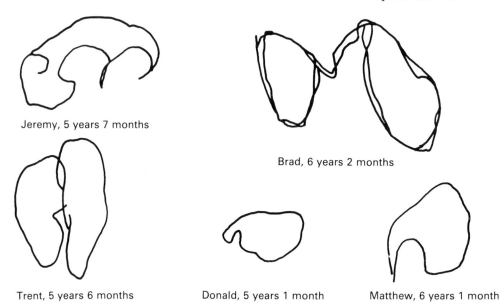

Jeremy, 5 years 7 months

Brad, 6 years 2 months

Trent, 5 years 6 months   Donald, 5 years 1 month   Matthew, 6 years 1 month

Figure 7.8   *Attempts at drawing the horseshoe.*

This task depends on spatial programming. The six and seven year olds performed this task with confidence, but made errors, while the older children produced an error-free performance, e.g. 53 eight year olds had zero error scores.

(vii) Tracing over the line. Models of the two figures were given to the child who was asked to trace over the line without deviating from it (Fig. 7.6c). Stress was placed on accuracy, not speed. One error score was recorded for every deviation from the printed line. In the case of errors extending over 5 mm in length, one error was recorded for each 5 mm deviation length. Time taken to complete the figure was recorded without the child's knowledge.

Spatial programming, fine kinaesthetic and visual error detection, and error corrective programming underlie the performance of the tracing task.

Performance style differed markedly across age groups. The types of tracing performance can be illustrated by examples shown in Fig. 7.9. Extended, long errors characterised the young child's tracing efforts, while the errors of eight year old children were shorter, and deviations were corrected sooner. By 10 years errors were infrequent and short in length.

The speed of performance decreased systematically with age. Although total time scores were not a reliable indication of tracing speed in the two youngest age groups [see *(v) Drawing*], the actual movement velocity could be seen to be fast.

(viii) Dotting — a manual, serial aiming task. The child was given a sheet of paper on which 11, 1 mm dots were printed in a pyramid configuration (see Fig. 7.10). The child was asked to touch each dot with a red, fine-tipped felt pen, starting at the single dot, then continuing by 'zigzagging' from side to side across each dot pair, finishing with the most widely placed dot pair. Both accuracy and speed of performance were stressed in the instructions. An error was scored when the child's mark was clearly separated from the printed dot. The time taken was also recorded with the child's knowledge. Success in this task depends primarily on spatial programming ability.

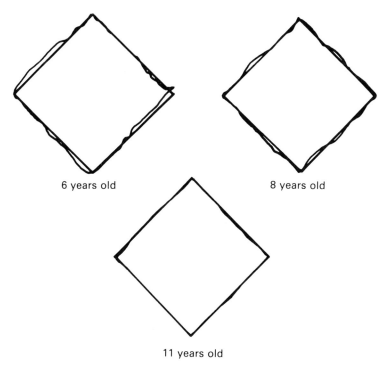

6 years old

8 years old

11 years old

Figure 7.9 *Tracing errors.*

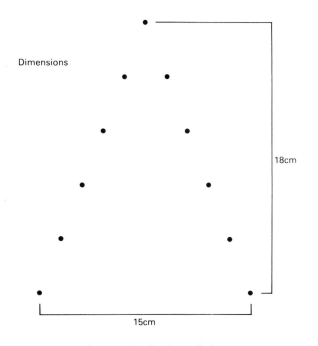

Dimensions

18cm

15cm

Figure 7.10 *Dotting task sheet.*

Children at all ages performed this task with confidence, though with varying degrees of accuracy.

Perceptual tasks

(ix) Kinaesthetic acuity and (x) Kinaesthetic perception and memory. These two tasks are fully described in Chapter 6.

(xi) Posture — static kinaesthesis. The aim of this task was to measure the ability of the child to monitor limb positions. The child lay on his back, thus the necessity to control body balance was eliminated. A toy 'pink panther' was used to demonstrate the two-dimensional test posture (see Fig. 7.11). The panther was held above the child, in the horizontal plane. The child was asked to put his own arms and legs into positions imitating the pink panther. Visual monitoring of limb position was prevented by instructing the child to keep his eyes on the pink panther. When the child reported that his limbs were placed in the required position, a photograph was taken, using a polaroid camera mounted on the ceiling directly above the child.

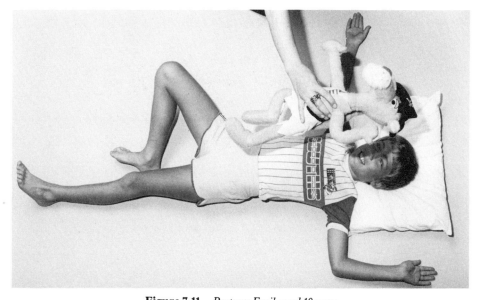

Figure 7.11   *Posture: Emil, aged 10 years.*

Each major joint which was placed in an incorrect position was counted as an error. Thus maximum error score was 12.

This task demands accurate perception of position information, i.e. static kinaesthesis.

A critical point can be raised regarding this task as a pure measure of kinaesthetic perception. The child is asked to actively assume the test position, thus motor control factors could affect the perceptual ability score. In normal children the influence of the motor factors would be of negligible importance as the necessary movements are simple and the child is given unlimited time to process the postural kinaesthetic information after assuming the posture. However, the task must be adapted to eliminate even this simple motor component when testing the disabled child; the movement is to be passively induced. The tester can move the child's limbs, one at a time, until the child signals that his limb is placed in the same position as pink panther has his limb, i.e. until the kinaesthetic information generated from his limb matches that of the required position. The passive task presentation would be considerably more time consuming than when the task is performed actively.

An unexpected qualitative difference in the performance of this task was evident when the two youngest age groups were compared with the older age groups. Many of the six- and seven-year-old children (53 and 39 respectively) assumed a three-dimensional posture, curling their limbs up, off the floor (Fig. 7.12). On the other hand, this did not occur in any of the older age groups. It is unlikely that the young children would have misunderstood the instructions since even repeated instructions, including specific pointers relating to the panther's limb position, could not eliminate this error. The reason is probably the inability of the youngest children to adequately monitor the kinaesthetic information generated by the limbs.

Figure 7.12 *Posture: Claire, aged six years.*

(xii) Velocity discrimination — visual–visual comparison. The child was seated in front of a table. The table top was made of a translucent glass screen. Below the glass screen, two rails were mounted on a wooden platform. The rails (43 cm long) running diagonally across the platform converged towards a point furthest from the child. A pencil torch was vertically attached to each rail. Two motors, independently controlled, were able to move the torches at five possible speeds (1.6, 3.6, 5.8, 7.6 and 9.4 cm/s). The lights from the torches were seen as two small dots on the surface of the screen. When the motors were activated, the two lights moved at different velocities away from the child. The child's task was to watch the lights moving on the screen and indicate as soon as he could which of the lights was travelling faster. The rails and torches were obscured from the child's view by the translucent screen. Six trials were given, with the relative velocities of the lights being varied in a predetermined order. The score was recorded as the distance travelled by one light to the point where the child gave his response (Fig. 7.13).

Figure 7.13 *Velocity discrimination: Claire, aged six years.*

(xiii) Velocity discrimination — kinaesthetic–kinaesthetic comparison. The same apparatus and scoring method were used as in the previous task, except that the lights were not switched on (Fig. 7.13). The child was asked to hold the pencil torches lightly, one in each hand. He was to indicate which of his hands was moved faster.

(xiv) Velocity discrimination — visual–kinaesthetic comparison. Apparatus and scoring were the same as in the two previous tasks, but only one torch light was switched on: the one corresponding to the child's non-preferred hand. With his preferred hand he gently held the corresponding torch. He was asked to watch the light and feel the movement of his arm. He was to say whether the light or the hand was travelling faster, as soon as he could make the judgement.

In the three velocity discrimination tasks performance depends on the ability to perceive and compare the velocity of two moving objects when the information is presented in the visual or kinaesthetic mode, or by a combination of both.

There were no observable changes in response style across the seven age groups in this task. However, one unexpected problem did emerge with the visual–kinaesthetic comparison in the two youngest age groups. In this cross-modal condition the children were asked to give their response verbally, to say whether the arm or the light was moving the faster. Many of the six and seven year old children signalled their decision first using gestures, and the verbal response followed some time after the gesture. It was apparently quicker and easier to wriggle a finger or jerk the head sideways than to translate the perceptual discrimination into a verbal response. It was the point at which the gesture was made which was accepted and recorded as the response. If the testers had rigidly adhered to their preconceived ideas of how the children should respond, rather than observing their behaviour and accepting the type of response the children chose, the performance of these children would have been severely underestimated. The importance of flexibility and open-minded observation when working with young children, indeed with all human subjects, is emphasised by this example.

 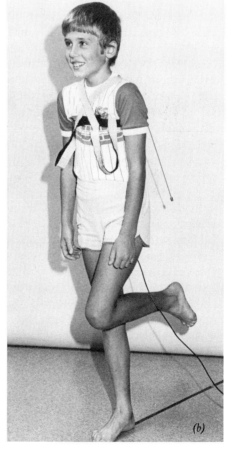

Figure 7.14 *(a) Balancing heel-to-toe: Damon, aged seven years. (b) Standing on one foot: Emil, aged 10 years.*

Balance

(xv) Static, whole body balance. The child was asked to stand with the left foot in front of the right, heel-to-toe, on a straight line marked on the floor, with his eyes open and without swaying for 10 seconds. Timing of the trial was started when the child achieved a steady posture. In the next trial the right foot was in front. These two trials were repeated with the child's eyes closed. Four trials of standing on one foot, first left then right, followed, two performed with vision, and two without vision. Sway was recorded by a sway meter strapped to the child's back. For each trial the error score was recorded, i.e. the duration of steady posture subtracted from the 10 second trial duration. For the total balance error score the eight individual error scores were summed (Fig. 7.14).

The ability to maintain steady posture and balance depends on the processing of kinaesthetic information (Marsden, Merton and Morton, 1981) and on error corrective programming.

Additional tasks

The following tasks were included in the present test battery but may be omitted from future tests. The tasks' descriptions and reasons for possible omission are given below.

(xvi) Ward game — aiming at a stationary target. The same apparatus and scoring procedure was used as in the Ward game with moving target *(i)*, except that the target assembly did not move from side to side but was stationary, and positioned centrally.

The similarity of the two Ward games made the stationary target game redundant. The correlation coefficient between the two games was high, ranging from $r = 0.65$ to 0.49 over the seven age groups. The two tasks were grouped along the same factor in the factor analyses. The major control processes underlying the two tasks are similar, although the temporal programming factor influenced the Ward game with moving target only.

(xvii) Simple reaction time and movement time. A visual stimulus was presented to the child who was asked to release the rest key and press the test key as fast as possible after seeing the light. Movement time was often considered as a pure measure of temporal control of movement. However, when watching the six- and seven-year-old children performing this task it was observed that spatial factors were also involved. The young children found it difficult to aim accurately for the key, often missing it at the first attempt. It was shown by Laszlo and Livesey (1977) that spatial accuracy demands in a reaction time task influenced the reaction time component of the response. Thus this task must be reconsidered as a spatio-temporal task, which, however, lacks a score denoting spatial performance. The test could not be used as a valid indicator of temporal programming and hence should be omitted from the final battery.

(xviii) Balance during walking. The child was asked to walk 10 steps, heel-to-toe, on a straight line marked on the floor. The time taken to complete the 10 steps was recorded as one of the performance scores, as well as recording the extent of sway during the trial. Performance on this task showed individual differences, but did not improve with age. Thus, the task was not considered useful as an index of normal motor development, but may prove valuable as an indicator of serious balance disorder in the disabled child.

(xix) Maintenance of steady force. The child was seated facing a force platform which was mounted on a stand. He was asked to put his fist on the platform, with his elbow fully extended, in the horizontal position. He was to push down on the platform as hard as he could. The maximal force exerted was recorded in gram units. He then relaxed the pressure, and after a short rest repeated the task, this time exerting only half maximal force, and holding the platform steady for 10 seconds. Continuous recording of the force maintained was read out on a paper chart.

This task was a measure of force programming. Improvement in force maintenance could not be demonstrated. The only change with age was in the maximal force that the child was able to exert; this increased with age.

Thus, as discussed in the previous task, force programming measured in this way is not a useful index in describing normal motor development. It could, however, prove to be a valuable diagnostic index when testing the physically disabled child.

Fig. 7.15 shows the test items placed into the framework of the closed-loop model.

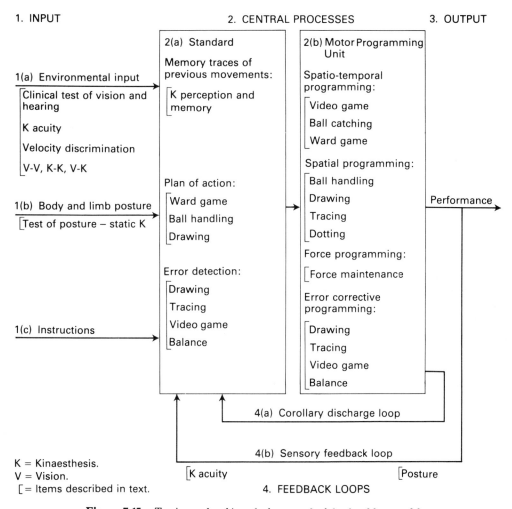

Figure 7.15 *Test items placed into the framework of the closed-loop model.*

ANALYSIS AND EVALUATION OF THE RESULTS

In the previous sections of this chapter the theoretical basis of the test, the choice of tasks and their administration are described. In this section formal data analysis is presented, and the results of the statistical analyses are related to the theoretical framework within which the test is constructed. The practical advantages and possible disadvantages of the test are also considered.

The data are examined to clarify a number of issues. Firstly, statistical evidence for developmental trends for the tasks included in the test battery should be discussed. Lack of improvement with age in a task would indicate that the task is not suitable as a developmental measure or that the scoring method used is not sensitive enough to measure the developmental trend. Secondly, the exact course of the developmental trends must be defined. If it is shown that children improve at similar rates in all tasks, and if all the tasks correlate with one another over the seven age groups, it could be argued that all the test items depend on one general motor factor. On the other hand, if stepwise, uneven development is found, with different tasks improving at different rates, the developmental trends would best be explained in terms of specific factors underlying motor development. The specific ages at which sudden changes in the performance of some tasks occur need to be established statistically, and the factors responsible for these changes need to be isolated. If specific factors develop at specific age levels, teaching and training methods in motor skills should be process-orientated, rather than relying on generalised training.

Further, it should be ascertained whether the analyses performed can account for all the findings, or do additional theoretical factors need to be considered?

Finally, attention should be paid to the practical aspects of the test battery and its possible usefulness as a tool in the diagnosis of specific motor disorders.

Establishing developmental trends

In Fig. 7.16 performance scores for each task are plotted against age groups to give an indication of the developmental trends. In each figure the result of the Analysis of Variance (Ferguson, 1981) is given, showing the significance level for age differences. Twenty subjects were randomly chosen from each age group. Their scores were used in the analyses of variance.

In all tasks significant age effects were found. For posture (Fig. 7.16i) the results of an additional analysis are included, omitting the nine year olds' results to ascertain that age differences are significant even without the unexpectedly low error scores at this age.

The means and standard deviations for tasks and ages are given in Table 7.2.

Significant age differences were not found for the time scores in the drawing and tracing tasks; children did not perform these tasks faster as they got older. The unreliability of the time scores at six and seven years, due to inconsistent performance, would bias the results in favour of age differences, yet no significant trend could be established.

Are the developmental trends continuous or stepwise?

Inspection of Fig. 7.16 gives some indication of stepwise development in most tasks, with

Table 7.2 Mean and standard deviation of tasks for all ages.

Task description	Age (years) Measurement	5.5–6.5 M	s.d.	6.5–7.5 M	s.d.	7.5–8.5 M	s.d.	8.5–9.5 M	s.d.	9.5–10.5 M	s.d.	10.5–11.5 M	s.d.	11.5–12.5 M	s.d.	$\overline{M}$ 23.1 (adult) M	s.d.
Ward moving	Mean score	4.0	0.54	3.7	0.55	3.4	0.67	3.5	0.49	3.0	0.40	2.9	0.50	3.1	0.42	2.7	0.30
Video game	No. of misses	47.9	12.94	38.7	11.11	40.5	9.56	29.6	12.12	26.7	11.70	31.9	10.43	23.6	9.03	24.7	11.10
Ball catching	No. of misses	20.8	9.6	11.0	8.7	4.5	5.0	3.5	3.4	1.4	1.9	0.8	1.0	0.4	0.7	0.4	0.8
Grasp	Time (s)	30.4	4.7	26.8	3.4	24.5	4.8	23.0	2.8	21.9	2.4	21.5	3.9	19.7	1.8	19.4	3.1
Drawing errors	Area error	256.07	70.77	234.00	55.55	199.54	60.99	177.17	64.59	176.96	49.02	143.95	53.27	139.80	41.12	91.35	43.86
⚏ Errors	No. of errors	3.90	3.36	1.7	1.79	0.7	1.02	0.8	1.40	0.5	0.79	0.2	0.67	0.2	0.72	0	0
∧ Errors	No. of errors	24.0	9.4	16.7	8.1	5.8	5.0	14.3	6.8	11.9	5.4	4.4	4.2	6.1	4.9	0.6	0.9
Drawing time	Time (s)	22.9	14.8	21.6	8.1	20.6	8.1	22.1	8.8	16.8	8.0	24.6	10.3	21.9	13.6	22.1	8.8
⚏ Time	Time (s)	44.0	16.0	39.5	10.7	45.3	14.4	34.8	8.1	31.3	11.2	49.4	19.4	39.1	19.2	31.4	9.8
∧ Time	Time (s)	54.5	21.9	50.5	14.4	49.4	17.3	47.7	12.2	41.5	15.9	51.8	15.2	43.5	19.0	48.6	29.5
Dotting errors	No. of errors	5.2	3.2	3.7	2.9	2.7	2.2	2.8	2.1	2.7	2.4	2.1	2.1	2.1	2.1	0.2	0.5
Dotting time	Time (s)	14.2	3.4	12.7	3.2	11.7	8.7	11.5	2.8	10.5	3.2	10.4	2.2	9.2	1.8	9.1	2.5
Kinaesthetic acuity	No. of errors	9.1	4.5	8.8	4.0	8.3	3.4	6.5	3.2	6.1	3.9	6.9	4.0	5.9	3.2	4.6	2.7
Kinaesthetic perception	Error degrees	55.2	22.9	59.0	23.7	55.2	21.8	44.5	15.8	45.2	15.8	45.0	16.2	37.4	18.0	22.6	13.1
Posture	No. of errors	3.0	1.9	2.4	1.8	2.7	1.6	1.0	1.3	1.7	1.0	2.3	1.5	1.5	1.2	1.1	0.9
Velocity V–V	Mean length	18.6	4.7	17.3	3.6	14.2	4.2	16.9	3.3	13.0	3.4	13.2	4.0	13.3	3.5	12.0	2.7
Velocity K–K	Mean length	18.3	4.9	15.9	4.2	14.1	4.2	14.4	3.5	11.9	3.6	13.1	3.9	12.7	3.1	12.1	3.2
Velocity V–K	Mean length	19.2	5.1	16.6	3.8	15.2	4.8	14.9	3.9	12.5	3.1	14.2	3.7	12.6	3.3	11.5	2.8
Balance time	Seconds error	29.3	14.3	23.7	10.8	14.9	11.3	13.8	7.5	9.0	7.6	7.3	6.76	3.5	4.7	3.24	3.62
Force	Drift in kg	0.12	0.16	0.15	0.18	0.30	0.40	0.20	0.20	0.15	0.20	0.30	0.45	0.14	0.20	–	–

⚏ = Drawing between lines; ∧ = Tracing over the line.

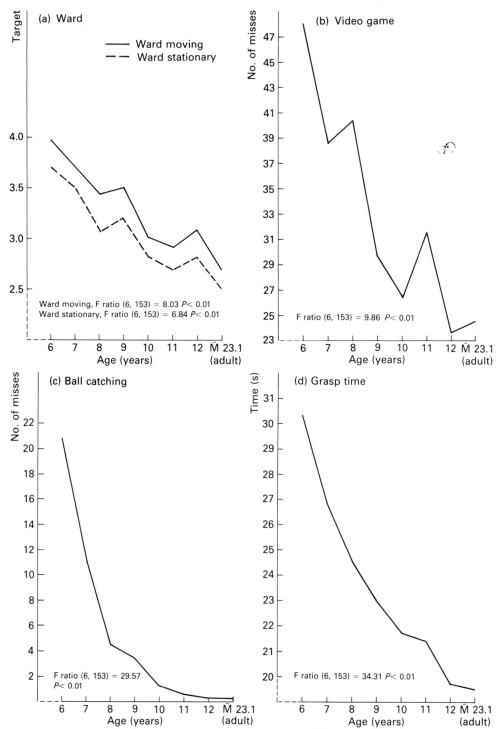

Figure 7.16   *Developmental trends; task performance scores plotted against age for each task.*

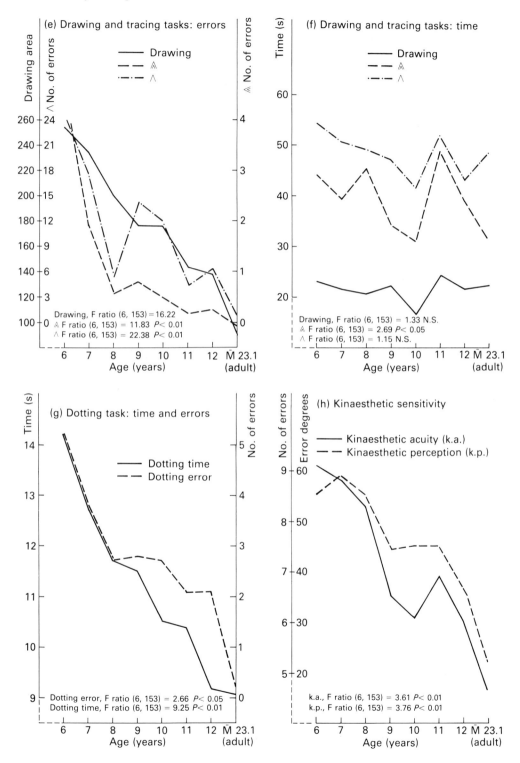

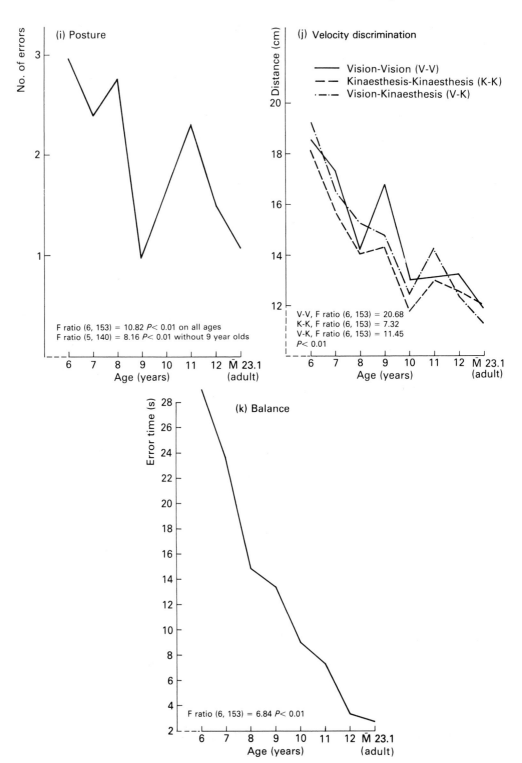

(i) Posture

No. of errors

F ratio (6, 153) = 10.82 *P*< 0.01 on all ages
F ratio (5, 140) = 8.16 *P*< 0.01 without 9 year olds

Age (years)
(adult)

(j) Velocity discrimination

Distance (cm)

—— Vision-Vision (V-V)
– – Kinaesthesis-Kinaesthesis (K-K)
·–·– Vision-Kinaesthesis (V-K)

V-V, F ratio (6, 153) = 20.68
K-K, F ratio (6, 153) = 7.32
V-K, F ratio (6, 153) = 11.45
P< 0.01

Age (years)
(adult)

(k) Balance

Error time (s)

F ratio (6, 153) = 6.84 *P*< 0.01

Age (years)
(adult)

sudden changes in the steepness of the performance curves, or definite plateaux between adjacent age groups.

The data need to be statistically analysed to confirm the existence of distinct developmental steps, and to verify the exact age levels at which the discontinuity in developmental trends occurs.

Table 7.3 summarises the results of the *t*-tests performed within tasks, comparing adjacent years. Data from 20 randomly selected subjects, from each year, were used in the *t*-tests. Inspection of Table 7.3 shows that in the column comparing six and seven year olds significant differences appeared for most tasks (13 significant *t*-values), and again in the next column (11 significant *t*-values) between ages seven and eight. The next two age groups, eight and nine, differed on only four tasks, and one of these differences, in the visual–visual velocity discrimination task, was due to a reversal of the developmental trend (see Fig. 7.16j). Nine and 10 year olds differed on six tasks, while the 10 and 11 year olds differed from each other on only three tasks. The results indicated that the six and seven year olds form two distinct developmental groups, the eight and nine year olds, and the 10 and 11 year olds can be considered as the next two groups, while the status of the 12 year olds is uncertain (5 significant differences are recorded between ages 11 and 12).

Table 7.3   *Differences between adjacent ages.*

	Age (years)					
Tasks	6–7	7–8	8–9	9–10	10–11	11–12
Ward moving	***$t=3.39$	*$t=2.32$		***$t=3.4$		
Video game	***$t=5.32$		**$t=4$			**$t=3.17$
Ball catching	***$t=7.68$	***$t=3.94$		*$t=2.43$		*$t=2.04$
Grasp	***$t=6.19$	***$t=5.48$				
Drawing errors	*$t=2.07$					
⅄ Errors	*$t=2.57$	**$t=3.56$				
∧ Errors		***$t=11.52$	***$t=5.73$		***$t=5.83$	*$t=2.37$
Drawing time					**$t=2.93$	
⅄ Time	*$t=2.36$	**$t=2.07$	**$t=2.9$		**$t=3.47$	
∧ Time						
Dotting errors	***$t=3.5$	**$t=2.6$				
Dotting time	***$t=3.38$					*$t=2.05$
Kinaesthetic acuity						
Kinaesthetic perception						
Velocity V–V	*$t=2.21$	**$t=2.9$	**$t=3.77$	**$t=3.58$		
Velocity K–K	***$t=4.1$	*$t=2.09$		*$t=2.48$		
Velocity V–K	***$t=4.1$	*$t=1.98$		*$t=2.48$		
Balance	**$t=3.31$	**$t=2.94$		*$t=2.03$		*$t=2.86$

Level of significance: $*=P<0.05$, $**=P<0.01$, $***=P<0.001$. *d.f. =38.*
⅄$=Drawing\ between\ lines;$ ∧ $=tracing\ over\ the\ line.$

This exploratory examination of the data was followed by a set of analyses of variance, comparing two adjacent age groups over all tasks (two factors, repeated measures on one factor, Ferguson, 1981) to verify the nature of the developmental trends further. In order to make comparisons across tasks possible, raw scores were converted to standard, or Z scores and these were used in the analyses (Miller, 1975). The number of tasks included in the analyses decreased with increasing age because tasks which showed a small between-subject variance at any one age were omitted from the analyses.

Table 7.4 *Developmental trends: two factor analysis of variance with repeated measures on one factor on standard scores.*

Ages in years compared	
6 versus 7	Age F=18.21 (d.f.=1, 58)** Tasks F= 7.86 (d.f.=16, 928)** Age×tasks interaction F=3.62 (d.f.=16, 928)**
7 versus 8	Age F=54.92 (d.f.=1, 58)** Tasks F= 4.39 (d.f.=16, 928)** Age×tasks interaction F=7.76 (d.f.=16, 928)**
8 versus 9	Age F= 0.57 (d.f.=1, 58) N.S. Tasks F= 0.39 (d.f.=16, 928) N.S. Age×tasks interaction F=1.08 (d.f.=16, 928) N.S.
9 versus 10	Age F=12.94 (d.f.=1, 58)** Tasks F= 0.52 (d.f.=16, 928) N.S. Age×tasks interaction F=0.91 (d.f.=16, 928) N.S.
10 versus 11	Age F= 1.21 (d.f.=1, 38) N.S. Tasks F= 1.24 (d.f.=14, 532) N.S. Age×tasks interaction F=0.8 (d.f.=14, 532) N.S.
10 versus 12	Age F= 1.29 (d.f.=1, 38) N.S. Tasks F= 2.86 (d.f.=14, 532)** Age×tasks interaction F=2.14 (d.f.=14, 532)**
11 versus 12	Age F= 4.34 (d.f.=1, 38)* Tasks F= 2.14 (d.f.=14, 532)** Age×tasks interaction F=0.91 (d.f.=14, 532) N.S.
12 versus $\overline{M}$ 23.1 (adult)	Age F=10.04 (d.f.=1, 38)** Tasks F= 4.44 (d.f.=11, 418)** Age×tasks interaction F=1.75 (d.f.=11, 418) N.S.

*Level of significance: *=$P<0.05$, **=$P<0.01$, N.S. =not significant. F=F ratio.*

Table 7.4 summarises the results gained from these analyses. The findings shown in Table 7.3 are confirmed. It can be stated, with confidence, that six and seven, eight to nine, and 10 to 11 year olds form four distinct groups. Again, the placement of the 12 year olds differed significantly from 11 year olds, but not from the 10 year olds. It is possible that the difference between ages 11 and 12 is attributable to the relatively high error scores gained by the 11-year-old sample. Indeed, 11-year-old children showed marked deterioration in performance on the video game, in kinaesthetic acuity and in the kinaesthetic–kinaesthetic and visual–kinaesthetic velocity discrimination condition compared to the 10 year olds' performance (Figure 7.16b, h and j). The 11-year-old children were also markedly slower than the 10-year-old children in the drawing and tracing tasks. The reason for the inferior performance level of the 11-year-old children versus the 10 year olds is not known at present, but a possible explanation can be put forward. It is conceivable that at this age a change occurs in the mode of kinaesthetic processing. It is not suggested that the children become less sensitive to kinaesthesis, but that their processing style, due to increased sensitivity towards kinaesthetic input, changes to a more analytical and more detailed mode of processing. However, by 12 years of age the increased sensitivity to kinaesthetic information allows efficient error correction. In the perceptual tasks (kinaesthetic acuity, kinaesthetic–kinaesthetic and kinaesthetic–visual velocity discrimination) the new processing style may introduce some uncertainty and this might be the reason for the drop in performance.

Hay (1978, 1979) argues that changes in information processing can be the reason for the performance decrement she found in an aiming task in seven-year-old children. Fine error corrective programming depends on efficient processing of kinaesthetic information. It was on those tasks of the Perceptual–Motor Abilities Test in which fine error corrective programming was most necessary that the 11-year-old children performed at a lower level than the 10 year olds. If the 11-year-old children are in the process of developing a 'more careful', more detailed analytical aproach to handling kinaesthetic information, then this new approach might explain the increase in time taken to complete the drawing and tracing tasks. At this stage of kinaesthetic development the increased sensitivity to kinaesthetic input would, in effect, increase the amount of information the child would need to consider before error corrective programmes can be initiated. Thus, at this age level kinaesthetic processing would take longer than either the cruder processing of the younger age group, or the more practised and skilful information handling of the older child. In the video game, the advantage of fine error detection would be outweighed by the delay introduced by slow processing of the information. Though error corrective programing would be initiated, the corrective movement would be made too late for interception of the target.

It is reasonable, on the basis of the performance scores, to group the three ages, 10, 11 and 12, together, but it is important to remember that each of these age groups reaches the same performance level through different abilities and strategies.

It could be argued that by 10 years asymptotic level is reached in a number of tasks, and hence the grouping of the three oldest groups is due to a ceiling effect reached in these tasks. The significant F ratio for the 'age main effect' between adults and 12 year olds negates this possibility.

Factors underlying the stepwise changes in developmental trends

The results thus far presented show that development of perceptual-motor efficiency follows an uneven, stepwise course. It is essential to examine the reasons responsible for the sudden, age-related increases in efficiency. It is hypothesised that with the steep improvement of a perceptual or motor ability at a certain age, the performance of tasks relying on underlying processes will change. The implication can be drawn that the sudden refinement in perceptual and motor processes are maturationally determined, and that the subsequent improvement in ability can be enhanced by practice on relevant, process-dependent tasks. If factor analyses show different factor structures at different age levels, examination of these factors could reveal the underlying process structure characteristic of the different stages of development. Taking the four distinct developmental stages which were identified previously (Tables 7.3 and 7.4), four factor analyses were performed, one each for ages 6, 7, 8 and 11 (100 subjects in each group), including performance scores for all the tasks in which between-subject variance is evident. Varimax rotated factor matrix, after Kaiser normalisation was used in the factor analyses (Nie *et al*, 1975b). The emerging factor structures are detailed in Table 7.5.

Table 7.5 *Factor analysis. Varimax rotated factor matrix after rotation with Kaiser normalisation.*

Six year olds
3 Factors:

Factor 1		Factor 2		Factor 3	
Eigenvalue = 2.66		Eigenvalue	= 1.52	Eigenvalue	= 1.28
	K–K = 0.91	Λ Error	= 0.75	Ward moving	= 0.74
Discrimination V–V	= 0.55	Å Error	= 0.57	Ward stationary	= 0.68
	V–K = 0.55	Dotting error	= 0.47	Ball catching	= 0.33
		Balance error	= 0.33		

Seven year olds
3 Factors:

Factor 1		Factor 2		Factor 3	
Eigenvalue = 2.33		Eigenvalue	= 1.52	Eigenvalue	= 1.19
	K–K = 0.87	Å Error	= 0.70	Ward moving	= 0.79
Discrimination V–K	= 0.61	Λ Error	= 0.64	Ward stationary	= 0.68
	V–V = 0.56	Dotting error	= 0.38	Ball catching	= 0.20
		Balance error	= 0.25		

Eight year olds
3 Factors:

Factor 1		Factor 2		Factor 3	
Eigenvalue = 2.38		Eigenvalue	= 2.10	Eigenvalue	= 1.37
	V–V = 0.88	Video game	= 0.61	Dotting error	= 0.50
Discrimination K–K	= 0.83	Ball catching	= 0.61	Grasp time	= 0.45
	V–K = 0.75	Ward moving	= 0.39	Ward moving	= 0.42
		Ward stationary	= 0.38	Ward stationary	= 0.40
				Drawing error	= 0.40

11 year olds
3 Factors:

Factor 1		Factor 2		Factor 3	
Eigenvalue = 2.09		Eigenvalue	= 1.79	Eigenvalue	= 1.12
	V–V = 0.81	RT	= 0.35	Kinaesthetic	
Discrimination K–K	= 0.80	Ward stationary	= 0.95	perception	= 0.56
	V–K = 0.80	Ward moving	= 0.67	Dotting time	= 0.50
				Grasp time	= 0.31

Velocity discrimination emerged as the first factor in all four analyses. It was evident that the judgement of movement velocity was dependent on a perceptual factor, independent of modality. That is, the encoding process was the same, whether the information was delivered visually, kinaesthetically or by a combination of these modalities. It is shown in Fig. 7.16j that this encoding process improved with age.

The analyses of variance (one factor, repeated measures; Ferguson, 1981) compared the three velocity discrimination tasks within each age group. The results of the analyses are given in Table 7.6. Only at ages nine and 11 do the conditions differ significantly from each other. At age nine the visual–visual judgement was slower than the kinaesthetic or mixed condition, while at age 11 the mixed condition scored at the lowest level (Table 7.2). It would be expected that the kinaesthetically based velocity judgements would be more difficult than the visually based judgements in the two youngest age groups since kinaesthetic acuity is poorly developed at that age (Chapter 6 and Fig. 7.16h). It seemed, however, that only in the development of spatial perception did visual precede kinaesthetic information processing, but that in velocity judgements the two information channels showed the same rate of development. Changes in the velocity of movements are signalled separately from spatial movement information by the kinaesthetic receptors (see Matthews, 1972, on the muscle spindle). It might be argued that the kinaesthetic input generated by velocity changes is easier to process than that generated by changes in the direction of the movement.

Table 7.6 *Velocity discrimination: one factor analysis of variance with repeated measures — between conditions: V–V; K–K; V–K.*

Age (years)		
6	Subjects	$F= 3.39$ (d.f.$= 19, 38$)**
	Conditions	$F= 1.56$ (d.f.$=2, 38$) N.S.
7	Subjects	$F= 6.23$ (d.f.$= 19, 38$)**
	Conditions	$F= 0.25$ (d.f.$=2, 38$) N.S.
8	Subjects	$F= 9.98$ (d.f.$= 19, 38$)**
	Conditions	$F= 2.14$ (d.f.$=2, 38$) N.S.
9	Subjects	$F= 4.05$ (d.f.$= 19, 38$)**
	Conditions	$F= 4.02$ (d.f.$=2, 38$)*
10	Subjects	$F= 3.02$ (d.f.$= 19, 38$)**
	Conditions	$F= 0.46$ (d.f.$=2, 38$) N.S.
11	Subjects	$F=12.27$ (d.f.$= 19, 38$)**
	Conditions	$F= 8.96$ (d.f.$=2, 38$)**
12	Subjects	$F= 2.57$ (d.f.$= 19, 38$)**
	Conditions	$F= 0.35$ (d.f.$=2, 38$) N.S.

Level of significance: $*=P < 0.05$, $**=P < 0.01$, *N.S. = not significant. F=F ratio.*

A very similar factor structure was obtained for six and seven year olds. Factor 2 can be considered as the 'steadiness' factor. Performance on all four tasks loading on this factor is greatly influenced by steady, unwavering execution of the movement or posture. Factor 3 appeared to be task- rather than process-orientated, relating to the handling of moving balls. Factor 3 could not be labelled the spatio-temporal programming factor as only three of the four tasks depending on the spatio-temporal programming ability load on this factor. The video game, which should be grouped with the other three tasks to reflect spatio-temporal programming ability, is the one task which does not involve rolling or catching balls.

At age eight years, Factors 2 and 3 clearly relate to programming processes. All four tasks which rely on spatio-temporal programming processes load on Factor 2, while all tasks dependent on spatial programming load on Factor 3.

Seemingly independent tasks are grouped under Factors 2 and 3 in the 11-year-old analysis.

Overall, the results of the factor analyses support the notion that proficiency in the programming parameters improves at different rates, and that at eight years performance on various tasks is determined by the level of development of these processes. From 11 years onwards, however, isolated programming factors do not play a decisive role in perceptual-motor performance.

Theoretical considerations

Consideration of the results presented in this chapter lead to the formulation of some general principles relevant to the perceptual-motor development of children between the ages 5–12 years.

The youngest two age groups perform both perceptual and motor tasks at a low level of efficiency. They seem to rely on trial and error methods rather than on planned task strategies. Kinaesthetic information processing is poor at this stage. At eight and nine years, children can be characterised by their stereotyped response style. Movements are often repeated without change in the response pattern. Performance at different tasks seems to be determined by processes involved in the spatio-temporal or spatial programming of movement. The rigid movement pattern prevents adaptive behaviour which is necessary when responding to changing environmental input as in the Ward game with moving target.

From 10 years and onward, two additional factors develop extensively: planning and error corrective programming. The behavioural evidence obtained from the test results relevant to the development of movement planning is supported by a recent neurophysiological study in which motor task-related brain-evoked potentials were recorded (Chiarenza *et al*, 1983). It was shown that 'skilled performance positive potentials', which precede a skilled movement, are present from 10 years, but do not appear at an earlier age. These authors conclude that below the age of 10 children do not use information about earlier responses for the formulation of movement 'strategies' (p 381) for subsequent performance. Response style becomes flexible, indicating that task strategies are well planned, and that the movement parameters are generated in accordance with planned task strategies. The significant improvement in the Ward game with moving target between ages nine and 10 (Table 7.3) can be quoted here as this task depends heavily on well-developed planning ability and concomitant spatio-temporal programming. Improvement in error corrective programming is made possible by the development of kinaesthetic sensitivity, which is necessary in error detection, and by improved motor programming ability. Evidence for error corrective programming can be found when considering the significant improvements shown in such tasks as the video game, tracing over a line, dotting and balance.

Changes in performance, due to the advance in planning and error corrective programming abilities, can be demonstrated with the drawing and tracing tasks. In the drawing task, planning the movement is followed by spatial programming and error corrective programming. By contrast, in the tracing tasks, planning of the movement is minimal. Error corrective programming demands vary between the two tracing tasks according to the error tolerance set by each task. In tracing between the lines, with 3 mm error tolerance, a less developed error corrective programming ability is necessary than when tracing over the line, where error tolerance is reduced to 1 mm. It can be seen when examining Fig. 7.16e that tracing between the lines, the task with low error corrective programming demands, develops at a faster rate than tracing over the line with high error corrective demands, and drawing, where both planning and possible error correction are important factors.

It is of interest to compare the performance of the different age groups in the two conditions of the video game as an example of development in ability to programme movements to suit changing task demands. Table 7.7 shows that from 10 years onwards children could perform the two conditions with equal facility, while the performance of the younger children differed significantly between the two conditions. They hit significantly more targets in Condition 1 than in Condition 2.

Table 7.7 *t-tests comparing Conditions 1 and 2 of the video game (d.f. = 38).*

Age (years)	t	P<
6	12.26	0.001
7	10.94	0.001
8	3.16	0.01
9	2.35	0.05
10	1.55	N.S.
11	1.95	N.S.
12	0.83	N.S.

N.S. = not significant.

In Condition 1 the target always appeared on the edge furthest from the child and travelled directly towards him. In Condition 2 targets were presented from three edges of the screen, and moved diagonally across the screen. The exact direction of the diagonal route could not be predicted by the child.

In Condition 1 the target could be intercepted by quickly moving the light pen across the screen and waiting for the target. Even the youngest two age groups could hit some targets, though by observing the children, hits often seemed more a matter of luck than skill. However, the haphazard strategy adopted in Condition 1 proved unsuccessful in Condition 2. With the development of spatio-temporal programming in the eight and nine year olds Condition 1 performance improved markedly, but in Condition 2, with unpredictable target movements, the hit rate was still significantly lower than in Condition 1. Only when error corrective programming abilities have sufficiently developed, from 10 years onwards, did the children perform the two conditions with equal facility. At these ages the spatio-temporal programme was generated in both conditions according to target demands and when necessary the light pen movement could be corrected both in direction and speed, if the child perceived that the target and pen would not meet.

Evidence for developmental trends in the third programming parameter, i.e. force programming, could not be obtained. The mean drift over the 10 second trial period in the six-year-old group was 120 g. The mean half maximal force at this age was 1500 g, thus the drift represents only 8% force deviation which is a negligible error.

In a recent article (Gachoud *et al*, 1983) the development of movement strategies in lifting objects was described. There was no change in the observed response between children aged five years and adults, yet when the skill was analysed in terms of movement strategies, expressed as differential force production between agonist and antagonist muscles, a clear development trend could be demonstrated. The fully developed motor strategy used by adults depends on an awareness of the potentials and limitations of the motor system and on experience with lifting objects of various sizes and weights. Such an awareness is developed to some extent by the age of nine, though not at age five. Gachoud *et al* (1983) showed that the developmental progression in force maintenance is not reflected in the overt response, but is evident when detailed electromyogram (EMG) output from both agonist and antagonist muscle groups is recorded. The recorded EMG pattern would be a direct reflection of the motor unit activation patterns, which in turn represents the motor programming strategy. Improvement with age would be evident in the motor unit activation pattern, showing increasing efficiency in the motor programme.

Kinaesthetic sensitivity, its importance in motor control and its role in error detection and hence correction, is fully discussed in Chapters 6 and 8. Kinaesthetic sensitivity develops gradually with age and kinaesthetic ability is necessary for the performance of all motor tasks. It could be mentioned here that marked improvement in kinaesthetic sensitivity occurs concurrently with the emergence of error corrective function (Fig. 7.16h).

Summarising the issues discussed in this section, the following conclusions can be reached:

1. Developmental trends are established for all test tasks other than the force maintenance task.
2. Evidence for a general motor abilities factor could not be obtained. On the contrary, specific motor programming abilities develop at different ages and these contribute to the age-related improvement in skilled performance.
3. The ability to plan a strategy for the performance of a task and an advanced error corrective programming ability develop last, and these abilities might be considered responsible for the flexible and adaptive performance style of the older child.

Sex differences and handedness

In one task only, static whole body balance, could significant sex differences be demonstrated at seven, eight and nine years ($t = 2.64$, d.f. 98, $P < 0.02$; $t = 2.02$, d.f. 98, $P < 0.05$; and $t = 3.15$; d.f. 21, $P < 0.01$ respectively). In measuring control of body sway Kohen-Raz and Hiriartborde (1979) also found that girls were better than boys at this task at five to nine years of age.

There is some evidence indicating sex differences in perceptual function. Freeman and Kelham (1981), in discussing a shape orientation matching task with seven-year-old children, found girls to be better at the task than boys. Laszlo *et al* (1980) presented evidence in support of the superiority of boys over girls aged 7–12 years in a pursuit tracking task. This superiority occurs only when distracting auditory stimuli are introduced into the test situation. The specific nature of the sex differences in perceptual abilities should be investigated in future research.

The motor skill literature (review by Maccoby and Jacklin, 1974) provides conflicting findings on sex differences in motor skills in children. Arguments are invoked to support either innate or culturally determined factors, in order to explain the observed sex differences.

The process-orientated testing approach proves to be a useful technique in resolving this conflict. Motor programming processes, as measured by novel tasks, develop at an equal rate and to an equal degree in boys and girls, indicating that there is no innate sex difference in motor abilities. In experiments and tests where sex differences are found in some tasks they may be due to culturally determined, motivational or practice effects.

Significant differences between right- and left-handed children could not be found in the present tests when the preferred hand is defined as the hand used in writing and drawing. Six- and seven-year-old children indicated their hand preference by picking up a pencil offered to them, while the older children were asked to show the hand which they normally used for writing and drawing.

During testing some of the children from the two youngest age groups used either hand, even during a single task, e.g. sometimes using their right and sometimes their left hand to roll the balls in the Ward game. The older children showed consistent hand preference throughout the test.

The absence of significant differences between right- and left-handed children when tested on this process-orientated test argues strongly against innate motor ability differences in these two groups.

PRACTICAL CONSIDERATIONS

The time taken to administer the test varied between 90 and 120 minutes, with the younger children needing the longest time. This time included a 10 minute break, half-way through the test, during which refreshments were offered. The total time of testing compared favourably with most other tests like those reviewed in Chapter 5.

Children were brought to the laboratory in pairs and each child was tested by one tester for the entire test battery.

Children found the testing session enjoyable and often described it as 'great fun', asking to be allowed to repeat it. They showed disappointment when they were told that repeated participation was not possible. On request they listed the tasks they liked best, with the Ward game, video game and ball catching gaining the most votes as favourites. The choice of the favourite task was independent of the success the child achieved in the task. The finding that children did not get upset by failure, even when failure was obvious, as in the ball catching task, must be considered as a favourable aspect of the test battery.

All the tasks were easily explained and even the youngest children could follow the instructions without undue difficulties, thus rapport established with the child was not undermined by difficult and repeated explanations.

The scoring procedures should also be mentioned. All scores were objective quantitative measures of performance (see Chapter 5). Performance scores of each trial in each task were recorded during testing, using individual scoring sheets for each task. Following completion of the testing session, the raw scores were totalled to give a single performance score for each task for each child. Each child's scores were recorded on a data summary sheet. Using this procedure, the large number of data points recorded during testing could be reduced in number without loss of information.

No further score transformation is necessary. A child's perceptual-motor status is established directly from the task scores. If a child gains low scores, for his age, on a group of tasks which depend on one perceptual or motor ability, the child is diagnosed as being deficient in that particular ability and therapy would consist of training him to improve that ability.

Finally, the clinical applicability of the test must be considered. The ease of administration of the test items, and the objective scoring procedures make the test suitable for the clinical setting. Only the ball catching task need be modified so that children confined to wheelchairs may be tested on this item.

The equipment used in the Perceptual-Motor Abilities Test is not portable. It is envisaged that the test could be set up in major assessment centres, and children would be referred to these centres for testing.

The results of the reported work on the Perceptual-Motor Abilities Test support the process-orientated approach as a potentially useful and appropriate test battery for the establishment of developmental trends for perceptual-motor processes, and for the assessment of perceptual-motor deficiencies. It is fully realised, however, that before a test manual can be produced some additional refinements relating to sampling and data analysis should be undertaken. In addition the reliability and validity of the test needs to be confirmed.

8 IMPROVEMENT IN SKILLED MOTOR PERFORMANCE THROUGH TRAINING OF ABILITIES

RELATING DIAGNOSIS AND THERAPY

There are four types of diagnostic approaches which can be distinguished: the task-orientated approach; the approach focused on general processes; an approach based on global diagnosis; and the process-orientated approach. Each of these methods leads to different therapeutic consequences.

Task-orientated tests (e.g. Gubbay, 1975; Stott, Moyes and Henderson, 1972) establish the child's performance level, relative to norms for his age, in a number of skills. The skills are chosen somewhat arbitrarily, often with the aim of including ecologically valid, everyday tasks. The tests describe the child's motor status either as an index of motor proficiency, or as a performance profile. This approach can identify the tasks on which the child has difficulties. Teaching or therapy can be directed at the motor tasks which were performed with least proficiency.

The diagnostic system advocated by Ayres (1972a) is aimed at defining process dysfunctions. Based on her theory of sensory integration, she claims that four sensory integrative dysfunctions underlie impairment of perceptual-motor behaviour. Dysfunction in each of these four domains leads to four distinct therapeutic programmes. The aim of the therapy is to correct neural malfunction. The strong criticism that can be levelled against this approach is exemplified in Cratty's review (1981). He points out that there is a lack of evidence supporting the theory of sensory integration. It is hypothesised in the theory, though not substantiated experimentally, that the practice of an activity can alleviate neural malfunction. As a result of the improved brain function, general improvement in the child's behaviour should become apparent, even in areas unrelated to the tasks the child practises during therapy.

Four independent dysfunctions were said to be identifiable with the aid of the Ayres' test and each dysfunction should yield distinctly different profiles. In practice, besides the expected four profiles, any number of score profiles emerge which are not predicted, and cannot be explained by the theory. In terms of therapy, the haphazard combination of test items on which a child might score badly negates the validity of prescribing any one of the four specific dysfunction-orientated training programmes.

Only the most global diagnostic demands are made by therapists who follow the undifferentiated, generalised training programmes. The Doman–Delacato system (Doman *et al*, 1960) can be mentioned here as an example of this approach. An extensive, uniform training schedule is prescribed on the basis of general diagnostic labels, such as severe brain injury. The training method is both energy- and time-consuming and improvement in behaviour resulting from the therapy is not measured.

The fourth diagnostic system is process-orientated (Chapter 7). This method focuses on individual perceptual-motor processes which are defined in the closed-loop model of perceptual motor function (Chapter 2). This approach aims at measuring abilities in relation to each process separately to achieve a causal diagnosis, and to describe the focal difficulty the child might experience in one or more perceptual-motor abilities. Therapy is focused on remediation of specific, underlying difficulties.

An unfortunate outcome of some systems of assessment is the attachment of a descriptive label to the child. Motor activity, as is pointed out in Chapters 1 and 2, forms the basis for the expression of psychological processes. A person's general functional capabilities, thoughts and feelings can only be expressed through movement. It follows that any descriptive label of motor dysfunction might have a wide-ranging impact on how a child's overall status is perceived by himself and others. It is unfortunate that some diagnostic terms used in this area carry emotive overtones. Clumsy is a derogatory term, and minimal brain dysfunction has connotations of low capabilities relevant to more than just the motor domain. Indeed, minimal brain dysfunction can have several meanings. Does it mean that the entire brain is minimally dysfunctional, or is a minimal, unspecified area of the brain functioning abnormally? Furthermore, labels are often attached to the child, not to his condition, i.e. the child is clumsy or the child is a 'minimal brain dysfunction child'.

The labelling of the child can have far-reaching and undesirable consequences, causing hopelessness and despair for the child and his parents. 'On the whole more harm than help arises from indiscriminant labelling of children as clumsy' (Holt, 1977, p 202). It is a more positive and desirable approach to restrict the diagnosis to the condition. Test procedures generate performance indices which could be used as descriptive terms of the child's condition. The child could be found to suffer from general motor disability, or of motor incapacity, or show slower than usual motor development. Admittedly, these terms are not precise, but they are no less so than 'clumsy' or 'minimal brain dysfunction'. Yet recognising the condition might be helpful in some cases. If a child is thought to be lazy, negligent and resisting help from the teacher, a report from the paediatrician or clinical psychologist gives authoritative recognition to the difficulties the child is experiencing. This might change the teacher's attitude towards the child, with a resultant decrease in tension and disapproval. The expectations of the teacher regarding the child's progress can become more realistic (Kinsbourne, 1980).

The task-orientated approach, by its nature, yields a limited evaluation of the child's performance, restricting assessment of motor difficulties to tasks included in the test battery. Therapeutic methods evolving from such an approach can be aimed at improving performance on the tasks on which the child showed low levels of proficiency. This approach falls short of the high standard of the 'medical model'. To illustrate, the medical practitioner is called to a child who suffers from severe abdominal pain. After examination and the necessary tests, the diagnosis of acute appendicitis is arrived at. The medical practitioner recommends immediate surgical intervention, appendectomy is performed, and in due course, the child recovers and the original symptoms are eliminated. In the case of a child suffering from a motor disability, a task-orientated assessment will confirm the motor disability (equivalent to confirming the severe abdominal pain), but will not diagnose the cause of the disability. In the treatment of any condition the most effective approach would approximate the medical model — by diagnosing, then treating the cause of the condition. The approach to assessment and therapy presented in this book has process-orientated methods as the goal. The following sections show how such an approach has proved to be of great benefit in particular cases of motor disability.

ESTABLISHING THE LINK BETWEEN PROCESS-ORIENTATED DIAGNOSIS AND THERAPY

The necessary steps to establish the link between diagnosis and therapy are listed below:

Step 1:   Establishing, through experimental verification, the theoretical framework on which the diagnostic test is to be based.
Step 2:   Defining, experimentally, the contribution made by each process described in the theory and clarifying the relationship between the processes.
Step 3:   Selecting test items, to measure abilities in relation to each process separately; the scores to represent a direct measure of ability, uncontaminated by extraneous factors.
Step 4:   Collecting normative data for each item and establishing the reliability and validity of the items.
Step 5:   Applying the test items to clinical samples to ascertain the suitability of the tasks for the physically handicapped child.

These five steps establish the test as a diagnostic tool.

Step 6:   Providing evidence that the abilities measured can be improved.
Step 7:   Devising training methods which can lead to improvement of the ability.
Step 8:   Quantifying the improvement.
Step 9:   Demonstrating the long-term effect of training-induced improvement in ability.
Step 10: Establishing that improvement in ability has beneficial effects on motor activities.

The last five steps provide the necessary evidence for establishing the viability and the usefulness of the proposed therapeutic programme.

   Within the framework of the closed-loop model of perceptual-motor behaviour all component processes have been investigated (Chapter 2), but only in regard to kinaesthetic abilities has the investigation proceeded through all the steps, and hence the diagnostic–therapeutic relationship fully established. In the next section, work relating to kinaesthetic abilities is described, tracing the development of the investigation from its theoretical beginnings to its applied conclusion.

KINAESTHESIS: ITS TRAINING AND RELATIONSHIP TO MOTOR CONTROL

In 1963 the role of kinaesthesis in skilled motor performance was a subject of extensive debate, but evidence was available mostly from experiments conducted on animals (Taub and Berman, 1963). Work on the functional characteristics of kinaesthesis in man was commenced in the author's laboratory in that year (Laszlo, 1966, 1967a,b, 1968) and is still in progress. The importance of kinaesthesis in the acquisition and performance of motor skills has been delineated. The relationships between kinaesthesis, vision and corollary discharge was also explored, and a closed-loop model of perceptual-motor behaviour was proposed. The work was extended to define further components of the model: the Standard and the Motor Programming Unit (Laszlo and Bairstow, 1971a). Concurrently with the detailed analysis of each component process, the relationship between the processes was also investigated. Thus the first two steps described in the previous section were satisfied.

The idea of testing kinaesthetic function emerged gradually as a natural extension of the experimental–theoretical work. As experimentation progressed and the crucial importance of kinaesthetic ability in motor control emerged, the oversight of this factor in the motor development literature became less and less acceptable. While the developmental progressions in other sensory systems, especially vision, were considered, kinaesthesis was hardly ever mentioned. Indeed, the word kinaesthesis, or its synonyms, was often conspicuous by its absence from the 'Index' pages of most books on motor development, one notable exception being Holle's (1976) *Motor Development in Children*, where the importance of kinaesthesis was emphasised and discussed in relation to practical issues.

The need for tests to measure kinaesthetic development became obvious. Such tests could be used in charting kinaesthetic development and could also be applied in the diagnosis of kinaesthetic dysfunction. To fulfil this need the Kinaesthetic Sensitivity Test was constructed (Chapter 6) which involved Steps 3–5 of the previous section. With the aid of the Kinaesthetic Sensitivity Test diagnosis of kinaesthetic difficulties became possible, and attention could now be focused on therapeutic methods aimed at improving kinaesthetic perception where this was found to be deficient.

Improvement in a perceptual ability can only occur if the ability is not a fixed characteristic of an individual, but is open to behavioural manipulation. Certainly, evidence is available to show that kinaesthetic abilities improve with age, as shown in Chapters 6 and 7. Also, Gibson (1953) described improvement in visual, tactile and auditory perception as a consequence of practice. Even without 'hard scientific evidence' it is recognised that wine tasters are trained, not born, and while a 'sensitive nose' is a prerequisite in perfume testing, 'noses' can be trained on the job by perfume manufacturers. Gibson and Gibson (1955) came to the conclusion that there is irrefutable evidence which shows that sensory thresholds are not innately fixed, and discrimination can often be enhanced with practice. There is no reason to suppose that the kinaesthetic modality is an exception to this rule.

Indeed, there is evidence that practice in kinaesthetically reliant skills can enhance kinaesthetic perception. In the course of collecting normative data on kinaesthetic abilities, a seven-year-old girl, Jodi, was tested on the kinaesthetic perception and memory task. She performed the task with ease and elegance, and between patterns volunteered the information that: 'This is easy — feels just like ballet.' When asked what she meant, since dancing and tracing a pattern with a stylus are very different tasks, she said: 'I don't care, they feel the same.' She was correct in her observation. The commonality between ballet and the pattern reorientation task did not lie in the type of movement, but in the common perceptual demand imposed by the two tasks. Jodi's comments were a stimulus to a series of studies in which the effect of ballet practice on kinaesthetic ability was investigated. It was also a clear demonstration that listening to a subject's comments can prove valuable at times.

In these follow-up studies (Bairstow and Laszlo, 1981) ballet dancers and gymnasts obtained significantly higher scores on the test of kinaesthetic perception and memory than individuals engaged in other sport activities. Ballet and gymnastics demand precise control in body and limb positioning and in the timing, force and accuracy of movements. Kinaesthetic information is the only channel through which the performer can concurrently monitor all aspects of these skills. During ballet and gymnastics training, kinaesthetic ability is also developed.

A further and even more direct measure of acquired reliance on kinaesthesis in the absence of vision was found when testing blind adults on the Kinaesthetic Sensitivity Test. These subjects showed amazing accuracy in kinaesthetic perception and memory. In fact, the best performance ever recorded was obtained from one of the blind subjects (mean error was 7°).

These studies support Gibson and Gibson (1955), and show that kinaesthetic ability can be affected and improved by practice of suitable motor skills. This satisfies Step 6.

Two studies of kinaesthetic training (Laszlo and Bairstow, 1983)

Study 1. Training in kinaesthetic acuity or discrimination

In this study 11 seven-year-old children were used, all of whom obtained low scores on the kinaesthetic acuity test. The four 10 minute training sessions followed the pretraining test, and each session was held on consecutive days.

The runway apparatus and masking box were used in training (Chapter 6 for details on the apparatus). In the first session the runways were set at a 20° difference from each other, with the masking box covering the runways. The child's hands, holding the two pegs, were guided up and down the runways as many times as was necessary for the child to decide which hand went up higher. Even with this large separation between the runways, the children often found this task very difficult. If the child was unable to correctly discriminate between the hands, the masking box was removed, and he was shown the large difference between the height of the runways. The masking box was then replaced, and without changing the runway settings, the trial was resumed. This time, the child knew which side was set higher, and he was asked whether he could 'feel' the difference. Typically, by the end of the 10 minute trial the child could confidently discriminate the 20° difference using kinaesthetic information alone and without visual cueing. The next session was started by 18° runway separation. Once the child could discriminate this difference with ease, the angle of separation was gradually reduced by 2° steps. During training care was taken to vary at random the side on which the runway was set higher. On the day following the fourth training session the children were retested on the standard kinaesthetic acuity test.

The results showed that the training improved kinaesthetic acuity. The pre-test and post-test scores differed significantly from each other ($t = 6.6$, d.f. 10, $P < 0.001$). The most surprising result was that the children reached adult performance level after the four 10 minute training sessions. Yet, only five days earlier their kinaesthetic acuity score was low; indeed, quite a number of them had performed randomly on the test. Some critics could argue that these poor performers were the children who either could not understand the instructions in the first test situation, or were not motivated to perform well. The first criticism was countered in Chapter 6, where it was pointed out that any difficulty the child might experience in understanding the instructions would become obvious during the preliminary, visually guided trials. Testing would not be started until evidence of clear understanding of task demands was obtained.

However, both critical points lose their import when the behaviour of the children in the first training session is considered. The amazed, even horrified exclamations that were voiced by the children when the masking box was removed and the 20° runway separation was visually exposed, were enough to quell the above criticisms. The children certainly knew what was expected of them, and they seemed to be highly motivated indeed!

Eight weeks after the training was completed, nine of the 11 children (two had left the school in the meantime) were tested on the kinaesthetic acuity task. Their scores were significantly better than prior to training ($t = 5.43$, d.f. 8, $P < 0.001$) though significant deterioration, between the immediate post-training and later results, was found. The children, eight weeks after training, performed at the 11-year-old level, not at the adult level as was shown immediately after training (Steps 7–9).

Study 2. Training in kinaesthetic perception and memory

Twenty children from a regular school, aged seven and eight years were included. Children who scored one standard deviation below the mean on the kinaesthetic perception and memory task were chosen to participate in the training programme. Six of these children performed at one standard deviation below the mean on both tasks. These six children were trained on both tasks while the other 14 received pattern training only.

Kinaesthetic acuity training was conducted as described in Study 1. In the first session of kinaesthetic perception and memory training the straight line pattern (pattern 1, Fig. 8.1) was shown to the child, who was told that this would be the only pattern on which he would practise that day. The pattern was put on the turntable, the masking box was placed over it, and the

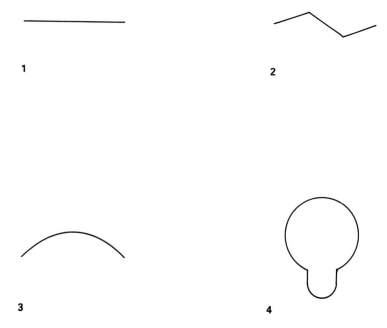

Figure 8.1 *Training patterns.*

child's hand, holding the stylus, was moved along the line four to six times. The line was then repositioned, with the child's hand resting beside the turntable, the masking box removed, and the child attempted to reorientate the line into its original position. Firstly, only horizontal and vertical settings were used since these positions were easier to perceive than the diagonal placements. Trials were then given randomly, varying the position of the line, until the child could reorientate the line with no more than a 15° error. This performance level with the straight line pattern was achieved by most children within the first 15 minutes of training. The session on the next day was started with practice of the diagonally placed straight line in order to consolidate the previous day's achievements. Next, training on the second pattern was started (pattern 2, Fig. 8.1). Once the child could reorientate a pattern within a 20° error limit the next pattern in the series was introduced. Altogether, six 15 minute training sessions were given. The six children who were trained on both tasks spent approximately 25 minutes each day on practising the tasks, starting with the runway training followed by the patterns. On completion of the training programme the children were retested on the task or tasks in which they were trained.

Significant improvement was found on the kinaesthetic perception and memory task for the 14 children trained on this task alone ($t = 5.22$, d.f. 13, $P < 0.001$) and on the acuity task in the six children who practised both tasks ($t = 5.71$, d.f. 5, $P < 0.01$) but their pattern reorientation performance did not improve significantly. The children might have felt tired after the runway practice. Pattern training should have been given on separate days.

confirmation was obtained for Step 9. The training methods devised to improve kinaesthetic acuity and kinaesthetic perception and memory proved to be successful, and the improvement was quantified by comparing pre- and post-training test performance. In kinaesthetic acuity the lasting effect of training was established. Unfortunately, the second kinaesthetic training study was carried out towards the end of the school year and hence follow-up retesting in this task was not possible.

The time necessary to improve kinaesthetic ability was only one hour for acuity, and no more than one-and-a-half hours for perception and memory. What could the children learn in such a short period of time? Woodworth (1938) argued that there is a direct perceptual motive 'to see clearly, to hear distinctly — to make out what it is one is seeing or hearing' (p 201). It seemed likely that this perceptual motive was relevant to kinaesthetic perception. The children showed pleasure in being helped to 'feel' the position and movement of their arms. Initially, in the first session the child was uncertain what he was meant to 'feel' from his arms. He knew what the task demands were, he could perform them easily when he was permitted to see what he was doing. However, in the absence of vision, he could not perform the task, either because he failed to recognise the information provided by the kinaesthetic sense, or because he could not differentiate it from other, albeit irrelevant, input which he was receiving at the time. With continued practice a sudden change occurred. The child would exclaim: 'I can feel my arms' or 'I know where my hands are'. The child often accompanied this statement with a happy smile of satisfaction. It was a clear example of the psychologist's 'Aha' phenomenon. Incidentally, the 'Aha' phenomenon was more sharply demonstrated in the acuity task than in the pattern task though it did occur during pattern reorientation as well, but to a lesser extent.

The sudden improvement could be explained by the controls introduced in the training situation. During training, extraneous input was kept to a minimum, and as the movements were passively induced there was no need for the child to control his movements actively. Thus, his attention could be focused on the kinaesthetic input. Under the conditions in which distractions from other sources of input were reduced, and motor output demands were eliminated, the kinaesthetic information was accentuated. The child became aware of the 'target' input, with a resulting improvement in kinaesthetic ability.

Sudden improvement in perceptual ability has been observed by Gibson as early as 1953. She described this, saying: 'the effectiveness of progressive practice suggests that a quality hitherto not responded to in isolation is being differentiated from the total stimulus input, and utilized as a cue variable' (p 423).

How could the child retain the high level of kinaesthetic ability outside the laboratory? Throughout everyday life kinaesthetic information is generated continuously. The child who has been made aware, through kinaesthetic training, of the position and movement of his body and limbs, could not fail 'to practise' his new perceptual skill and hence maintain his perceptual ability.

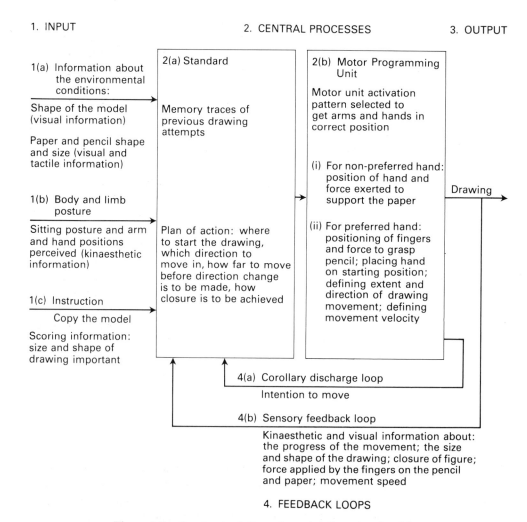

Figure 8.2 *Copying simple figures from visually presented models.*

The importance of kinaesthesis in drawing skills

In Chapter 2 the importance of kinaesthetic information in error detection and correction in the performance of motor skills was discussed. It was also said that during the execution of a skill, kinaesthetic information is stored and the memory of past experience is necessary for the trial-by-trial improvement during acquisition of the skill. It can be assumed, therefore, that adequate kinaesthetic abilities are necessary in the satisfactory performance of drawing tasks since drawing skill is heavily dependent on accurate motor control.

A drawing task, in the present instant, copying from a given model, can be represented within the framework of a closed-loop model. This is shown in Fig. 8.2.

Examination of Fig. 8.2 reveals the stages in the drawing task which depend on kinaesthesis. At the input stage (1a), body, arm and hand positions, adopted at the start of the task are perceived primarily through kinaesthesis, although some visual information might also be used. The Standard (2a) can evaluate this information, and if necessary initiate postural adjustments to support the drawing action. There are kinaesthetic memory traces in the Standard relevant to previous drawing attempts. The Standard, incorporating available information relevant to the drawing task, instructs the Motor Programming Unit (2b) to generate the appropriate motor commands. During the course of the subsequent movement, kinaesthetic information is processed by the Standard and any discrepancy between the model figure and the movement being performed is detected. Error detection can then lead to error corrective programming. It could be argued that in drawing, the visually perceived pencil line is a more important source of error information than movement-generated kinaesthetic input. However, by the time the pencil line becomes visible on the paper, it is too late to correct it. The kinaesthetic information about the ongoing progress of the movement is conveyed to the Standard. The delay between kinaesthetic and visual input is exaggerated in young children who tend to hold the pencil in such a way that their hand obscures a considerable part of their drawing. The importance of vision lies more in correctly positioning the drawing on the paper and in checking the final output than in monitoring ongoing movement. The role of vision can easily be demonstrated. The reader could place a piece of paper in front of him, pick up a pencil and with his eyes closed draw a square and a diamond, or write a sentence. On opening his eyes, he would discover that his drawings or writing is quite accurate, but that the placement of the figures might be off centre, they might overlap, or that the lines of the sentence might slope upwards or downwards. Yet, when kinaesthetic input is eliminated experimentally, paper-pencil skills cannot be performed. In the absence of kinaesthesis the subject cannot grasp the pencil, nor can he move it with sufficient accuracy to draw or write. Even the simpler task of 'writing letters in the air with the index finger' is difficult and the accuracy of the movement is greatly reduced (Laszlo and Bairstow, 1971a).

The concept of kinaesthetic readiness

Further evidence of the importance of kinaesthetic perceptual ability in drawing and writing skills can be found in the correlational data reported by Bairstow and Laszlo (1981). Significant positive correlations were found between paper-pencil skills and kinaesthetic sensitivity (Chapter 6) in six- and seven-year-old children attending regular schools.

With the aid of the Kinaesthetic Sensitivity Test the developmental norms of kinaesthetic abilities could be established. It became apparent that 33% of children in the six- and seven-year-old age groups show only rudimentary kinaesthetic abilities, i.e. that kinaesthetic abilities normally develop at a much slower rate than visual and auditory abilities. The low level of kinaesthetic abilities in these children hinders the acquisition and performance of skills which demand a high degree of accuracy, such as printing.

Some authors state (Crosby and Liston, 1976) that 10–15% of children have neurologically based problems when entering 'normal' primary schools. It is difficult to accept that up to 15% of the normal school population in the first years of schooling suffer from non-specific neural disorders, impeding their progress. It is more acceptable to explain the difficulties experienced by some of the children in terms of normal developmental trends in kinaesthetic abilities, rather than postulating neurological abnormalities. One in every three of the children entering school and attending the first two classes has not attained kinaesthetic readiness necessary for the acquisition and performance of fine paper-pencil skills. The discrepancy between curricular demands and kinaesthetic readiness can penalise one-third of our children aged six to seven years. The reason for this discrepancy is due to the lack of knowledge of normal kinaesthetic developmental trends prior to the availability of the Kinaesthetic Sensitivity Test.

Study of the effect of kinaesthetic training on drawing skills (Laszlo and Bairstow, 1983)

The choice of copying geometric figures seems an appropriate task in the investigation of the effect kinaesthetic training might play in the performance of perceptual-motor skills. Two reasons support this choice: firstly, kinaesthetic abilities are shown, in the foregoing discussion, to be necessary to the successful performance of the task; and secondly, the educational value of the task cannot be overestimated, especially when the time and effort spent on teaching paper-pencil skills in the first few years of primary school curriculum is considered. The task of copying geometric figures is selected as being representative of paper-pencil skills, and also for convenience of scoring.

The children were six and seven year olds, except one boy, Matthew, who was repeating Year 2. He was 8.5 years old at the time. He repeated Year 2 because he could not achieve an acceptable level in paper-pencil skills.

The 24 children were selected from 65 seven-year-old pupils, all of whom were tested on the Kinaesthetic Sensitivity Test. Three groups of eight children were chosen. The children who were allocated to the two experimental groups (Groups 1 and 2) obtained low scores on one or both tasks in the test. These two groups did not differ from each other in kinaesthetic sensitivity. The children selected for the control group scored at above average level on both kinaesthetic tasks when tested on the Kinaesthetic Sensitivity Test.

All 24 children were given a drawing test. They were asked to copy a square, a diamond and a triangle from models shown to them, one at a time. They were told to reproduce the models exactly, in both size and shape. During this test, the masking box was placed over their hands, thus visual information was obscured, and only kinaesthetic feedback was available.

The children in Group 1 were trained in both kinaesthetic abilities and drawing skill. Kinaesthetic training was given in the task or tasks in which the child gained low scores when tested on the Kinaesthetic Sensitivity Test. The methods of training were the same as described in the previous studies. In each session kinaesthetic training was followed by drawing practice. Here the child was shown a card with a line drawing on it and was asked to copy the model three times. The masking box was placed over the child's hands and the experimenter positioned the

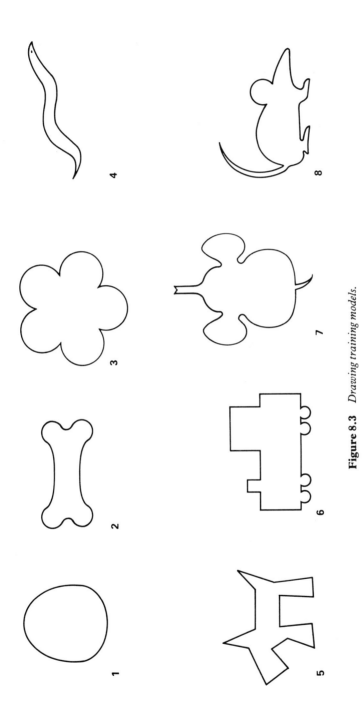

Figure 8.3 *Drawing training models.*

pencil on the paper to locate a suitable starting point. After completing the drawing, the child was allowed to look at it. The children often thought their attempts were funny and joked and laughed about their pictures while discussing their mistakes. Each model was copied three times, one model given per training session. The pictures gradually increased in difficulty. From the third practice session onwards the children could choose the picture they were to copy; the pictures are shown in Fig. 8.3.

Group 2 and control group children were given drawing training only; they were not trained in kinaesthesis.

All the children participated in six training sessions and were then retested on the Kinaesthetic Sensitivity Test and the drawing test, again using the square, diamond and triangle figures.

This completed the work for Group 1 and control group children. The children in Group 2, however, were given five kinaesthetic training sessions. Each child was trained on the task or tasks in which they gained low scores in the test. On completion of the kinaesthetic training, the children were retested on the drawing test alone.

The experimental design is summarised and the test results are listed in Table 8.1.

Table 8.1 *Table of experimental manipulations and results.*

	Experimental manipulations				
	Test 1	Training 1	Test 2	Training 2	Test 3
Group 1	Kinaesthetic Sensitivity Test and Drawing Test	Kinaesthetic task(s) and drawing	As Test 1	–	–
Group 2	As for Group 1	Drawing	As Test 1	Kinaesthetic task(s)	Drawing Test
Control Group	As for Group 1	Drawing	As Test 1	–	–

	Results							
	Test 1 versus 2						Test 2 versus 3	
	Kinaesthetic acuity		Kinaesthetic perception and memory		Drawing		Drawing	
	t	P<	t	P<	t	P<	t	P<
Group 1	2.19	0.05	3.49	0.01	3.55	0.01	–	–
Group 2	1.61	N.S.	0.8	N.S.	1.02	N.S.	3.36	0.01
Control group	1.07	N.S.	2.4	0.05*	1.94	N.S.	–	–

The control group was significantly worse in retest.
N.S. = not significant.

The results section of Table 8.1 shows that kinaesthetic training alone improves the drawing performance of those children who were poor in kinaesthetic abilities prior to training. Practice in drawing, in contrast, did not lead to improvement in this skill.

The finding that improvement in kinaesthetic ability results in improvement in drawing skill, while training in the drawing skill itself does not, lends strong support to the process-orientated diagnostic–therapeutic approach. The task-orientated approach would indicate that the child should be trained in drawing if he is found to be weak at this task. The results of this study contradict this contention (see Group 2 drawing test 1 versus 2 results). The difficulty teachers experience with some children in achieving improvement in paper-pencil skills through specific training of this skill can also be mentioned as evidence against the efficacy of the task-orientated training. On the other hand, correction of a dysfunction in an underlying process yields significant improvement in the target task after training over a short time period (see Group 2 drawing test 2 versus 3 results).

A brief explanation for the inclusion of the control group might be appropriate. It is often said that special attention paid to a child has a non-specific beneficial effect on behaviour and that it can lead to improvement in a number of diverse skills. Thus, the control group was included to counter criticism that the improvement in the drawing task found in this study might be the result of the special attention the child has received.

There is another critical point that could be raised against the validity of the findings of this study and the arguments advanced in favour of the process-orientated training approach. It could be suggested that children who can draw well do not need training and that the specific training offered in this study could not improve the high level of performance already reached by these children. However, copying geometric figures is a task most adults find difficult. There is certainly room for improvement in accuracy even for the 'talented' seven year old (Fig. 7.16e).

One further observation might be reported as being relevant to the results obtained from, and the behaviours shown by, the children during the second application of the Kinaesthetic Sensitivity Test. Children in Groups 1 and 2 seemed to enjoy the challenge presented by the test and the obvious ease and confidence with which they could perform it. The control group children, on the other hand, found the acuity task 'boring' when performed for the second time. In the kinaesthetic perception and memory task they attempted to find a new strategy in performing the pattern reorientation task, thinking that they must have done something wrong the first time to be asked to repeat the test a second time. On questioning these children some described their 'better way' of doing the test, e.g. 'the biggest lump is always up top'. The inappropriate strategies lead to significant deterioration in the retest scores.

The last two steps, 9 and 10, can now be undertaken to establish the link between process-orientated diagnosis and therapy.

Five months after the completion of the training study the teachers were approached and asked for a progress report on the paper-pencil skill development of the 24 children who took part in the study. The teachers were unaware of the type of training each child received during the experiment, hence their report could not be biased by expectations. The eight control group children and three children from the experimental groups were judged to have progressed in drawing and printing at a normal, expected rate, while 10 children from the experimental groups were said to have improved 'out of sight', i.e. at a highly accelerated rate. Three children who were included in the study had left the school in the meantime and their progress could not be checked.

Thus the long-term effect of kinaesthetic ability training is verified (Step 9), and evidence is provided that improvement in an underlying ability has a significant and lasting effect on overt behaviour — behaviour or skills which depend for efficient performance on the ability which was trained (Step 10).

It is an often described finding (e.g. Hearn, 1969; Saunders, 1962) that a large proportion of 'dyslexic' children have difficulty in acquiring and performing the skills of printing and writing. It is suggested here that in some of these children the writing difficulty is the primary problem, with dyslexia following as a secondary consequence. The child, if kinaesthetically underdeveloped, might battle on bravely to print well-formed letters, without observable success. He is unaware of his perceptual problems and comes to the false conclusion that he is inferior to his class mates when it comes to letters. Rather than blaming himself entirely for his failure to manage his 'printing', he develops a hearty dislike of all printed material, with the resultant low motivation and application to learning the skill of reading. The improvement in kinaesthetic sensitivity, following kinaesthetic training, enhances his printing skill and removes his general fear of printed material, providing the impetus to the acquisition of reading skill. In fact, the teachers did report improvement in reading in some of the children from the experimental groups.

Two illustrative case studies

The first case to be described is that of eight-year-old Matthew, mentioned previously. He was one of the children allocated to Group 1 of the training study, discussed earlier.

Matthew was brought to the attention of the educational psychologist at the age of seven years, while attending Year 2 class. He experienced considerable difficulties in writing and printing skills and performed poorly in some sports activities. The counsellor referred him for neurological examination. The neurological examination did not reveal an abnormality and he was diagnosed as a minimal brain dysfunction child. He continued in Year 2 and was given extensive remedial teaching in drawing and printing and general physical education. At the end of his school year, on the recommendation of his class and remedial teachers and the educational psychologist, it was decided that Matthew should repeat Year 2. It was hoped that with further remedial teaching Matthew might achieve adequate performance on paper-pencil skills to be able to advance into Year 3 after his repeat year. His class teacher reported that this decision upset him greatly and he changed from a happy, popular, outgoing child into an unhappy, withdrawn boy. Rather than improving his school performance he became progressively worse in all school subjects.

The training study was commenced nearly half-way through the school year in which Matthew was repeating Year 2. His case history was not known when he was selected into Group 1 of the training study. He was allocated to the group due to his low scores on both kinaesthetic tasks of the Kinaesthetic Sensitivity Test. In fact, Matthew performed both tasks randomly and could be described as suffering from 'dyskinaesthesia'.

He improved markedly in kinaesthetic abilities and when retested reached adult level in kinaesthetic acuity and 10-year-old level in kinaesthetic perception and memory. Matthew's pre- and post-training drawing test performances are shown in the left hand frame of Fig. 8.4.

In the follow-up study, five months after training, the teacher reported a 'miraculous' improvement in Matthew's progress. He became the printing champion of the class! The teacher was pleased not only with his progress in paper-pencil skills, but with the general change in Matthew. He showed extreme pride in his success, progressed fast in all school subjects and regained his sunny outgoing personality.

It must be strongly emphasised that no assertion is made to imply that kinaesthetic abilities underlie general cognitive function or that they are a prerequisite for a happy, well-balanced personality. Improvement in kinaesthetic abilities can only influence those skills which rely on these abilities directly for skilful performance. The general improvement found in Matthew's school achievements and disposition are the consequence of being able to perform the tasks which he thought he might never master. Prior to kinaesthetic training, Matthew was fully

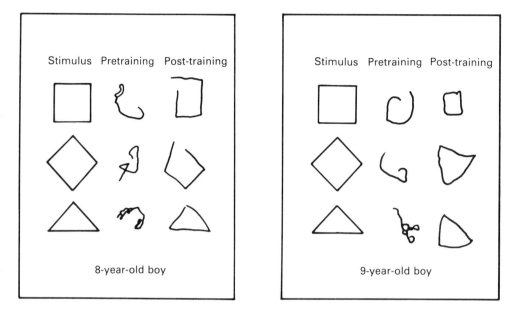

Figure 8.4 *The effect of kinaesthetic training on drawing performance.*

aware of his inability to learn printing and drawing skills. This disability set him apart from his class mates, and earned him the label of 'clumsy' and 'stupid'. What Matthew could not realise was that he was neither 'stupid' nor 'clumsy', but that he suffered from a perceptual disorder, no more degrading than being short sighted. The sudden discovery, after kinaesthetic training, that he is capable of handling pencil and paper, and indeed that he is the best in the class in printing, removed his doubts about himself; he regained his self-esteem and self-confidence.

The second case to be reported is that of nine-year-old Mike. Mike's history resembles that of Matthew's to some degree. Mike found drawing and printing difficult and failed to achieve progress in these skills. He was also referred for neurological examination, and was found to be clear of neurological abnormalities and diagnosed as clumsy at the age of seven years. Remedial teaching in paper-pencil skills and in general motor activities failed to result in improvement. Mike's response to failure differed from that of Matthew. By the end of Year 2 he refused to attempt any drawing or printing work. In fact, he would not handle any kind of writing implement. He was transferred to a special school from Year 3 onwards. His progress at the special school was slow, and his aversion to paper-pencil skills continued.

Mike's performance on the Kinaesthetic Sensitivity Test was random, showing a poor ability to process kinaesthetic information in both tasks. He was trained in both kinaesthetic acuity and kinaesthetic perception and memory in seven sessions. Improvement in the latter tasks was not evident until the fifth session, but rapid improvement was shown thereafter. He achieved kinaesthetic abilities, as shown on retesting, commensurate with his age. His pre- and post-training drawing test performance is given in the right hand frame of Fig. 8.4.

Two weeks after the last training session, Mike's mother received a card from Mike for Mother's Day. Mike drew a picture and wrote the address and a five line message of good wishes and thanks. The writing was clearly legible and the letters were of even size. The most important point about the card was that it gave evidence that Mike had started writing again. The case could not be followed up further because the family moved to another State.

Examination of these two case studies provides an opportunity to compare the efficacy of the diagnostic and therapeutic methods employed in task- versus process-orientated approaches.

Both boys manifested the same overt symptom: extreme difficulty in acquiring paper-pencil skills. Due to the prevailing school system, this symptom assumed importance in the second year of their school careers. Both children were exposed to the task-orientated diagnostic–therapeutic method. Neurological examination resulted in general diagnostic labels, minimal brain dysfunction for one, clumsiness for the other. These diagnostic classifications did not define specific therapy. Thus, the therapeutic method employed was, by necessity, focused on the overt symptom, i.e. remedial teaching in paper-pencil skills and supportive physical education training. The remedial programme involved the boys and their remedial teachers in daily sessions for more than one academic year without noticeable improvement in the target task. This lack of success resulted in different, but grave consequences for the two boys. One had to repeat a school year, and the other was removed from the general educational stream. Both suffered pronounced loss of confidence and self-esteem, and their academic development was retarded.

When the process-orientated approach was adopted both boys were diagnosed as suffering from dyskinaesthesia. This specific diagnosis required specific therapy, i.e. kinaesthetic training. The method of kinaesthetic training involved the child and his therapist in four hours work (at the most) over a two-week period. Alleviation of the overt symptom followed without further intervention; both boys improved in their paper-pencil skills significantly.

Thus the task-orientated approach proved to be effort- and time-consuming, without succeeding to reduce the problem, whereas the process-orientated method was shown to be effort- and time-efficient and led to success in eliminating the overt symptom. The previous discussion was concerned with the management of perceptual difficulties. In the following section the process-orientated approach is extended to a possible therapy programme relevant to a motor programming variable.

SPATIAL PROGRAMMING DIFFICULTIES AND DRESSING: A PROPOSED TRAINING METHOD

It is shown that all 10 steps necessary for establishing the link between diagnosis and therapy in a process-orientated system have been carried out for kinaesthetic abilities. However, for the other test items in the Perceptual-Motor Abilities Test (Chapter 7) only the first three steps and part of the fourth step are completed. It might be useful to select one underlying motor process and attempt to describe the proposed diagnostic–therapeutic approach for the associated ability. The influence of the selected motor process on an everyday skill can be described and the effect of training of the ability considered. A description of a hypothetical case could indicate the type of training programmes which can be generated to improve specific motor abilities. In the following illustrative example spatial programming is the selected process (Chapter 2) and dressing the everyday activity.

'Jim' is referred by his parents and educational psychologist for suspected clumsiness. He is eight years old and is said to be clumsy in a number of motor skills. On discussing the problem with Jim, he complains about the difficulty he experiences in dressing himself and in writing. He states that his inefficiency in these two skills worry him a great deal.

Routine neurological examination does not reveal neurological abnormalities, nor are there any visual or auditory deficiencies.

He is then tested on the Perceptual-Motor Abilities Test. On the two kinaesthetic sensitivity tasks he achieves scores that are slightly above the mean for his age, and performs the posture and all three velocity discrimination tasks adequately. His perceptual ability is well within normal range. However, his scores are very low on the tasks relying on finely graded spatial programming, i.e. Ward game, drawing, tracing and dotting. On tasks demonstrating only moderately exacting spatial programming he performs satisfactorily, i.e. ball catching and ball handling. He shows above-average skill in the balancing tasks.

The test results indicate that Jim has not developed spatial programming ability commensurate with his age. In all other aspects of perceptual-motor development he can be regarded as normal for his age. Both dressing and writing are tasks which depend heavily on spatial programming ability for efficient performance. The diagnosed low level of this ability could explain the problems experienced by Jim when trying to perform these tasks.

If Jim was to be tested on a task-orientated test battery he would possibly be diagnosed as a 'clumsy' child, and a general motor training programme would be suggested to alleviate his 'condition'. The general programme would include a number of exercises such as trampolining, ball games and swimming, which would have little direct effect on his dressing and writing skills. Alternatively, he might be told to practise these two skills, a suggestion of dubious value since he must already have been practising them prior to testing, achieving little improvement.

In contrast, the process-orientated test procedure yields a causal diagnosis, on the basis of which a well-defined training programme can be devised, aiming at improvement in the ability diagnosed as being deficient. Thus, to achieve improvement in spatial programming, a set of tasks is devised which impose increasingly fine spatial programming demands. Both whole body and manipulative tasks would be included in the training programme. Whole body tasks to be used are:

1. Throwing a ball into a large basket, and gradually decreasing the size of the basket as performance improves.
2. Hitting a suspended ball with a large bat, gradually decreasing ball size and bat width.

The manual tasks chosen are:

1. Posting box.
2. Pegboard task starting with round pegs, then square and hexagonal pegs to be placed in the appropriate holes.
3. Connecting circles printed at equal distances from each other by drawing straight lines between them. The circles are numbered to indicate the order in which they are to be connected to reveal a picture. The size of the circles would be gradually decreased from the 4 mm starting size to a 1 mm dot; concurrently the distance between the targets would become more varied. The pictures obtained could differ from trial to trial.
4. Handling nuts and bolts, starting with large ones and graduating to small-sized nut–bolt assemblies.

These training tasks rely primarily on spatial programming ability and require minimal planning of the movement.

   The rate of advance from easy to difficult tasks cannot be predetermined but must depend on the improvement Jim achieves in each task during the training sessions. In order to reduce monotony, one whole body and one manual task should be included in each training session.

   When a skilled performance level is reached in the training tasks, Jim should be retested on the test items in which he was deficient when first tested. If the retest results show marked improvement in spatial programming ability, i.e. scores expected for an eight year old, as shown by the normative data, further training is not necessary. The tasks which caused the greatest difficulty to Jim, dressing and writing, both depend heavily on spatial programming. As Jim's spatial programming ability improves, he should experience improvements in these two tasks, along with many other tasks which also rely on spatial programming.

   It is predicted that the advantages of the process-orientated approach over that of the task-orientated approach, discussed in relation to kinaesthetic ability, would also apply to motor programming abilities.

A Kinaesthetic Sensitivity Test training kit and manual can be ordered from Senkit Pty Ltd, PO Box 77, Willetton, Western Australia 6155.

REFERENCES

Abravanel, E. (1981) Integrating the information from eyes and hands: a developmental account. In
Walk, R. D. & Pick, H. C. (Eds) *Intersensory Perception and Sensory Integration*, pp 71–108. New
York: Plenum Press.

Adams, J. A. (1971) A closed-loop theory of motor learning. *Journal of Motor Behavior* **3**: 111–150.

Alderson, G. J. K. (1972) The perception of velocity. In Whiting, H. T. A. (Ed) *Readings in Sports
Psychology*, pp 116–155. London: Kimpton.

Alderson, G. J. K., Sully, D. J. & Sully, H. G. (1974) An operational analysis of a one-handed catching
task using high speed photography. *Journal of Motor Behaviour* **6**: 217–226.

Anderson, N. H. (1980) Information integration theory in developmental psychology. In Wilkening, F.,
Becker, J. & Trabasso, T. (Eds) *Information Integration by Children*, pp 1–45, New Jersey: Erlbaum.

Anokhin, P. K. (1969) Cybernetics and the integrative activity of the brain. In Cole, M. & Maltzman, I.
(Eds) *A Handbook of Contemporary Soviet Psychology*, pp 830–896. London: Basic Books.

Ashby, A. A. (1983) Developmental study of short-term memory characteristics for kinaesthetic
movement information. *Perceptual and Motor Skills* **57**: 649–650.

Ayres, A. J. (1972a) *Southern California Sensory Integration Tests*. Los Angeles: Western Psychological
Services.

Ayres, A. J. (1972b) *Sensory Integration and Learning Disorders*. Los Angeles: Western Psychological
Services.

Bairstow, P. J. (1983) Development of motor skills. In Harre, R. & Lamb, R. (Eds) *The Encyclopedic
Dictionary of Psychology*. Oxford: Basil Blackwell.

Bairstow, P. J. & Laszlo, J. I. (1976) The nerve compression block technique: a reply to Kelso, Stelmach
and Wanamaker. *Journal of Motor Behavior* **8**: 147–153.

Bairstow, P. J. & Laszlo, J. I. (1978a) Perception of movement patterns. Recognition from visual arrays
of distorted patterns. *Quarterly Journal of Experimental Psychology* **30**: 311–317.

Bairstow, P. J. & Laszlo, J. I. (1978b) Perception of movement patterns. Recall of movement. *Perceptual
and Motor Skills* **47**: 287–305.

Bairstow, P. J. & Laszlo, J. I. (1979a) Perception of movement patterns. Tracking of movement. *Journal
of Motor Behavior* **11**: 35–48.

Bairstow, P. J. & Laszlo, J. I. (1979b) Perception of size of movement patterns. *Journal of Motor
Behavior* **11**: 167–178.

Bairstow, P. J. & Laszlo, J. I. (1980) Motor commands and the perception of movement patterns.
Journal of Experimental Psychology: Human Perception and Performance **6**: 1–12.

Bairstow, P. J. & Laszlo, J. I. (1981). Kinaesthetic sensitivity to passive movements in children and
adults, and its relationship to motor development and motor control. *Developmental Medicine and
Child Neurology* **23**: 606–616.

Bairstow, P. J. & Laszlo, J. I. (1982) Complex movement patterns: learning, retention and sources of
error in recall. *Quarterly Journal of Experimental Psychology* **34**: 183–197.

Basmajian, J. V. (1962) *Muscles Alive: Their Functions Revealed by Electromyography*. Baltimore:
Williams & Wilkins.

Bayley, N. (1969) *Manual for the Bayley Scales of Infant Development*. New York: Psychological Corporation.

BCP Observation Booklet (1973) *Santa Cruz Special Education Management System*. Palo Alto, California: VORT Corporation.

Benesh, R. & McGuiness, J. (1974) Benesh movement notation and medicine. *Physiotherapy* **60**: 176–178.

Benjamin, J. (December 1976) The Northwick Park A.D.L. Index. *Occupational Therapy*: 301–306.

Berger, M. (1983) Tests: Intelligence. In Harre, R. & Lamb, R. (Eds) *The Encyclopedic Dictionary of Psychology*. Oxford: Basil Blackwell.

Bernstein, N. (1967) *The Co-ordination and Regulation of Movements*. Oxford: Pergamon Press.

Birch, H. G. & Lefford, A. (1963) Intersensory development in children. *Monograph of the Society for Research in Child Development* **28**: No. 89.

Birch, H. G. & Lefford, A. (1964) Two strategies for studying perception in 'brain-damaged' children. In Birch, H. G. (Ed) *Brain Damage in Children: The Biological and Social Aspects*. New York: Williams & Wilkins.

Boice, R. (1983) Observational skills. *Psychological Bulletin* **93**: 3–29.

Bonnet, C. & Kolehmainen, K. (1969) Prediction of the future position of a moving object. *Scandinavian Journal of Psychology* **10**: 65–70.

Borjesson, E. & Von Hofsten, C. (1973) Visual perception of motion in depth: application of a vector model to three-dot motion patterns. *Perception and Psychophysics* **13**: 169–179.

Bower, T. G. R. (1972) Object perception in infants. *Perception* **1**: 15–30.

Bower, T. G. R., Broughton, J. M. & Moore, M. K. (1970a) The demonstration of intention in the reaching behavior of neonate humans. *Nature* **228**: 679–681.

Bower, T. G. R., Broughton, J. M. & Moore, M. K. (1970b) The coordination of visual and tactual input in infants. *Perception and Psychophysics* **8**: 51–53.

Bronson, G. (1974) The postnatal growth of visual capacity. *Child Development* **45**: 873–890.

Brooks, V. B. (1979) Motor programs revisited. In Talbot, R. E. & Humphrey, D. R. (Eds) *Posture and Movement: Perspective for Integrating Sensory and Motor Research on the Mammalian Nervous System*, pp 13–49. New York: Raven Press.

Brooks, V. B. (1981) Task related cell assemblies. In Pompeiano, O. & Marsan, C. A. (Eds) *Brain Mechanisms and Perceptual Awareness*. New York: Raven Press.

Brown, J. F. (1931a) The visual perception of velocity. *Psychologische Forschung* **14**: 199–232.

Brown, J. F. (1931b) The thresholds for visual movement. *Psychologische Forschung* **14**: 249–268.

Brown, R. H. (1961) Visual sensitivity to differences in velocity. *Psychological Bulletin* **58**: 89–103.

Brown, A. L. (1978) Knowing when, where, and how to remember: a problem of metacognition. In Glaser, R. (Ed) *Advances in Instructional Psychology*. Hillsdale, New Jersey: Erlbaum.

Brown, S. H. C. & Cooke, J. D. (1981) Amplitude- and instruction-dependent modulation of movement related electromyogram activity in humans. *Journal of Physiology* **316**: 97–107.

Bruininks, R. H. (1978) *Bruininks–Oseretsky Test of Motor Proficiency*. Circle Pines, Minnesota: American Guidance Service.

Bruner, J. S. (1970) The growth and structure of skill. In Connolly, K. (Ed) *Mechanisms of Motor Skill Development*. New York: Academic Press.

Bruner, J. S. (1973) Organization of early skilled action. *Child Development* **44**: 1–11.

Bruner, J. S. & Koslowski, B. (1972) Visually preadapted constituents of manipulatory action. *Perception* **1**: 3–12.

Bryant, P. (1974) *Perception and Understanding in Young Children*. London: Methuen.

Burns, Y. & Watter, P. (1974) Identification and developmental assessment of children with neurological impairment. *Australian Journal of Physiotherapy* **20**: 5–14.

Bushnell, E. W. (1981) The ontogeny of intermodal relations: vision and touch in infancy. In Walk, R. D. & Pick, H. C. (Eds) *Intersensory Perception and Sensory Integration*, pp 5–36. New York: Plenum Press.

Butterworth, G. (1981) The origins of auditory–visual perception and visual proprioception in human development. In Walk, R. D. & Pick, H. C. (Eds) *Intersensory Perception and Sensory Integration*, pp 37–70. New York: Plenum Press.

Campbell, R. L. & Richie, D. M. (1983) Problems in the theory of developmental sequences. *Human Development* **26**: 156–172.

Carlton, L. G. (1981) Visual information: the control of aiming movements. *Quarterly Journal of Experimental Psychology* **33**A: 87–93.

Carroll, J. B. (1983) Studying individual differences in cognitive abilities: through and beyond factor analysis. In Dillon, R. F. & Schmeck, F. F. (Eds) *Individual Differences in Cognition*, pp 1–33. New York: Academic Press.

Carter, C. O. & Fairbank, T. J. (1974) *The Genetics of Locomotor Disorders*. Oxford: Oxford University Press.

Castner, B. M. (1932) The development of fine prehension in infancy. *Genetic Psychology Monographs* **12**: 105–193.

Chess, S., Korn, S. J. & Fernandez, P. B. (1971). *Psychiatric Disorder of Children with Congenital Rubella*. London: Butterworths.

Chiarenza, G. A., Papakostopoulos, D., Giordana, F. & Guareschi-Cazzullo, A. (1983) Movement-related brain macro potentials during skilled performances. A developmental study. *Electroencephalography and Clinical Neurophysiology* **56**: 373–383.

Clark, J. E. (1978) Memory processes in the early acquisition of motor skills. In Ridenow, M. V. (Ed) *Motor Development: Issues and Applications*. Princeton, New Jersey: Princeton.

Cleghorn, T. E. & Darcus, H. D. (1952) The sensibility to passive movement of the human elbow joint. *Quarterly Journal of Experimental Psychology* **4**: 66–77.

Cohen, R. L. (1962) An investigation of velocity synthesis. *Scandinavian Journal of Psychology* **3**: 97–111.

Cohen, M. M. (1981) Visual–proprioceptive interaction. In Walk, R. D. & Pick, H. C. (Eds) *Intersensory Perception and Sensory Integration*, pp 175–215. New York: Plenum Press.

Connolly, K. J. (1981) Maturation and the ontogeny of motor skills. In Connolly, K. J. & Prechtl, H. F. R. (Eds) *Maturation and Development: Biological and Psychological Perspectives*. London: Heinemann.

Connolly, K. J. & Jones, B. (1970) A developmental study of afferent–reafferent integration. *British Journal of Psychology* **61**: 259–266.

Cordo, P. J. & Nashner, L. M. (1982) Properties of postural adjustments associated with rapid arm movements. *Journal of Neurophysiology* **47**: 287–302.

Cotman, C. W. & Nieto-Lampedro, M. (1982) Brain function, synapse renewal, and plasticity. *Annual Review of Psychology* **33**: 371–401.

Crago, P. E., Houk, J. C. & Rymer, W. Z. (1982) Sampling of total force by tendon organs. *Journal of Neurophysiology* **47**: 1069–1083.

Cratty, B. J. (1967) *Social Dimensions of Physical Activity*. Englewood Cliffs, New Jersey: Prentice-Hall.

Cratty, B. J. (1981) Sensory-motor and perceptual-motor theories and practices: an overview and evaluation. In Walk, R. D. & Pick, H. C. (Eds) *Intersensory Perception and Sensory Integration*, pp 345–373. New York: Plenum Press.

Cratty, B. J. & Martin, M. (1969) *Perceptual-Motor Efficiency in Children*. Philadelphia: Lea & Febiger.

Crosby, R. M. N. & Liston, R. (1976) *The Waysiders: Reading and the Dyslexic Child*. New York: John Day.

D'Amato, M. R. (1970) *Experimental Psychology: Methodology, Psychophysics and Learning*. New York: McGraw-Hill.

Davis, F. B. (1974) *Standards for Educational and Psychological Tests*. Washington, DC: American Psychological Association.

Desmedt, J. E. & Godaux, E. (1978) Ballistic contractions in fast and slow human muscles: discharge patterns of single motor units. *Journal of Physiology* **285**: 185–196.

Desmedt, J. E. & Godaux, E. (1979) Voluntary motor commands in human ballistic movements. *Annals of Neurology* **5**: 415–421.

Diewert, G. L. & Stelmach, G. E. (1977) Intramodal and intermodal transfer of movement information. *Acta Psychologica* **41**: 119–128.

Di Franco, D., Muir, D. W. & Dodwell, P. C. (1978) Reaching in very young infants. *Perception* **7**: 385–392.

Dileo, J. H. (1971) *Young Children and Their Drawings*. London: Constable.

Dodwell, P. C., Muir, D. & Di Franco, D. (1976) Responses of infants to visually presented objects. *Science* **194**: 209–211.

Doman, R. J., Spitz, E. B., Zucman, E. & Delacato, C. H. (1960) Children with severe brain injuries: neurological organization in terms of mobility. *Journal of the American Medical Association* **174**: 257–262.

Donnelly, M. C. & Connolly, K. J. (1983) Motor development: a hypothesis and a simulation concerning voluntary reaching in infancy. *Human Movement Science* **2**: 15–33.

Dorfman, P. W. (1977) Timing and anticipation: a developmental perspective. *Journal of Motor Behavior* **9**: 67–79.

Dorland's Medical Dictionary (1965) Philadelphia: W. B. Saunders.

Ebbenson, E. B., Parker, S. & Konecni, V. J. (1977) Laboratory and field analysis of decisions involving risk. *Journal of Experimental Psychology: Human Perception and Performance* **3**: 576–589.

Ellingstad, V. S. (1967) Velocity estimation for briefly displayed targets. *Perceptual and Motor Skills* **74**: 943–947.

Ellingstad, V. S. & Heimstra, N. W. (1969) Velocity–time estimation as a function of target-speed and concealment extent. *Human Factors* **11**: 305–312.

Elliot, R. (1970) Simple reaction time: Effects associated with age, preparatory interval, incentive-shift and mode of presentation. *Journal of Experimental Child Psychology* **9**: 86–107.

Evarts, E. V. & Granit, R. (1976) Relations of reflexes and intended movements. In Homma, S. (Ed) *Understanding the Stretch Reflex, Progress in Brain Research*, pp 1–14. Amsterdam: Elsevier.

Evarts, E. V. & Tanji, J. (1976) Reflex and intended responses in motor cortex pyramidal tract neurons of monkey. *Journal of Neurophysiology* **39**: 1069–1080.

Evarts, E. V., Fromm, C., Kroller, J. & van Jennings, A. (1983) Motor cortex control of finely graded forces. *Journal of Neurophysiology* **49**: 1199–1215.

Fantz, R. L. (1961a) The origin of form perception. *Scientific American* **204**: 66–72.

Fantz, R. L. (1961b) A method for studying depth perception in infants under six months of age. *Psychological Record* **11**: 27–32.

Fentress, J. C. (1981) Sensorimotor development. In Aslin, R. N., Alberts, J. R. & Petersen, M. R. (Eds) *Development of Perception. Psychological Perspectives. Volume I. Audition, Somatic Perception and the Chemical Senses*, pp 293–318. New York: Academic Press.

Ferguson, G. A. (1981) *Statistical Analysis in Psychology and Education* (5th edn). New York: McGraw-Hill.

Fetz, E. E. & Cheney, P. D. (1980) Postspike facilitation of forelimb muscle activity by primate corticomotoneuronal cells. *Journal of Neurophysiology* **44**: 751–772.

Field, J. (1977) Coordination of vision and prehension in young infants. *Child Development* **48**: 97–103.

Fischer, K. W. (1980) A theory of cognitive development: the control and construction of hierarchies of skills. *Psychological Review* **87**: 477–531.

Fitts, P. M. & Posner, M. I. (1967) *Human Performance*. Belmont, California: Brooks/Cole Publishing.

Fleishman, E. A. (1966) Human abilities and the acquisition of skill. In Bilodeau, E. A. (Ed) *Acquisition of Skill*. New York: Academic Press.

Fleishman, E. A. (1972) On the relation between abilities, learning and human performance. *American Psychologist* **27**: 1017–1032.

Foot, H. C. (1969) Visual prediction of the point of coincidence of two moving targets. *Ergonomics* **12**: 723–733.

Forsstrom, A. & Von Hofsten, C. (1982) Visually directed reaching of children with motor impairments. *Developmental Medicine and Child Neurology* **24**: 653–661.

Fox, R. & McDaniel, C. (1982) The perception of biological motion by human infants. *Science* **218**: 486–487.

Frankenburg, W. K. & Dodds, J. B. (1967). The Denver Developmental Screening Test. *Journal of Pediatrics* **71**: 181–191.

Franks, I. M. & Wilberg, R. B. (1982) The generation of movement patterns during the acquisition of a pursuit tracking task. *Human Movement Science* **1**: 251–272.

Freeman, N. H. & Kelham, S. E. (1981) The interference of a baseline with children's orientation judgement need not entirely mask their contextual responsiveness. *Quarterly Journal of Experimental Psychology* **33**A: 145–154.

Freund, H.-J. (1983) Motor unit and muscle activity in voluntary motor control. *Physiological Review* **63**: 387–436.

Frith, C. D. & Lang, R. J. (1979) Learning and reminiscence as a function of target predictability in a two-dimensional tracking task. *Quarterly Journal of Experimental Psychology* **31**: 103–109.

Fromm, C. & Evarts, E. V. (1982) Pyramidal tract neurons in somatosensory cortex: central and peripheral inputs during voluntary movements. *Brain Research* **238**(1): 186–191.

Gachoud, J. P., Mounoud, P., Havert, C. A. & Viviani, P. (1983) Motor strategies in lifting movements: a comparison of adult and child performance. *Journal of Motor Behavior* **15**: 202–216.

Gallahue, D. L. (1982) *Understanding Motor Development in Children*. New York: John Wiley.

Gandevia, S. C. & McCloskey, D. I. (1976) Perceived heaviness of lifted objects and effects of sensory inputs from related non-lifting parts. *Brain Research* **109**: 399–401.

Gelman, R. (1978) Cognitive development. *Annual Review of Psychology* **29**: 297–332.

Georgopoulos, A. P., Kalaska, J. F. & Massey, J. E. (1981) Spatial trajectories and reaction time of aimed movements: effects of practice, uncertainty and change in target location. *Journal of Neurophysiology* **46**: 725–743.

Geppert, U. & Kuster, U. (1983) The emergence of 'wanting to do it oneself': a precursor of achievement motivation. *International Journal of Behavioral Development* **6**: 355–369.

Gerhard, D. J. (1959) The judgement of velocity and the prediction of motion. *Ergonomics* **2**: 287–304.

Gesell, A. (1941) *The First Five Years of Life*, 1st edition. London: Methuen.

Gesell, A. (1954) *The First Five Years of Life*, 2nd edition. London: Methuen.

Gesell, A. & Amatruda, C. S. (1969) *Developmental Diagnosis. Normal and Abnormal Child Development*, New York: Harper & Row.

Gesell, A. & Ilg, F. L. (1946) *The Child from Five to Ten*. London: Hamilton.

Gibson, E. J. (1953) Improvement in perceptual judgements as a function of controlled practice or training. *Psychological Bulletin* **50**: 401–431.

Gibson, J. J. (1954) The visual perception of objective motion and subjective movement. *Psychological Review* **61**: 304–314.

Gibson, J. J. (1958) Visually controlled locomotion and visual orientation in animals. *British Journal of Psychology* **49**: 182–194.

Gibson, J. J. (1962) Observations on active touch. *Psychological Review* **69**: 477–491.

Gibson, J. J. (1966) *The Senses Considered as Perceptual Systems*. Boston: Houghton-Mifflin.

Gibson, J. J. (1968) What gives rise to the perception of motion? *Psychological Review* **75**: 335–346.

Gibson, E. J. (1983) Commentary on the development of perception and cognition. In Tighe, T. J. & Shepp, B. E. (Eds) *Perception, Cognition and Development: Interactional Analysis*, pp 307–321. New York: Academic Press.

Gibson, J. J. & Gibson, E. J. (1955) Perceptual learning: differentiation or enrichment. *Psychological Bulletin* **62**: 32–41.

Gibson, J. J., Smith, O. W., Steinschneider, A. & Johnson, C. W. (1957) The relative accuracy of visual perception of motion during fixation and pursuit. *American Journal of Psychology* **70**: 64–68.

Godschalk, M., Aremon, R. N., Nijo, H. G. T. & Kuypers, H. G. J. M. (1981) Behavior of neurones in monkey peri-arcuate and pericentral cortex before and during visually guided arm and hand movements. *Experimental Brain Research* **44**(1): 113–116.

Gogel, W. C. & McNulty, P. (1983) Perceived velocity as a function of reference mark density. *Scandinavian Journal of Psychology* **24**: 257–265.

Goodkin, R. & Diller, L. (1973) Reliability among physical therapists in diagnosis and treatment to gait deviations in hemiplegics. *Perceptual Motor Skills* **37**: 727–734.

Goodman, E. S. (1979) Mirror-drawing performance as a function of instructional set and conflict. *Perceptual and Motor Skills* **48**: 1063–1069.

Gordon, N. & McKinlay, I. (1980) *Helping Clumsy Children*. Edinburgh: Churchill Livingstone.

Gorman, J. J., Cogan, D. G. & Gellis, S. S. (1957) An apparatus for grading the visual acuity of infants on the basis of optikokinetic nystagmus. *Pediatrics* **19**: 1088–1092.

Gottsdanker, R. M. (1952a) The accuracy of prediction motion. *Journal of Experimental Psychology* **43**: 26–36.

Gottsdanker, R. M. (1952b) Prediction-motion with and without vision. *American Journal of Psychology* **65**: 533–543.

Gottsdanker, R. M. (1955) A further study of prediction-motion. *American Journal of Psychology* **68**: 432–437.

Gottsdanker, R. M. (1956) The ability of the human operator to detect acceleration of target motion. *Psychological Bulletin* **53**: 477–487.

Gottsdanker, R. M. & Edwards, R. V. (1957) The prediction of collision. *American Journal of Psychology* **70**: 110–113.

Gottsdanker, R. M., Frick, J. W. & Lockard, R. B. (1961) Identifying the acceleration of visual targets. *British Journal of Psychology* **52**: 31–42.

Grieve, D. W., Miller, D., Mitchelson, D., Paul, J. & Smith, A. J. (1975) *Techniques for the Analysis of Human Movement*. London: Lepus.

Griffiths, R. (1970) *The Abilities of Young Children. A Comprehensive System of Mental Measurement for the First Eight Years of Life*. London: Child Development Research Centre.

Gubbay, S. S. (1975) *The Clumsy Child. A Study of Developmental Apraxia and Agnosic Ataxia*. London: W. B. Saunders.

Halverson, H. M. (1932) An experimental study of prehension in infants by means of systematic cinema records. *Genetic Psychology Monographs* **10**: 110–286.

Halverson, H. M. (1954) Motor development. In Gesell, A. (Ed) *The First Five Years of Life*. London: Methuen.

Hammerton, M. & Tickner, A. H. (1970) Structural and blank backgrounds in a pursuit tracking task. *Ergonomics* **13**: 719–722.

Haubenstricker, J. (1978) A critical review of selected perceptual-motor tests and scales currently used in the assessment of motor behavior. In Sanders, D. L. & Christina, R. W. (Eds) *Psychology in Motor Behavior and Sports — 1977*, pp 536–543. Champaign, Illinois: Human Kinetics.

Hay, L. (1978) Accuracy of children in an open-loop pointing task. *Perceptual and Motor Skills* **47**: 1079–1082.

Hay, L. (1979) Spatial–temporal analysis of movements in children: motor programs versus feedback in the development of reaching. *Journal of Motor Behavior* **11**: 189–200.

Haywood, K. M. (1977) Eye movements during coincidence-anticipation performance. *Journal of Motor Behavior* **9**: 313–318.

Hearn, R. S. (1969) Dyslexia and handwriting. *Journal of Learning Disability* **2**: 37–42.

Held, R. & Bauer, J. A. (1968) Visually guided reaching in infant monkeys after restricted rearing. In Haber, R. N. (Ed) *Contemporary Theory and Research in Visual Perception*. New York: Holt, Rinehart and Winston.

Heller, M. A. & Myers, D. S. (1983) Active and passive tactual recognition of form. *Journal of General Psychology* **108**: 225–229.

Helmstadter, G. C. (1964) *Principles of Psychological Measurement*. London: Methuen.

Helson, H. (1949) Design of equipment and optimal human operation. *American Journal of Psychology* **62**: 473–497.

Henderson, S. E. (1977) Role of feedback in the development and maintenance of a complex skill. *Journal of Experimental Psychology: Human Perception and Performance* **3**: 224–233.

Henderson, S. E. & Hall, D. (1982) Concomitants of clumsiness in young children. *Developmental Medicine and Child Neurology* **24**: 448–460.

Herkowitz, J. (1978a) Developmental task analysis: the design of movement experiences and evaluation of motor development status. In Ridenow, M. V. (Ed) *Motor Development: Issues and Applications*. Princeton, New Jersey: Princeton.

Herkowitz, J. (1978b) Assessing the motor development of children: presentation and critique of tests. In Ridenow, M. V. (Ed) *Motor Development: Issues and Applications*, pp 167–187. Princeton, New Jersey: Princeton.

Hoff, P. A. (1971) Scales of selected aspects of kinaesthesis. *Perception and Psychophysics* **9**: 118–120.

Holding, D. H. (1976) An approximate transfer surface. *Journal of Motor Behavior* **8**: 1–9.

Holle, B. (1976) *Motor Development in Children*. Oxford: Blackwell Scientific.

Holt, K. S. (Ed) (1975) Importance of movement in child development. In *Movement and Child Development*, Clinics in Developmental Medicine, No. 55. Spastics International Medical Publications, London: William Heinemann Medical.

Holt, K. S. (1977) *Developmental Paediatrics*. London: Butterworth.

Holt, K. S. (1982) Developmental screening, diagnosis and guidance. *Child Health* **1**: 9–22.

Hottinger, W. L. (1973) Motor development: conception to age five. In Corbin, C. B. (Ed) *A Textbook of Motor Development*, pp 6–28. Dubuque, Iowa: Brown.

Howard, I. P. (1971) Perceptual learning and adaptation. *British Medical Bulletin* **27**: 248–252.

Hulliger, M. & Vallbo, A. B. (1979) The responses of muscle spindle afferents during voluntary tracking movements in man. Load dependent servo assistance? *Brain Research* **166**: 401–404.

Hulliger, M., Nordh, E. & Vallbo, A. B. (1982) The absence of position response in spindle afferent units from human finger muscles during accurate position holding. *Journal of Physiology* **322**: 167–179.

Johansson, G. (1950) Configurations in the perception of velocity. *Acta Psychologica* **7**: 25–79.

Johansson, G. (1975) Visual motion perception. *Scientific American* **232**: 76–89.

Johnson, O. G. (1976) *Tests and Measurements in Child Development: Handbook II*. San Francisco: Jossey-Bass.

Kay, H. (1957) Information theory in the understanding of skills. *Occupational Psychology* **31**: 218–224.

Kay, H. (1970) Analysing motor skill performance. In Connolly, K. (Ed) *Mechanisms of Motor Skill Development*, pp 139–151. New York: Academic Press.

Keele, S. W. (1973) *Attention and Human Performance*. Pacific Palisades, California: Goodyear Publishing.

Keele, S. W. & Hawkins, H. L. (1982) Explorations of individual differences relevant to high level skill. *Journal of Motor Behavior* **14**: 3–21.

Keil, F. C. (1981) Constraints on knowledge and cognitive development. *Psychological Review* **88**: 197–227.

Keogh, J. (1973) Development in fundamental motor tasks. In Corbin, C. B. (Ed) *A Textbook of Motor Development*, pp 57–74. Dubuque, Iowa: Brown.

Kinsbourne, M. (1980) Foreword. In Gordon, N. & Kinsbourne, M. (Eds) *Helping Clumsy Children*. Edinburgh: Churchill Livingstone.

Klein, R. M. (1976) Attention and movement. In Stelmach, G. E. (Ed) *Motor Control: Issues and Trends*. New York: Academic Press.

Kohen-Raz, R. & Hiriartborde, E. (1979) Some observations on tetra-ataxiametric patterns of static balance and their relation to mental and scholastic achievements. *Perceptual and Motor Skills* **48**: 871–890.

Kremenitzer, J. P., Vaughan, H. G., Kurtzberg, D. & Dowling, K. (1979) Smooth-pursuit eye movements in the newborn infant. *Child Development* **50**: 442–448.

Laabs, G. J. (1974) The effect of interpolated motor activity on the short-term retention of movement distance and end location. *Journal of Motor Behavior* **6**: 279–288.

Lackner, J. R. (1981) Some aspects of sensory-motor control and adaptation in man. In Walk, R. D. & Pick, H. C. (Eds) *Intersensory Perception and Sensory Integration*. New York: Plenum Press.

Lashley, K. S. (1951) The problem of serial order in behavior. In Jeffries, L. A. (Ed) *Cerebral Mechanisms in Behavior*, pp 112–146. New York: John Wiley.

Laszlo, J. I. (1966) The performance of a simple motor task with kinaesthetic sense loss. *Quarterly Journal of Experimental Psychology* **18**: 1–8.

Laszlo, J. I. (1967a) Training of fast tapping with reduction of kinaesthetic and tactile sensations and with combined reduction of kinaesthetic tactile, visual and auditory sensation. *Quarterly Journal of Experimental Psychology* **19**: 344–349.

Laszlo, J. I. (1967b) Kinaesthetic and exteroceptive information in the performance of motor skills. *Physiology and Behavior* **2**: 359–365.

Laszlo, J. I. (1968) The role of visual and kinaesthetic cues in learning a novel skill. *Quarterly Journal of Experimental Psychology* **20**: 191–196.

Laszlo, J. I. & Baguley, R. A. (1971) Motor memory and bilateral transfer. *Journal of Motor Behavior* **3**: 235–240.

Laszlo, J. I. & Bairstow, P. J. (1971a) Accuracy of movement, peripheral feedback and efference copy. *Journal of Motor Behavior* **3**: 241–252.

Laszlo, J. I. & Bairstow, P. J. (1971b) The compression block technique: a note on procedure. *Journal of Motor Behavior* **3**: 313–317.

Laszlo, J. I. & Bairstow, P. J. (1980) The measurement of kinaesthetic sensitivity in children and adults. *Developmental Medicine and Child Neurology* **22**: 454–464.

Laszlo, J. I. & Bairstow, P. J. (1983) Kinaesthesis: its measurement, training and relationship to motor control. *Quarterly Journal of Experimental Psychology* **35**: 411–421.

Laszlo, J. I. & Baker, J. E. (1972) The role of visual cues in movement control and motor memory. *Journal of Motor Behavior* **4**: 71–77.

Laszlo, J. I. & Livesey, J. P. (1977) Task complexity, accuracy, and reaction time. *Journal of Motor Behavior* **9**: 171–177.

Laszlo, J. I. & Pritchard, D. A. (1969) Transfer variables in tracking skills. *Journal of Motor Behavior* **1**: 317–328.

Laszlo, J. I. & Pritchard, D. A. (1970) Recovery of lost transfer effects. *Journal of Motor Behavior* **2**: 44–51.

Laszlo, J. I. & Ward, G. R. (1978) Vision, proprioception and corollary discharge in a movement recall task. *Acta Psychologica* **42**: 477–493.

Laszlo, J. I., Baguley, R. A. & Bairstow, P. J. (1970) Bilateral transfer in tapping skill in the absence of peripheral information. *Journal of Motor Behavior* **2**: 261–271.

Laszlo, J. I., Bairstow, P. J. & Baker, J. E. (1979) Dependence on feedback following practice. *Perceptual and Motor Skills* **48**: 1225–1226.

Laszlo, J. I., Shamoon, J. S. & Sanson-Fisher, R. W. (1969) Reacquisition and transfer of motor skills with sensory feedback reduction. *Journal of Motor Behavior* **1**: 195–209.

Laszlo, J. I., Bairstow, P. J., Ward, G. W. & Bancroft, H. (1980) Distracting information, motor performance and sex differences. *Nature* **283**: 377–378.

Lee, D. N. (1976) A theory of visual control of braking based on information about time-to-collision. *Perception* **5**: 437–459.

Lefebvre-Pinard, M. (1983) Understanding and autocontrol of cognitive functions: implications for the relationship between cognition and behavior. *International Journal of Behavioral Development* **6**: 15–75.

Lipsitt, L. P. (1979) Critical conditions in infancy: a psychological perspective. *American Psychologist* **34**: 973–980.

Livesey, J. P. & Laszlo, J. I. (1979) Effect of task similarity on transfer performance. *Journal of Motor Behavior* **11**: 11–21.

London, I. D. (1954) Research on sensory integration in the Soviet Union. *Psychological Bulletin* **51**: 531–588.

Ludvigh, E. J. (1955) Visual and stereoscopic acuity for moving objects. *Symposium on Physiological Psychology*, School of Aviation Medicine, Pansacola, Florida.

Ludvigh, E. & Miller, J. W. (March 1953) A study of dynamic visual acuity. US Naval School of Aviation Medicine, Research Report No. NM001 075.01.01.

Maccoby, E. E. & Jacklin, C. N. (1974) *The Psychology of Sex Differences*. California: Stanford University Press.

MacKay, D. G. (1982) The problems of flexibility, fluency and speed–accuracy trade-off in skilled behaviour. *Psychological Review* **89**: 483–506.

Mackworth, N. H. & Kaplan, I. T. (1968) Visual acuity when eyes are pursuing moving targets. In Haber, R. N. (Ed) *Contemporary Theory and Research in Visual Perception*. New York: Holt, Rinehart and Winston.

Macpherson, J. M., Marangoz, C., Miles T. S. & Wiesendanger, M. (1982) Microstimulation of the supplementary motor area in the awake monkey. *Experimental Brain Research* **45**(3): 410–416.

Malina, R. M. (1973) Factors influencing motor development during infancy and childhood. In Corbin, C. B. (Ed) *A Textbook of Motor Development*, pp 31–53. Dubuque, Iowa: Brown.

Mandler, G. (1962) From association to structure. *Psychological Review* **69**: 415–427.

Marsden, C. D., Merton, P. A. & Morton, H. B. (1981) Human postural responses. *Brain* **104**: 513–534.

Marteniuk, R. G. (1976) *Information Processing in Motor Skills*. New York: Holt, Rinehart and Winston.

Masters, J. C. (1981) Developmental psychology. *Annual Review of Psychology* **32**: 117–151.

Matthews, P. B. C. (1972) *Mammalian Muscle Receptors and their Central Actions*. London: Edward Arnold.

McCarthy, D. (1972) *McCarthy Scales of Children's Abilities*. New York: The Psychological Corporation.

McClenaghan, B. A. & Gallahue, D. C. (1978) *Fundamental Movement: A Developmental and Remedial Approach.* Philadelphia: W. B. Saunders.

McCloskey, D. I. (1974) Muscular and cutaneous mechanisms in the estimation of the weights of grasped objects. *Neuropsychologia* **12**: 513–520.

McCloskey, D. I. (1978) Kinaesthetic sensibility. *Psychological Reviews* **58**: 763–813.

McDonnell, P. (1975) The development of visually guided reaching. *Perception and Psychophysics* **18**: 181–185.

McGinnis, J. M. (1930) Eye-movements and optic nystagmus in early infancy. *Genetic Psychology Monographs* **8**.

Meyer, D. E., Smith, J. E. & Wright, C. E. (1982) Models for the speed and accuracy of aimed movements. *Psychological Review* **89**: 449–482.

Meyers, C. E. & Dingman, H. F. (1960) The structure of abilities at the preschool ages: hypothesized domains. *Psychological Bulletin* **57**: 514–532.

Michel, G. F. (1983) Development of hand-use preference during infancy. In Young, G., Carter C., Segalowitz, S. & Trehub, S. (Eds) *Manual Specialization and the Developing Brain: Longitudinal Research.* New York: Academic Press.

Milani-Comparetti, A. & Gidoni, E. A. (1967) Routine developmental examination in normal and retarded children. *Developmental Medicine and Child Neurology* **9**: 631–638.

Millar, S. (1972) The development of visual and kinaesthetic judgements of distance. *British Journal of Psychology* **63**: 271–282.

Miller, S. (1975) *Experimental Design and Statistics.* London: Methuen.

Muijen, A. R. W. (1969) Rhythmic registration of movement, apparent movement and apparent rest. *Acta Psychologica* **29**: 134–149.

Mulder, G. (1983) The information-processing paradigm: concepts, methods and limitations. *Journal of Child Psychology and Psychiatry* **24**: 19–35.

Nakayama, K. & Loomis, J. M. (1974) Optical velocity patterns, velocity-sensitive neurons, and space perception: a hypothesis. *Perception* **3**: 53–80.

Nashner, L. M. & Cordo, P. J. (1981) Relation of automatic postural responses and reaction–time voluntary movements of human leg muscles. *Experimental Brain Research* **43**: 395–405.

Neisser, U. (1967) *Cognitive Psychology.* Englewood Cliffs, New Jersey: Prentice-Hall.

Neisser, U. (1976) *Cognition and Reality.* San Francisco: Freeman.

Nessler, J. (1973) Length of time to view a ball while catching it. *Journal of Motor Behaviour* **5**: 179–185.

Neuhauser, G. (1975) Methods of assessing and recording motor skills and movement patterns. *Developmental Medicine and Child Neurology* **17**: 369–386.

Newell, K. M. (1976) Motor learning without knowledge of results through the development of a response recognition mechanism. *Journal of Motor Behavior* **8**: 209–217.

Nie, H. H., Hull, C. H., Jenkins, J. G., Steinbrenner, K. & Bent, D. H. (1975a) *Standards for Educational and Psychological Association* (2nd edn.). New York: McGraw-Hill.

Nie. H. H., Hull, C. H., Jenkins, J. G., Steinbrenner, K. & Bent, D. H. (1975b) *Statistical Package for the Social Sciences.* New York: McGraw-Hill.

O'Connell, A. L. & Gardner, E. B. (1972) *Understanding the Scientific Bases of Human Movement.* Baltimore: Williams and Wilkins.

Oseretsky, N. A. (1948) A scale for studying the capacity of children. *Journal of Clinical Psychology* **12**: 37–47.

Over, R. & Over, J. (1967) Kinaesthetic judgements of the direction of line by young children. *Quarterly Journal of Experimental Psychology* **19**: 337–340.

Paillard, J. (1960) The patterning of skilled movements. In Field, J. (Ed) *Handbook of Physiology I. Neurophysiology,* Volume 3. Washington, DC: American Psychological Society.

Paine, P. A. Pasquali, L. & Spegiorin, C. (1983) Appearance of visually directed prehension related to gestational age and intrauterine growth. *Journal of Genetic Psychology* **142**: 53–60.

Pepper, R. L. & Herman, L. M. (1970) Decay and interference effects in the short-term retention of discrete motor act. *Journal of Experimental Psychology Monograph Supplement* **83**: No. 2, Part 2.

Pew, R. W. (1969) The speed–accuracy operating characteristic. *Acta Psychologica* **30**: 16–26.

Pew, R. W. (1974a) Human perceptual-motor performance. In Kantowitz, B. H. (Ed) *Human Information Processing: Tutorials in Performance and Cognition.* Hillsdale, New Jersey: Erlbaum.

Pew, R. W. (1974b) Levels of analysis in motor control. *Brain Research* **71**: 393–400.

Pew, R. W. & Rupp, G. L. (1971) Two quantitative measurements of skill development. *Journal of Experimental Psychology* **90**: 1–7.

Pick, H. L. (1983) On the relation between perceptual and cognitive development. In Tighe, T. J. & Shepp, B. E. (Eds) *Perception, Cognition and Development: Interactional Analysis.* New York: Academic Press.

Pick, H. L. & Pick A. D. (1970) Sensory and perceptual development. In Mussen, P. H. (Ed) *Carmichael's Manual of Child Psychology,* pp 773–847. New York: John Wiley.

Poulton, E. C. (1981) Human manual control. In Brooks, V. B. (Ed) *Handbook of Physiology.* Bethesda: American Psychological Society.

Rancoux, A., Culee, C. & Rancoux, M. (1983) Development of fixation and pursuit eye movements in human infants. *Behavioral Brain Research* **10**: 133–139.

Rarick, G. L. & Dobbins, D. A. (1975) Basic components in the motor performance of children six to nine years of age. *Medicine and Science in Sports* **7**: 105–110.

Richardson, F. E. (1916) Estimation of speeds of automobiles. *Psychological Bulletin* **13**: 72.

Riesen, A. H. (1982) Effects of environments on development in sensory systems. *Contributions to Sensory Physiology* **6**: 45–77.

Roach, E. G. & Kephart, N. C. (1966) *The Purdue Perceptual-Motor Survey.* Columbus: Merrill.

Rosenbaum, D. A. (1975) Perception and extrapolation of velocity and acceleration. *Journal of Experimental Psychology: Human Perception and Performance* **1**: 395–403.

Rosenbloom, L. (1975) The consequences of impaired movement — a hypothesis and review. In Holt, K. S. (Ed) *Movement and Child Development,* Clinics in Developmental Medicine, No. 55. Spastic International Medical Publications, London: William Heinemann Medical.

Runeson, S. (1974) Constant velocity — not perceived as such. *Psychological Research* **37**: 3–23.

Runeson, S. (1975) Visual prediction of collision with natural and non-natural motion functions. *Perception and Psychophysics* **18**: 261–266.

Ryan, T. A. (1940) Interrelations of the sensory systems in perception. *Psychological Bulletin* **37**: 659–678.

Sanderson, F. H. & Whiting, H. T. A. (1978) Dynamic visual acuity: a possible factor in catching performance. *Journal of Motor Behavior* **10**: 7–14.

Sanes, J. N. & Evarts, E. V. (1984) Motor psychophysics. *Human Neurobiology* **2**: 217–225.

Saunders, R. E. (1962) Dyslexia: the phenomenology. In Money, J. (Ed) *Reading Disability,* pp 35–39. Baltimore: Johns Hopkins Press.

Schaible, H.-G. & Schmidt, R. F. (1983) Responses of fine medial articular nerve afferents to passive movements of knee joints. *Journal of Neurophysiology* **49**: 1118–1126.

Schiff, W. & Detwiler, M. L. (1979) Information used in judging impending collision. *Perception* **8**: 647–658.

Schiller, P. H. (1952) Innate constituents of complex responses in primates. *Psychological Review* **59**: 177–191.

Schmidt, R. A. (1968) Anticipation and timing in human motor performance. *Psychological Bulletin* **70**: 631–646.

Schmidt, R. A. (1975) A scheme theory of discrete motor skill learning. *Psychological Review* **82**: 225–260.

Schmidt, R. A. (1982) *Motor Control and Learning. A Behavioral Emphasis.* Champaign, Illinois: Human Kinetics.

Scott, G. M. (1955) Measurement of kinaesthesis. *Research Quarterly* **26**: 324–341.

Sharp, R. H. & Whiting, H. T. A. (1974) Exposure and occluded duration effects in a ball-catching skill. *Journal of Motor Behavior* **6**: 139–147.

Sheikh, K., Smith, D. S., Meade, T. W., Goldenberg, E., Brennan, P. J. & Kinsella, G. (1979) Reliability and validity of a modified Activities of Daily Living (ADL) index in studies of chronic disability. *International Rehabilitation Medicine* **1**: 51–58.

Siegal, A. W., Bisanz, J. & Bisanz, G. L. (1983) Developmental analysis: a strategy for the study of psychological change. In *Contributions to Human Development,* pp 53–80. Basel: Karger.

Siegler, R. S. & Richards, D. (1979) Development of time, speed and distance concepts. *Developmental Psychology* **15**: 288–298.

Slater-Hammel A. T. (1955) Estimation of movement as a function of the distance of movement perception and target distance. *Perceptual and Motor Skills* **5**: 201–204.

Slater-Hammel A. T. (1960) Reliability, accuracy and refractoriness of a transit reaction. *Research Quarterly* **31**: 217–228.

Slinger, R. T. & Horsley, V. (1906) Upon the orientation points in space by the muscular, arthroidal, and tactile senses of the upper limbs in normal individuals and in blind persons. *Brain* **29**: 1–27.

Smothergill, D. W. (1973) Accuracy and variability in the localization of spatial targets at three age levels. *Developmental Psychology* **8**: 62–66.

Spinelli, D. N. & Jensen, F. E. (1979) Plasticity: the mirror of experience. *Science* **203**: 75–78.

Stevens, J. C. & Mack, J. D. (1959) Scales of apparent force. *Journal of Experimental Psychology* **58**: 405–413.

Stott, D. H., Moyes, F. A. & Henderson, S. E. (1972) *Test of Motor Impairment.* Guelph, Ontario: Brook Educational Publishing.

Stott, D. H., Moyes, F. A. & Henderson, S. E. (1984) *Test of Motor Impairment.* Guelph, Ontario: Brook Educational Publishing.

Sugden, D. A. (1980) Movement speed in children. *Journal of Motor Behavior* **12**: 125–132.

Tanji, J. & Evarts, E. V. (1976) Anticipatory activity of motor cortex neurons in relation to direction of an intended movement. *Journal of Neurophysiology* **39**: 1062–1068.

Tanji, J., Taniguchi, K. & Saga, T. (1980) Supplementary motor area: neuronal response to motor instructions. *Journal of Neurophysiology* **43**: 60–68.

Tanner, J. M. (1978) *Foetus into Man.* London: Open Books.

Taub, E. (1977) Movement in non-human primates deprived of somatosensory feedback. In Keogh, K. (Ed) *Exercise and Sports Sciences Reviews,* Volume 4. Santa Barbara, California: Journal Publishing Affiliates.

Taub, E. & Berman, A. J. (1963) Avoidance conditioning in the absence of relevant proprioceptive and exteroceptive feedback. *Journal of Comparative Physiological Psychology* **56**: 1012–1016.

Teeple, J. (1978) Physical growth and maturation. In Ridenow, M. V. (Ed) *Motor Development: Issues and Applications,* pp 3–27. Princeton, New Jersey: Princeton.

Thelen, E. & Fisher, D. M. (1983) From spontaneous to instrumental behavior: kinematic analysis of movement changes during very early learning. *Child Development* **54**: 129–140.

Thompson, H. (1954) Adaptive behaviour. In Gesell, A. (Ed) *The First Five Years of Life.* London: Methuen.

Todd, J. T. (1981) Visual information about moving objects. *Journal of Experimental Psychology: Human Perception and Performance* **7**: 795–810.

Touwen, B. C. L. (1979) *Examination of the Child with Minor Neurological Dysfunction.* Clinics in Developmental Medicine, No. 71, London: William Heinemann Medical.

Twitchell, T. E. (1965) The automatic grasping responses of infants. *Neuropsychologia* **5**: 247–259.

Vallbo, A. B., Hagbarth, K-E., Torebjork, H. E. & Wallin, B. G. (1979) Somatosensory, proprioceptive and sympathetic activity in human peripheral nerves. *Physiological Reviews* **59**: 919–957.

Volkman, F. C. & Dobson, M. V. (1976) Infant responses of ocular fixation to moving visual stimuli. *Journal of Experimental Child Psychology* **21**: 86–99.

Von Hofsten, C. (1979) Development of visually guided reaching: the approach phase. *Journal of Human Movement Studies* **5**: 160–178.

Von Hofsten, C. (1980) Predictive reaching for moving objects by human infants. *Journal of Experimental Child Psychology* **30**: 369–382.

Von Hofsten, C. (1983) Catching skills in infancy. *Journal of Experimental Psychology: Human Perception and Performance* **9**: 75–85.

Von Hofsten, C. & Lindhagen, K. (1979) Observations on the development of reaching for moving objects. *Journal of Experimental Child Psychology* **28**: 158–173.

Wade, M. G. (1976) Developmental motor learning. In Keogh, S. & Hutton, R. S. (Eds) *Exercise and Sport Science Reviews,* pp 375–394. Santa Barbara, California: Journal Publishing Affiliates.

Wade, M. G. (1982) Motor skills development in young children: current views on assessment and programming. In Katz, L. (Ed) *Current Topics in Early Childhood Education,* Volume IV, pp 55–71. Norwood, New Jersey: Ablex Publishing.

Wade, M. G. & Davis, W. E. (1983) Motor skill development in children: current views on assessment and programming. *Current Topics in Early Childhood* **4**: 55–70.

Welch, R. B. & Warren, D. H. (1980) Immediate perceptual response to intersensory discrepancy. *Psychological Bulletin* **88**: 638–667.

Welford, A. T. (1976) *Skilled Performance: Perceptual and Motor Skills.* Glenview, Illinois: Scott, Foresman.

White, B. L. & Held, R. (1966) Plasticity of sensori-motor development in the human infant. In Rosenblith, J. F. & Allinsmith, W. (Eds) *The Causes of Behavior: Readings in Child Development and Educational Psychology,* pp 60–70. Boston: Allyn & Bacon.

White, B. L., Castle, P. & Held, R. (1964) Observations on the development of visually-directed reaching. *Child Development* **35**: 349–364.

Whiting, H. T. A. & Cockerill, I. M. (1974) Eyes on hand — eyes on target? *Journal of Motor Behavior* **6**: 27–32.

Whiting, H. T. A., Gill, E. B. & Stephenson, J. M. (1970) Critical time intervals for taking in flight information in a ball catching task. *Ergonomics* **13**: 265–272.

Wickens, C. D. (1974) Temporal limitations of human processing: a developmental study. *Psychological Bulletin* **81**: 739–755.

Wickens, C. D. & Gopher, D. (1977) Control theory measures of tracking as indices of attention allocation strategies. *Human Factors* **19**: 349–365.

Wiesendanger, M. (1969) The pyramidal tract, recent investigations on its morphology and function. *Ergebnisse der Physiologie, Biologischen Chemie und experimentellen Pharmacologie* **61**: 72–136.

Williams, H. G. (1973) Perceptual-motor development: children. In Corbin, C. B. (Ed) *A Textbook of Motor Development,* pp 111–148. Dubuque, Iowa: Brown.

Winter, D. A. (1976) The locomotor laboratory as a clinical assessment system. *Medical Progress Through Technology* **4**: 95–106.

Wohwill, J. (1960) Developmental studies of perception. *Psychological Bulletin* **57**: 249–288.

Wolff, P. (1972) The role of stimulus-correlated activity in children's recognition of nonsense forms. *Journal of Experimental Child Psychology* **14**: 427–441.

Woodworth, R. S. (1938) *Experimental Psychology.* New York: Henry Holt.

Yonas, A., Bechtold, A. G., Frankel, D., Gordon, F. R., McRoberts, G., Norcia, A. & Sternfels, S. (1977) Development of sensitivity to information for impending collision. *Perception and Psychophysics* **21**: 97–104.

Zaporozhets, A. V. (1965) The development of perception in the preschool child. *Monographs of the Society for Research in Child Development* **30**: Whole No. 100.

AUTHOR INDEX

SUBJECT INDEX